"Using key sections of the National Catechetical Directory, *Sharing the Light of Faith,* to introduce each of the chapters imparts a Catholic flavor to this book. Although the contents concern the teaching of religion, they embrace much more than teaching in the narrow sense of academic programs. *Creative Catechist* clarifies some obscure elements in the Directory by introducing practical and concrete dimensions. Brilliant analyses and syntheses mark nearly every chapter.

"Reflective questions and suggested projects accompany each chapter. Diagrams effectively summarize the content and organization of sections."

Robert Y. O'Brien
The Living Light

"A blend of insight, questions for reflection, recommendations for response, practical catechetical skills and activities pulled from traditional and contemporary sources help make this book a valuable resource for individual catechists and for those who train them on the diocesan, parish, parochial school, and college levels. Through illustrations and carefully prepared text, the authors share their belief that catechesis is a creative response to the Holy Spirit's call to a life filled with 'sensitive, caring questioning and a willingness to grow' and to invite others into that process."

Religious Education Association
Religious Education

"'Being a good catechist is one of the most creative, exciting, rewarding—as well as challenging—experiences anyone can have.' That is the core of the catechetical creed proposed by the nationally recognized master catechist team Janaan Manternach and Carl Pfeifer in their recently revised book, *Creative Catechist.*

"Drawing on the church's twenty centuries of catechetical experience, the authors blend their principles with a variety of practical catechetical skills and activities pulled together from traditional and contemporary sources."

Aids in Ministry

"This superb book is recommended for catechists. It is an excellent and comprehensive work for personal reflection by the individual catechist and for teachers' training programs. It has a well-balanced section on the content of catechesis and many other chapters outlining creative approaches. The writers, who have already done so much good for American catechesis, show throughout the work their awareness of and sensitivity to the real situation of the average catechist. This book is indispensible for the DRE and will be very helpful to every catechist."

NCEA, Religious Education
Forum Newsletter

Revised
and Expanded

CREATIVE
CATECHIST

A COMPREHENSIVE, ILLUSTRATED GUIDE
FOR TRAINING RELIGION TEACHERS

Janaan Manternach & Carl J. Pfeifer

TWENTY-THIRD PUBLICATIONS
Mystic, Connecticut

Photo Credits

Jeff Brass 58, 121; Cleo Freelance Photo 31; Robert Finken, 107; Mark J. Goebel 36; Carl J. Pfeifer 52, 76, 125, 142; Patricia Roberts 87, 90; James L. Shaffer 47, 81, 95; Michael Siluk 71; Strix Pix 7, 11, 16, 41, 64, 114, 133, 139.

Acknowledgments

Excerpts from *Sharing the Light of Faith: National Catechetical Directory for Catholics of the United States,* copyright © 1979, by the United States Catholic Conference, Department of Education, Washington, D.C., are used by permission of copyright owner. All rights reserved.

P. 4: A.A. Milne, *The World of Pooh* (New York: E.P. Dutton & Co., 1957). P. 33: Shel Silverstein, *The Missing Piece* (New York: Harper & Row, 1976). P. 51: Miska Miles, *Annie and the Old One* (Boston: Little Brown and Co., 1971). P. 60 "David Sutton, Crime Fighter," *The Washington Post,* April 12, 1977. P. 113: Cindy Herbert, "The Theft," *I See A Child* (Garden City, New York: Doubleday, 1974). P. 124: "She's not going to play the accordian again, is she?" *Pastoral Music,* August/September 1977.

Third printing 1995

Twenty-Third Publications
185 Willow Street
P.O. Box 180
Mystic, CT 06355
(203) 536-2611
800-321-0411

ISBN 0-89622-490-2
Library of Congress Catalog Card No. 91-90951

CONTENTS

INTRODUCTION

The original edition of *Creative Catechist* (1983), and its revised and upgraded edition (1991), have proven helpful to thousands of catechists and religion teachers. We trust that this new edition will be even more helpful.

We have now included references to the *Catechism of the Catholic Church*, published in 1994 (see Chapter 26). This makes it easier to find items in the *Catechism* that relate to the chapters of *Creative Catechist,* or to use *Creative Catechist* as a guide to reading the *Catechism* more directly in relation to your catechetical ministry.

While the *Catechism* is not meant to be a practical guide to creative catechesis, it indirectly affirms our most basic catechetical creed, which informs the whole of *Creative Catechist.*

•We believe that catechesis is a very creative activity.

•We believe that catechists are creative people who want to become more creative.

•We believe that being a good catechist is one of the most creative, exciting, rewarding—as well as challenging—experiences anyone can have.

•We believe that you are creative and that you can and want to become more creative.

These beliefs are the result of more than thirty years of teaching children, teenagers, and adults, and twenty years of working with catechists. We have discovered that creativity is not some rare, esoteric gift enjoyed by a few people like poets, musicians, actors, sculptors, dancers. Rather, it is something that comes with being alive, sensitive, caring, questioning, open to the Holy Spirit, willing to learn from the past and to explore the present. To be creative is to be willing to grow and to encourage growth in others. And "growing in faith" is what catechesis is all about.

Creativity is rooted in basic principles and expresses itself in a variety of practical ways. In one sense the most practical of all things is a good principle. So, *Creative Catechist* is a blending of sound catechetical principles and a wide variety of practical catechetical skills and activities. The principles are drawn from the church's twenty centuries of catechetical experience. The skills and activities are also pulled together from traditional and contemporary sources. Each of our chapters includes:

•A significant and appropriate quotation from the *National Catechetical Directory*

•A theological-pedagogical essay on some aspects of catechesis

•Questions designed for reflection and discussion

•Creative exercises to help you better understand the principles presented, and to help you develop the recommended skills

•Helpful books and other resources that are grouped together under "Resources" for handy reference.

These and other features make *Creative Catechist* useful in the following ways:

•For personal reflection. Individual catechists will discover here valuable resources for personal reflection and prayer, as well as for classroom skills.

•For group in-service. Dioceses, parishes, and grade-level groupings will find that this is a complete manual for initial and on-going catechist training and certification.

•For catechetics courses. Colleges and other professional institutions will find here an excellent theoretical and practical textbook for catechetics courses.

•As a resource tool. DREs and master catechists will discover that this is an excellent resource for workshops, lectures, and other catechetical presentations.

•For parent meetings. The principles and practical applications in our book will help parents understand the catechetical approaches being used with their children, and will also help them to grow in faith as a family.

Most importantly, we wrote *Creative Catechist* to help you tap your own creativity and that of those you teach. We wrote it to help you grow in faith and to increase those skills that will lead others to grow in faith with you. Creative catechesis is what creative catechists do. That is why our focus is on you.

We will be more than satisfied if you discover in yourself more of the creativity already there and let it blossom so that you may become an even more creative catechist.

Janaan Manternach

Carl J. Pfeifer

PART I

CATECHESIS: WHAT? WHY? WHERE?

THE GOAL OF CATECHESIS: FAITH GROWTH

Catechesis is an esteemed term in Christian tradition. Its purpose is to make a person's faith become living, conscious, and active, through the light of instruction.

Faith grows and matures. Such faith is a grace, a gift of God. Growth in faith is intimately related to one's response to this gift.

National Catechetical Directory, 32, 33

The Old Grey Donkey, Eeyore, stood by himself in a thistly corner of the forest, his front feet well apart, his head on one side, and thought about things. Sometimes he thought sadly to himself, "Why?" and sometimes he thought, "Inasmuch as which?" and sometimes he didn't quite know what he was thinking about. So when Winnie-the-Pooh came stumping along, Eeyore was very glad to be able to stop thinking for a little, in order to say "How do you do?" in a gloomy manner.

"And how are you?" said Winnie-the-Pooh.

Eeyore shook his head from side to side.

"Not very how," he said. 'I don't seem to have felt at all how for a long time."

—*Winnie-the-Pooh*

Like Eeyore, many, many catechists have seemingly not felt at all "how" for a long time. They are confused or befuddled, frustrated and gloomy. This feeling is registered in comments such as, "I sometimes wonder just what I'm trying to do when I walk into religion class. The approach the textbooks suggest is so different from the way I learned catechism."

In our work with catechists, we have heard over and over again observations like that or questions like these.

"When should children know all the basic truths Catholics must believe?" "Shouldn't they learn the Ten Commandments and the traditional prayers?" "I can get the children to memorize the doctrines and prayers, but I suspect it doesn't mean much to them. How can I make it all more meaningful?"

Catechesis and Faith

The answers are partially found in the desires expressed by the questioners. For example, "We want children to grow up believing (and affirming) what Catholics believe (and affirm)." "We want children to really love God as someone who makes a difference." "We would like children to believe what the church believes about itself and we'd like to know ourselves what it believes." However the answer is phrased, most catechists indicate that they want *growth in faith,* not only for youngsters, but for themselves as well. They want to grow in "knowing, loving, and serving God" as Catholics.

This is exactly what the official documents of the church affirm. The purpose of catechesis is "to make faith become living, conscious, and active, through the light of instruction" (Vatican II, *Bishops,* 14). Rome's *General Catechetical Directory* reaffirms that catechesis "leads both communities and individual members of the faithful to maturity of faith" (21).

And our own National Catechetical Directory, *Sharing the Light of Faith*, simply quotes the above text from the Second Vatican Council as its definition of the goal of catechesis (32).

Catechesis aims at a faith that is living and maturing, affecting people's everyday responses, and grounded in the church's tradition.

Catechists sense what the church officially affirms in answer to the question, "What are we trying to do?" But like most answers to questions, this answer raises another set of questions: "What is faith?" "How does one encourage a living, maturing faith?"

Faith as Experience

Faith has several meanings. Most important of all is to realize that faith is not primarily a set of basic truths, teachings, or doctrines of the church. Rather, faith is a personal giftedness that grows as a person trusts and depends upon him or herself, upon others and upon God. Faith is a reality that grows out of and is experienced within the fabric of daily living.

For example, Janaan recalls the following experience in which her faith made a real difference.

My dad died on May 2, 1979. I had not seen him for five months, because he lived in Iowa and I live in Arlington, Virginia. His death was sudden and unexpected. My initial reaction was 'no, no, no!' That was followed by helpless crying, because I had not been able to tell him good-bye. I

had not been there to give him a final hug and to support him in those last awe-ful moments. While this was happening to me, I began to pray spontaneously, silently. This steadied me, and although the pain of shock and loss lingered, I was in control and felt willing to accept what was: my dad was dead!

It is this kind of faith in God and in himself that prompted Abraham to leave his home and security and set out into the unknown, completely trusting in God's promise because he, himself, was part of the promise. Mary experienced that kind of commitment within herself when she responded to God's invitation to be the mother of the messiah. Jesus himself walked through life up to Calvary placing himself in the care of his Father because he and the Father are one. Millions of Christians have continued to believe in themselves because of God and have continued to believe in God because of themselves.

That is ultimately what is meant by a living, maturing faith. In the book of the prophet Micah, we are told:

...this is what Yahweh asks of you:
only this, to act justly,
to love tenderly
and to walk humbly with your God (6:8).

In the deepest sense, such faith is the goal of catechesis. Faith as a profound experience involves several dimensions. It is a *relationship* with God, with Jesus Christ, a relationship of trust and affection, of surrender and commitment. The relationship with Christ enables

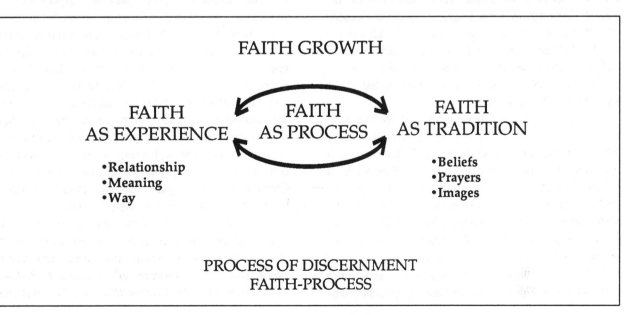

the believer to experience new *meaning* in life.

Knowing and loving Jesus Christ is the key to unlocking life's mysteries.

Faith helps the believer make sense out of his or her life. Finally, the meaningful relationship with Christ is that faith allows the believer to find a *way* to live happily, humanly, in accord with Christ's own way.

The rich experience of faith is summed up simply in the ancient prayer, "Day by Day" of *Godspell.* Originally authored by Saint Richard of Chichester in the thirteenth century, it has us pray for a continually growing, maturing faith:

Day by day, day by day,
O dear Lord, three things I pray:
to see thee more clearly,
love thee more dearly,
follow thee more nearly,
day by day.

Faith as Tradition

It is obvious that such experienced faith cannot be taught, nor can it be found in a book. But there is a sense in which Catholics talk about "handing on the faith" or "teaching the faith," or simply "the faith" or "the Catholic faith." When we talk about faith in those terms, we are talking about something important, but only insofar as it fosters the relationship that is described by the prophet Micah.

"The faith," in the sense of a *belief system,* is found in biblical stories, liturgical symbols and rituals, prayers, moral stances, creeds and doctrines, as well as the example of dedicated Catholics. These elements of the church's developing living tradition express the experienced faith of Christian communities down through the centuries. There is no question that catechists and parents want their children to come in contact with that bundle of beliefs that the church preserves, hands on, and continually develops.

But what does a knowledge of church teachings and ritual have to do with the experience of God in daily life? It adds to our identification with Catholicism. In it is preserved the experience and meaning of centuries of Catholics before us. It creates in us awareness of what Jesus Christ and the Gospels meant for our forefathers and mothers. Since the community of believers, the church, is the context in which our faith normally grows, the traditional expressions of faith are vital sources of nourishment and guidance. The teachings and worship of the church also provide for community testing of individual experiences and for individual testing of the community's experiences. The church's traditional forms of prayer provide a base for contemporary prayer forms. The example of great Christians provides models of what it means to live a life rooted in the Christ of the Gospels. The Bible remains the norm of our faith.

It is important that parents and catechists keep in touch with this rich heritage both for their own and their children's edification and inspiration. The teachings, prayers, and moral insights of a tradition need to be cherished by a community of believers, even as new insights and practices take over. This is part of what it means to be schooled in "the faith." To understand "the faith" as it is grounded in a tradition is part of the objective of religious education at home, in school, or in church.

Faith as Process

But knowledge of the traditional faith of the church is little more than academic information unless it enriches and influences people's lived experience of themselves, others, and God. For this reason, catechesis can never be simply handing on or teaching traditional expressions of Catholic belief, morality, and worship. Such teaching, important as it is, must be related to what is happening in people's lives as they learn what it means to be human in a complex society that is made up of a variety of traditions, a variety of experiences, a variety of needs.

Parents and catechists foster a maturing, growing faith by gradually initiating themselves and others into a *faith-process* sometimes known as a *process of discernment.* What this means in practice is that the catechist normally begins with people and their experiences and probes for answers to significant questions. What does it mean to be happy and sad, to grow and to diminish, to question and to answer, to succeed and fail? How does one cope with the evils of ignorance, poverty, loneliness, oppression, injustice, joblessness, boredom? How does one make an adventure out of leisure, adolescence, old age, incompleteness? How does one help others cope or respond creatively?

Such experiences and questions are then looked at consciously in the light of the Gospel, in the light of Christ's call, in the light of Christ's own experience of humanness. Out of this interplay of experience and Christian tradition a meaning may be sensed, a call heard, a decision made, a spirituality formed. The goal is to make sense out of life through the teachings of the Gospel and to make sense out of the Gospel through the teachings of life. The faith-process of relating *life* and

Catholic tradition aims at the experienced faith or trust described above as the goal of catechesis.

Parents often do this spontaneously. When a child is captivated with wonder at a flower, or at the birth of an animal, the mother or father may speak simply of God's creation, God's presence, God's gifts. Religion texts structure this kind of faith process according to themes that bridge people's daily lives and important biblical or traditional themes.

The experience of freedom, for example, is the key to grasping the biblical theme of "exodus" and the Catholic doctrine of "salvation." That biblical theme and church doctrine, in turn, are guides to what true freedom really is.

The traditional meaning of "grace" rests on the experience of being loved and expands that experience to the surprising awareness of being loved by God.

The meaning of the Eucharist makes sense only in the light of the experience of togetherness in community—a togetherness that is deeper and more demanding than the gathering that takes place at the Sunday liturgy. The Eucharist has the power to enable the kind of togetherness with Jesus and with people that makes a difference.

Exercising this faith process of relating significant segments of daily experience with related aspects of our Catholic Christian tradition initiates people into a process that may be life-long. It is one of trying to make sense out of life in the light of the church's tradition while attempting to probe more deeply into that tradition in the light of one's changing experience. Some draw attention to this dynamic growth process by saying that "faith is a verb."

That faith process, if put into motion, gives us grounds to hope that catechesis will lead to an experienced faith in God that is open to life while rooted in tradition.

What's It All About?

What, then, are we trying to do as parents at home or catechists in a classroom or priests in the pulpit? We are trying to help others (as well as ourselves) grow in a maturing faith within the Catholic Christian tradition. Such a goal involves at least three aspects of what we mean by "faith." Most important in the final analysis is 1) *faith as experience,* a deep trust in God who is intimately in-

volved in everyday experience, and a commitment to God's ways. A significant help toward that for Catholics is familiarity with 2) *faith as tradition,* the cumulative insights of Christians before us whose experience of God in faith finds expression in doctrines, stories, rituals, prayers, and example. The practical key toward enabling growth in the experience of faith within the Catholic faith tradition 3) is the *faith process* of consciously relating daily experience with that tradition.

All three senses of faith are part of the goal of catechesis. That's what it's all about: encouraging growth in faith as *experience, tradition,* and *process.*

Questions for Reflection and Discussion

1. In your own words, in terms of your own life, what does "faith" mean?

2. What would be an example in your life of how your Catholic faith really makes a difference?

3. What does your relationship with Christ have to do with your grasp of life's meaning? How does knowing and loving Jesus help you find your way in life?

4. What is the biggest challenge to your faith? What doubts rise up from time to time in your consciousness?

5. What do you think would be a good symbol or image for faith?

Ways to Respond

1. Draw pictures. Begin by thinking of what your Catholic faith means in your life. Then share your insights in a group of three or four. Come to a consensus on an image, symbol, or picture that best expresses what you all mean by faith. Draw your picture, symbol, or image. Then add one or two words that give further expression to the visual statement. Reflect together on what your "poster" says to you all. You might also do this activity alone.

2. Write creeds. Take time to think of what you as a Catholic Christian really believe. Write your own personal creed, beginning "I believe...." If you are working with others, share your creeds, reading and explaining them to each other.

3. Write autobiographies. Take time to write a story of your faith. What person(s) or experience(s) have most influenced the way you believe today? What customs, practices in your childhood gave life and meaning to your faith?

4. Collect stories of faith. Search through issues of your local newspapers and through magazines for stories of faith. Clip them and file them for use in your teaching. Share and discuss them with others on your teaching team.

The Context of Catechesis: Community

Catechists situate catechesis within the community of believers. The church, the Body of Christ, is always the context for catechesis. The meaning and vitality of catechesis grow especially in the parish, the praying, believing, and serving community of faith. The parish gives spiritual, moral, and material support to regular, continuing catechesis.

National Catechetical Directory, 60

"Harlequin, Harlequin," shouted his friends, "come on out!" Slowly Harlequin pulled on his worn gray clothes and joined his friends.

They were all very excited as they walked toward the town square—all but Harlequin. "My costume is yellow," one shouted. "Mine is velvet," boasted another. "Wait till you see mine," chimed in another. Harlequin said nothing. He turned and ran back home.

Slowly it dawned on his friends what was bothering Harlequin. "He doesn't have a costume," one of them said. They realized Harlequin had nothing special to wear to the carnival because he was too poor.

So the friends decided to cut pieces of cloth from their own jackets and dresses. They took the assorted pieces of many colors to Harlequin's house. Harlequin was amazed to see them. He was grateful, but puzzled, as they heaped the pieces of cloth into his hands.

Then Harlequin had an idea. "Mother, do you think if we sewed these scraps onto my old suit, it would make a good costume?" "I think it would be beautiful," she answered.

Harlequin's mother sewed all night. By morning the costume was ready. It was beautiful indeed.

"It's wonderful," Harlequin shouted as he put it on.

He ran to the town square. As people danced and frolicked, they noticed a figure in a fantastic costume. No one recognized Harlequin in his colorful coat.

Then Harlequin's friends noticed pieces of their own costumes. "That piece of blue is mine," said one. "And that shiny red stuff is mine," said another. All at once the puzzle fell together. "It's Harlequin!" they all shouted.

Harlequin was the happiest of them all. He was clothed in the love of his friends.

Community and Faith

This old tale, retold beautifully by Remy Charlip and Burton Supree in *Harlequin and the Gift of Many Colors* (New York: Parent's Magazine Press, 1973), suggests something basic about life. We all come to our fullest personal growth through interaction with others who care about us. His friends' creative caring helped Harlequin experience his own creativity and fulfillment.

In similar fashion our personal faith grows normally within a community of believers. The faith of others around us fosters individual growth in faith. Solitary faith is abnormal. Believers need other believers. Even the ancient monks of the desert stayed close to Christian communities nearby.

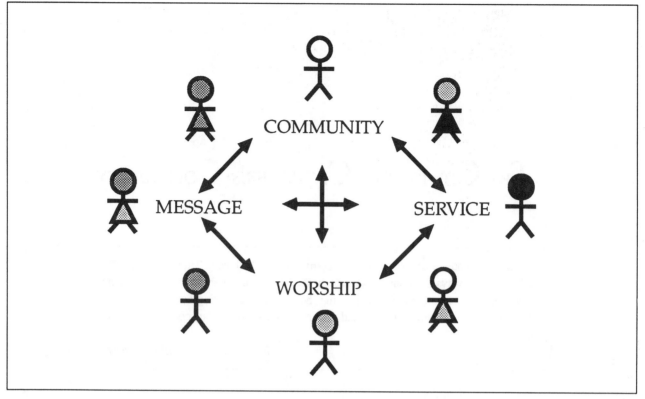

The goal of catechesis, then, is not just individual growth in personal faith. Catechesis aims at personal faith growth within a community of faith. Each of us needs to be enriched with swatches of the faith "colors" of other believers.

The renewed Rite of Christian Initiation of Adults (RCIA) exemplifies the role of the community in evangelization and catechesis. The RCIA is built on the conviction that the journey to faith, baptism, and steadily maturing faith involves the entire local community of believers. The entire process of welcoming and sustaining new Christians is no longer a matter of the parish priest instructing prospective converts in the basic teachings of the church. Rather the parish community as a whole is to be involved in initiating new candidates into the Catholic way of living together, worshipping together, sharing faith, and responding in compassionate service to all who are in need.

Community as Catechist

While gifted catechists from within the community play a vital role in the initiation process, the most important catechist is the community itself. The parish community catechizes by its lifestyle, liturgy, service, hospitality, as well as by formal and informal sharing of God's Word. The community—beginning with the family community— shares the inquirers' journey much as the stranger walked with the two dispirited disciples on the road to Emmaus (Luke 24:13-25). Believers share their experience and their Catholic tradition, bringing both to bear on the questions and needs of the inquirers. The community itself is the chief catechist in this process.

The shared search by inquirers and community also provides the major curriculum in the RCIA process. The community itself becomes the most effective catechism. The local Catholic community needs to measure its steps to the sometimes halting, sometimes eager steps of the inquirers—respecting their rhythm, dealing with their questions, sharing their experiences. In the process, the life of shared faith, worship, and service to the community illumines the questions, needs, and desires of the inquirers. From observing, listening, and sharing the candidates best learn what Catholics believe, how they worship, and what is expected of them in living out their faith.

To view the local parish community as the most effective catechist and most meaningful catechism is an ideal just beginning to be taken seriously in our country. In many Third World countries the catechetical importance of the community of faith is an established reality. The *comunidades eclesiales de base* (CEB)—base church communities—in Latin America are the best known example of this.

What the RCIA sets forth for the catechumenate pro-

cess is meant to provide a model for catechesis long after the catechumenate is concluded. Its community-centered catechesis is recognized as the model for all catechesis. The RCIA model is a challenging, quite radical ideal based on a demanding vision of church as God's richly gifted people.

Communal Dimensions

A similar ideal is found in the *National Catechetical Directory* (NCD). This directory indicates that the catechetical activity of nurturing faith has important communal dimensions. "Its components include sharing faith life, experiencing liturgical worship, taking part in Christian service, and participating in religious instruction" (39). In the same section the directory points out that "every pastoral activity has a catechetical dimension."

The document draws upon the four-fold dimension of Christian community life found already in the earliest Jerusalem communities described in the Acts of the Apostles. These original Christian communities exhibited a strong sense of community fellowship *(koinonia)*. They celebrated their shared faith in worship, particularly the "breaking of bread," or eucharist *(leiturgia)*. They lived out their faith in a compassionate Lord by imitating his life of compassionate service *(diakonia)*. And they expressed the meaning of their faith experience in preaching and teaching *(kerygma, didache)*.

Today we speak of these four traditional components of catechesis as community, worship, service, and message. They also designate the four basic catechetical tasks. The four tasks are grounded in the mission of Christ in forming a people of God *(community)*, namely as "priest" *(worship)*, as "prophet" *(message)*, and as "servant-king" *(service)*. In other words the whole life of the faith community has profound implications for catechesis. The community of faith is the normal catechist for its members, who together provide the most convincing catechism or curriculum for faith growth.

Practical Implications

The community model proposed by the RCIA, CEBs, and the NCD suggests three immediately practical challenges for parish catechetical programs.

The first challenge has to do with *overall catechetical planning*. Planning for catechesis needs to be placed within the broader context of total parish planning. What happens at Sunday liturgy can have a significant impact on the catechetical programs. So too can the many social ministry activities in the parish. And so also can the more purely social events that are designed to build community. All these ministries need to be planned in relation to one another and with awareness of important events within the neighborhood, town, nation, and world at large.

Liturgy, service, and community building need to be planned with awareness of their catechetical potential. Catechetical programs, in turn, need to be planned with conscious awareness of the other parish ministries and needs. Integrated parish planning is vital if the catechetical potential of the community of believers is to be actualized. One parish, for example, focused its adult religious education program on parish involvement in the construction of a church building. They discovered that building a church structure provides rich opportunity for exploring the theological and pastoral implications of such a structure.

A second challenge is to explore alternative models of catechesis. In recent years a variety of alternative models have been developed in many parishes, sometimes as total approaches to catechesis, replacing classroom or school models. Perhaps more often the alternative models coexist with the school or one-a-week parish religious education programs, expanding, supplementing, and enriching them.

Here are some of the more common alternative catechetical models, all of which show a strong community dimension. Some parishes use more than one to provide greater balance.

• *Study/prayer/action groups* Small groups gather regularly for study, often Bible study and/or prayer and/or action, often for justice and peace.

• *Vacation church school* One or two week summer sessions blend study, prayer, action, and play.

• *Liturgy of the Word* Children separate from adults during the Liturgy of the Word each Sunday for catechesis and prayer, rejoining them for the Liturgy of the Eucharist.

• *Lectionary-based catechesis* The Sunday lectionary readings provide the basis for weekly reflection, study, and worship—often beginning during the Sunday Liturgy of the Word and continuing later.

• *Children's catechumenate* An RCIA-based process of initiating into the parish community children of catechetical age who have not been baptized, or who have been baptized but never received catechesis or celebrated confirmation, first eucharist or first reconciliation.

• *Family-centered catechesis* Catechesis, organized in family groupings, is led by parents, typically taking place in homes.

• *Intergenerational catechesis* Often blending lectionary-based and family-centered catechesis, all age groups focus on same texts each week.

• *Small Christian communities* Individuals and families share their life and faith in small communities bound by some degree of lasting commitment.

The third challenge more directly affects each individual catechist, presuming he or she is informed of the overall parish planning. The NCD describes the cate-

chist's role: "To proclaim Christ's message, to participate in efforts to develop community, to lead people to worship and prayer, and to motivate them to serve others" (213). That role description reflects the community model of catechesis.

This challenge touches down on the catechist's *regular lesson planning*. Each lesson needs to be planned with an awareness of what is happening in the parish beyond the walls of one's own class. Parish happenings—such as Sunday liturgies, sacramental celebrations, service projects, social events—can be integrated into lessons taught at the various age levels.

Lessons Reflect Parish Life

For example, at times lessons may be prepared out of their textbook sequence in order to tie the learning more immediately to some parish experience. A lesson on the Holy Spirit might, for example, be best taught in relation to the celebration of Confirmation or the feast of Pentecost rather than according to its place in the textbook sequence.

Each lesson can be enriched if it is tied in with parish events. Activities done in religion class can flow naturally over into parish worship. For example, banners made in class can be used at the Sunday Masses. So too, on occasion, can class dramatizations or other creative expressions. Lessons on compassion or social justice can be more meaningful when tied directly to parish social ministries. In this way both catechesis and the other parish ministries can enrich each other through more careful planning of lessons. (For more helps, see Chapter 15.)

Once catechists recognize the potential for faith growth that lies with the parish community at large, a whole world of lesson enrichment may develop. As the NCD affirms, *every pastoral activity in the parish has catechetical implications*.

As the community-of-faith model of catechizing becomes more of a reality, people begin to discover in one another signs of faith growth that reflect themselves. It is like the friends of Harlequin recognizing snatches of their own colors. They were enriched by the very fact of enriching Harlequin, who in turn was enriched by their gifts. It is a beautiful ideal: individuals growing in faith through their interaction with the community of faith in which they live, worship, serve, and teach. And the other side of the ideal is that the whole community grows in faith through the giftedness of its growing members.

Such is the goal of catechesis: enabling faith growth in individuals within and through the community of faith.

Questions for Reflection and Discussion

1. Have you ever experienced the care of friends as Harlequin did? What happened? How did you feel?

2. How does the life and worship of your parish affect your own faith growth? How might the impact be increased?

3. What sense does it make to you to speak of parish life as a curriculum or catechism of Catholic faith?

4. What concrete examples of community, worship, service, and message do you experience in your parish?

5. What challenges does this community model of catechesis suggest to you?

6. How do you plan your lessons in relation to parish experiences? How could your planning be more integrated into parish life?

Ways to Respond

1. Explore the symbol. Read the story of Harlequin. (If you can't get the book, at least reread the excerpt in this chapter.) Together with other catechists reflect on how his coat of many colors is a symbol of what church really means and can in fact be.

Talk about the story and your reactions to its symbolism in terms of the church. Ask one another what this symbol and the way it came to be through the creativity of Harlequin, his mother, and his friends may suggest about the communal dimensions of growth in faith.

Then create together an actual "coat of many colors" symbol for yourselves.

2. Analyze your parish. Consider together your parish and its varied activities. Look carefully at expressions of community life and sharing. Look at the parish worship and social ministry. From what you observe, try to formulate what Catholics believe, how they worship. and how they are called to love. In other words study your parish activities as you would study a catechism or a catechist.

Write down and share your observations. Consider together what might be changed or improved to make the community impact on catechesis more effective.

3. Adapt your textbook schedule. Carefully create and analyze a calendar of your parish's many activities during the year. Then carefully look over the sequence of lessons in your textbook, noting the content, topics, and themes. Compare the textbook themes with the most important parish events: social, liturgical, service, etc. Adjust the sequence of textbook lessons to mesh more meaningfully with these parish events.

The Process of Catechesis: Integration

> Catechesis is not limited to one methodology. Although certain norms or criteria apply to all catechesis, they do not determine a fixed methodology, nor even an order for presenting the truths of faith. For instance, catechesis can begin with God and proceed to Christ, or do the reverse; it can proceed from God to humanity, or from humanity to God, and so on.
>
> Whatever the method, catechists are responsible for choosing and creating conditions which will encourage people to seek and accept the Christian message and integrate it more fully in their living out of the faith.
>
> *National Catechetical Directory,* 176

Joan's mother could hardly hide the pride she felt at her daughter's first-grade wisdom. "Last week," she told us, "after the final religion class of the year, I thought I would test Joan. I asked her what she had learned all year."

We listened with some apprehension. We remembered this woman from a previous visit to Woodbridge, Virginia. At that time she was very concerned about her first-grader's religious education, and she was a bit skeptical about our approach.

"What did Joan say she learned?" we asked.

"I think this is just marvelous," the mother began. "Joan said, 'Mommy, I learned that Jesus is alive. And he's right here in Woodbridge!"

We were as excited as Joan's mother over her first-grader's insight. Little Joan's words reveal with disarming simplicity the very heart of the process that has come to characterize contemporary catechesis.

"Jesus is alive" is a three-word summary of the core of Christian tradition. "And he's right here in Woodbridge" is a heartfelt integration of that tradition into her own world of experience.

Joan's simple expression exemplifies a process that is essential to growth in a maturing, living faith: the integration of daily experience with the church's living tradition.

Grounded in Scripture

This catechetical *process of discernment and integration* is grounded in the traditional conviction of the Hebrew and Christian Scriptures: God's Word is present and active in the whole of life as well as in the religious traditions of God's own people.

The Hebrew prophets exemplify the effort in faith to make sense of life in the light of religious traditions, and to see new meaning in those very traditions because of new experiences in the life of the people. Miriam, for example, discerns in the Hebrew escape from Pharaoh the powerful presence of the God of Abraham, Isaac, and Jacob. But she and Moses also glimpse something new about the God of their ancestors, namely, that God loves freedom and works to free people held in bondage. Centuries later, Isaiah and Jeremiah and Ezekiel draw on that earlier insight to make sense of the exile in Babylon. They firmly believed the traditional faith that God loved freedom and worked to free people held in bondage. They proclaimed a new exodus, a new escape from bondage. But from their new experience they recognized that there was a deeper, spiritual freedom that God loved more than just freedom from chains and dictators.

The followers of Jesus turned to the Hebrew Scriptures, our Old Testament, to make sense out of their experience of Jesus of Nazareth. In the process they discovered a radically new meaning in those sacred traditions because of their experience of Jesus. They described Jesus, for example, as the "suffering servant" proclaimed centuries earlier by Isaiah. They saw his passage through death to new life as a "new exodus." In so doing they discovered a new depth of meaning in the words and imagery of the prophets.

Christian catechesis and spirituality initially grew out of that same process of interpretation and integration. The process of discernment remained central to Christian spirituality throughout the centuries, but it was lost to catechesis after the first two or three centuries after Christ. It has been reintroduced in our century as the fundamental *process of catechesis*.

Process Reintroduced

The *National Catechetical Directory* (NCD) builds on several decades of development in catechetics and on the teaching of the Second Vatican Council in formulating the discernment process of integrating life and tradition.

For many years now catechists have recognized that God's Word comes to us through signs. These signs make up the basic content of catechesis, since they mediate to us God's Word. In our country, catechists during the fifties spoke of four such signs: Bible, liturgy, doctrine, and witness. Catechetical textbooks quickly reflected these four content areas.

Further developments in the sixties helped rediscover a traditional, but long neglected, sign of God's Word: ordinary life experience. Catechists began to speak of five signs: *Bible, liturgy, doctrine, witness,* and *life.*

Religion texts focused enthusiastically on this fifth experiential sign. In the late 1960s and 1970s, building on Vatican Council II, the biblical process of discernment, and the rich tradition of spirituality, they began to integrate the four "sacred" signs with the one "secular" sign. The goal was to associate experiences of daily life with the living tradition of the church found in the Bible, liturgy, doctrine, and witness.

The *National Catechetical Directory* encourages this essential faith process. It slightly changes the terminology of the signs, calling "life" the *"natural signs,"* and it regroups the traditional four into three: *"biblical signs," "liturgical signs,"* and *"ecclesial signs"* (which include doctrine and witness). Through the integration of these signs in a dynamic process, the church at large and individuals within the church can come to discern God's Word—the unique source of catechesis—in their daily experience and in their religious tradition.

This discernment process continues to be the heartbeat of catechesis in the eighties and nineties. Now, however, there is greater awareness of the community dimension of the process and its implications for commitment to social justice.

Basis for Lesson Plans

Besides providing basic principles for designing catechetical curricula and programs, the discernment process

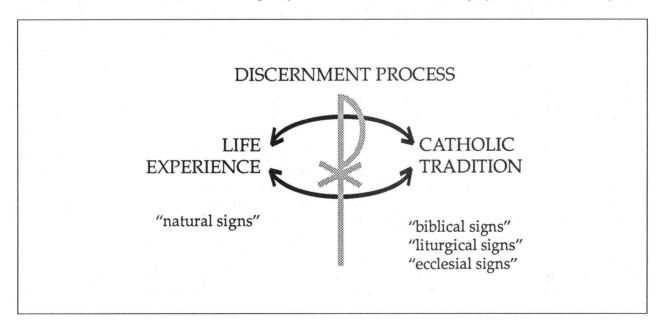

DISCERNMENT PROCESS

LIFE
EXPERIENCE

CATHOLIC
TRADITION

"natural signs"

"biblical signs"
"liturgical signs"
"ecclesial signs"

becomes as well the basis for creating lesson plans within the curriculum. Typical lesson plans center on themes that bridge human experience and the church's tradition. And they usually develop in three movements. Terminology in the various textbooks varies, but the lesson plan structure and process is essentially the same.

The first movement normally deals with some dimension of human experience. The second relates the experience to some aspect of Catholic tradition: a Bible story, liturgical symbol, doctrinal teaching, or example of Christian witness. The third movement is the integration of the two previous steps through some kind of active response. Some textbooks call these movements 1) Learning About Our Lives, 2) Learning About Our Faith, and 3) Learning How to Live Our Faith. Others use slightly different terms. For further insights into lesson plans and planning, see Chapter 15.

To help these movements come alive in the minds and hearts of those they teach, you need to engage yourself and your students in four essential learning strategies: reflection, dialogue, prayer, and action.

Essential Strategies

Reflection The ancient Greek philosophers were fond of saying that "an unexamined life is not worth living." Today there is growing interest in "critical thinking." As Christians we all experience how life can pass us by without our grasping its meaning for us. To understand the daily mysteries of human experience we must reflect on and question life. Reflection and questioning is also required to understand our Catholic heritage. We cannot integrate daily life and Christian tradition without going beneath the surface of both. And such integration is vital to the catechetical process.

Search out creative methods and media to help people reflect, question, and integrate. Challenge students to think deeply about what they are experiencing in daily living in relation to what they know of their rich Catholic tradition.

Dialogue The importance of dialogue or sharing stems from the belief that the church is a community of people, each of whom is gifted in a unique way by the Holy Spirit. The Spirit gives differing gifts to individuals, not for their personal gratification so much as for the building up of the body of Christ, the community of faith that is the church.

It is important that you foster in catechesis an honest sharing of individual gifts. When the fruits of personal reflection are shared in the church of Christ, it is for the benefit of all. Without honest dialogue the full implications of God's Word for today's church and world will not be grasped. No one person, no single group, has a monopoly on the guidance of the Holy Spirit.

Helping people learn to respect one another and listen, as well as to share, is vital to the discernment process and to catechesis. Remember (as was explored in Chapter 2) that the community is often its own most effective catechist and curriculum.

Prayer The third essential learning strategy is prayer. Without prayer faith will not grow. Prayer allows for the deepest integration of the human and divine, of daily life and our Catholic tradition. Prayer offers the opportunity for the insights of each day to surface in individual and group awareness so they can be related to the living Christ and his message. Gerard Sloyan taught us at Catholic University that the very purpose of religious education is to help people learn to pray. Certainly in the long tradition of individual and group discernment prayer has always been recognized as an essential element.

In the catechetical process prayer may occur at any point. What is important is that the prayer arise from life experience and be enriched by the traditional spirituality of the church. Whatever the specific form you use, prayer is an integral part of the catechetical process.

Action The fourth essential learning strategy is action. Not only must faith show itself in the way we live, but our actions are also critical means of growing in faith and grasping its meaning in our lives. It is common human experience that we do not really understand something until we do it. How we act reveals not only to others but to ourselves who we are, what we believe and value. Reflection, dialogue, and prayer should not only precede and direct our actions, but should also follow what we do, so we can discover why we act the way we do. It is not just a matter of applying what we learn, but of learning from what we do. Third World theologians rightly stress the importance of orthopraxis (right actions) along with orthodoxy (right beliefs) in evaluating faith.

So, in catechesis, action is as important a learning strategy for faith-growth as are reflection, dialogue, and prayer.

Shared Praxis

In his important books about catechesis, *Christian Religious Education* (Harper & Row, 1980), and *Sharing Faith: A Comprehensive Approach to Religious Education and Pastoral Ministry* (Harper & Row, San Francisco, 1991) Thomas Groome affirms—though at times with different terminology—what we have been describing. In place of "discernment process" Groome speaks of a "shared praxis approach" to religious education. Drawing upon comprehensive interdisciplinary research, he describes his shared praxis approach as "a group of Christians sharing in dialogue their critical reflection on present action in light of the Christian Story and its Vision toward the end of lived Christian faith."

Groome stresses the essentially communal nature of religious education. He says that through group process, life experience ("present action") and tradition ("Christian Story and Vision") are brought together in a dynamic interrelation which he calls a "dialectical hermeneutic." He, too, stresses the need for reflection and

dialogue. His awareness of the place of prayer in the process is present but not as explicit. His distinction between Story and Vision within the Christian tradition is helpful for highlighting the role of tradition as interpreting human experience ("Story") and critiquing it ("Vision"), calling us to live out the consequence of God's call in our actions.

In place of the more usual three-movement development, Groome's shared praxis approach involves five movements, which differ slightly in his two books. The difference seems to be chiefly a matter of emphasis and terminology. What we call a lesson's "theme" or "topic," Groome calls a "particular focus." For example, a religious education process might deal with prayer, or commandments. His first two movements, naming and reflecting critically on "present action" and the participant's stories and visions, seem to parallel what we describe as a first movement exploring life experience, "Learning About Our Lives." Groome's third movement, making accessible the Christian Story and Vision, is the same as our second movement of sharing Catholic tradition, "Learning About Our Faith."

Where we describe our third movement as integrating and responding to God's word in both our experience and our Catholic tradition, "Learning How to Live Our Faith," Groome has two movements: dialectical hermeneutic between the Christian Story and Vision and the participants' stories and visions, and a decision/response for lived Christian faith.

LEARNING STRATEGIES

LIFE EXPERIENCE ⟷ CATHOLIC TRADITION

REFLECTION
DIALOGUE
PRAYER
ACTION

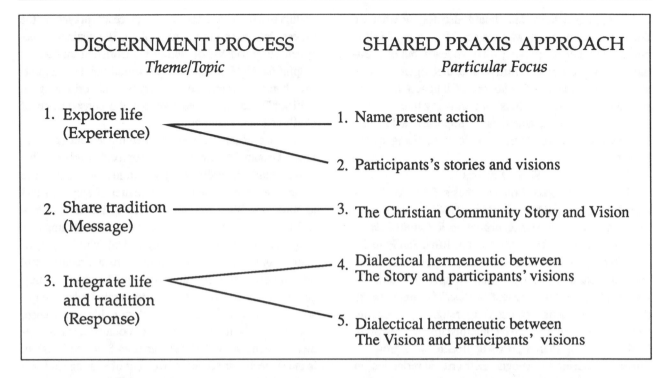

DISCERNMENT PROCESS *Theme/Topic*	SHARED PRAXIS APPROACH *Particular Focus*
1. Explore life (Experience)	1. Name present action
	2. Participants's stories and visions
2. Share tradition (Message)	3. The Christian Community Story and Vision
3. Integrate life and tradition (Response)	4. Dialectical hermeneutic between The Story and participants' visions
	5. Dialectical hermeneutic between The Vision and participants' visions

Groome's "shared praxis" approach is an important statement of the essential catechetical process. In itself it seems a helpful refinement that makes explicit the now commonly used catechetical process and language that has emerged in the past decade or two. Groome himself states that there is much in common between his shared praxis approach and the approach found in standard religious education programs. In fact, he defines "shared praxis" to some extent as "a drawing together of many trends and insights that have been evident in religious education over the past eighty years."

For years we have pointed to a story in Luke's Gospel as a marvelous example of the catechetical process. Groome, interestingly, highlights the same story, that of Jesus and the two disciples on the road to Emmaus (Luke 24:13-35). We recommend that you reread it thoughtfully in the light of your catechetical task.

Notice the feelings of the two disheartened disciples as they talk about the tragic experiences of the last days of Jesus of Nazareth. Observe Jesus, the unrecognized fellow traveler. He joins the two, sharing their journey, walking with them. Sensing their pain, he questions them about what happened. Then he listens as they share with him their experience and questions. After they have poured out their stories, he dips into their tradition, the Hebrew Scriptures. Starting with Moses, he cites text after traditional text, bringing them to bear directly on the two disciples' experience of the past several days. They discover new meaning in that painful experience through the prophetic teachings Jesus shares with them. At the same time, they discover a richer meaning in those long known texts because of the past three days' happenings.

They are already beginning to sense new hope, a renewed vision, as they invite the intriguing stranger for supper. There as they share a meal they recognize the traveler "in the breaking of bread." Rushing back to Jerusalem they tell the community that they saw the Lord and ate with him. They realize now that he was with them along the way as the stranger.

Such is the process of catechesis as the master himself exemplifies it. The Gospel story is much more sophisticated and developed than the words of first-grader Joan. But the insight and process of both are quite similar: "I learned Jesus is alive and he's right here in Woodbridge!"

Questions for Reflection and Discussion

1. How would you describe to someone God's presence and activity in your life?

2. To what or to whom do you normally turn in order to make sense out of what is happening in your life? Why?

3. What is the make-up of the lesson plans in the program you are using? To what extent is it the same as what is described in this article?

4. What has been your experience of faith-sharing in your family? In your parish? What value does honest sharing have for you? Why?

5. How can it be claimed that the goal of catechesis is to help people learn to pray? Do you agree with Sloyan? Why? Why not?

6. What do you think of Thomas Groome's "shared praxis" approach? Why is terminology so important?

Ways to Respond

1. Study your textbook. After reading this chapter, turn to your textbook and go through it to discover how it exemplifies or differs from the essential process we described. Examine the following components:

• *Contents*   What evidence is there of the integration of traditional teaching and life experience?

• *Introduction*   Does it describe this process of integration (in the same or different terminology)?

• *Cover and visual designs*   Do the cover and inside visuals suggest an attempt at catechetical integration? What about the page design? Do pictures and words suggest a relationship between daily life and Catholic tradition?

• *Lesson plans*   To what extent do the lesson plans give evidence of the process described in this chapter?

• *Activities*   Do the activities lead people to reflection, dialogue, prayer, and action?

If at all possible, share and discuss your findings with other catechists.

2. Examine your conscience. Take some time alone or in a group setting with other catechists. Begin by reflecting on your last few religion classes. To what extent do these classes reflect the kind of process and learning strategies described in this chapter? After reflecting on your classes, share together what you discovered. Then try to discover how you might help one another implement the process and strategies more effectively.

3. Study the Gospel. Since the story of Jesus and his two friends on the road to Emmaus is mentioned in the text as a good model of the discernment process or the shared praxis approach, you and your co-catechists might want to read and discuss the story in greater depth.

You will need a New Testament. Locate the story, Luke 24:13-35. Each read it quietly. Note down step by step, verse by verse, how Jesus "catechizes" the two disciples. What do they do? What does Jesus do? What happens? Be as specific and detailed as you can, working directly from the Bible text.

When you have finished your individual analyses, share your findings and talk about them in the light of what is stated in this chapter. Compare the steps and strategies you found in the Gospel story with the process, the steps, and strategies here. Then discuss the way Jesus dealt with the two, his attitude toward them, and how he reacted to them and their situation. How does Jesus' attitude and actions provide a model for you as a catechist?

4

THE HISTORY OF CATECHESIS: DEVELOPMENT

> The church continues the mission of Jesus, whose teaching has come down to us through the apostles. The ministry of catechesis serves the church in that mission. Great importance has always been attached to catechesis, but its methods and emphases have varied in different times and places, from apostolic times to the present, according to changing circumstances and needs.
>
> *National Catechetical Directory*, 8

It was a steamy August afternoon in Kansas in the early 1960s. One of America's great catechists, Aloysius J. Heeg, S.J., sat in his room after teaching a class on how to teach catechism. He was chatting with one of his students, who had grown up with Father Heeg's famous first communion catechism, *Jesus and I.*

On Father Heeg's desk was a book he was currently reading, *The Good News Yesterday and Today,* by a great European catechist, Josef Andreas Jungmann, S.J.

The student noticed Jungmann's book and asked Father Heeg what he thought of it. It was almost thirty years old but had just been translated into English.

"I haven't finished it yet," Fr. Heeg answered thoughtfully, "but I must admit, I'm not sure what he's getting at. I know I'll need to read it a second time."

This example of a student catechist learning from a great catechist who himself was learning from another great catechist's experience and insights is both instructive and inspiring.

We have found the history of catechesis helpful in understanding our task as catechists. As you will see, this history recalls the experiences of real men and women who shared the same call to help individuals and communities grow in faith. History can also help us grasp why we may be teaching and learning our faith the way we do.

1. Early Christian Centuries (1st to 5th Centuries)
"Catechesis" is a New Testament term. It is used in Luke's Gospel (1:4), in the Acts of the Apostles (18:25), and in Paul's letters to the Romans (2:18) and Galatians (6:6). In each case the word refers to oral teaching or instruction, especially in the law of God and the way of Christ.

Catechesis in the early church was primarily teaching about how to live as a Christian. Accepting Christ and his Good News required a profound change of heart and lifestyle for converts, both from Judaism and from the Greek and Roman religions.

Early Christian catechesis focused on the "two ways," that of life or death, light or darkness. The underlying law of life was seen as Jesus' law of love, inspired by his Spirit, the Spirit of love.

This essential instruction in the Christian way was initially given in home churches by the apostles and other teachers. Gradually the catechesis became an integral part of the initiation ritual or catechumenate. The normal place for catechesis then, besides the home, was the liturgy, particularly through homilies. During the catechumenate the new Christians were given two basic texts to learn as summaries of the Christian way and teachings: the Lord's Prayer or Our Father, and the Apostles' Creed.

Within this liturgical context early catechesis tended to be strongly biblical. St. Augustine urged catechists to use a narrative approach tracing the history of salvation in the Bible.

Augustine also introduced several other approaches that had a longer lasting impact on subsequent catechesis. He arranged catechetical instruction according to the three virtues of faith, hope, and charity. With faith he linked the Apostles' Creed, with hope the Lord's Prayer, and with charity the Law of Love, which he summarized under the Ten Commandments. He also tried to help people remember by arranging groupings of sevens, like the seven petitions of the Lord's Prayer.

Catechesis in the early church clearly linked belief with life, took place primarily in the home and in liturgical celebrations, and drew heavily upon the biblical narrative. It was predominantly oral teaching.

2. Medieval Catechesis (6th to 15th Centuries)

Gradually the practice of the lengthy initiation into the church through the catechumenate declined. There were mass conversions of "barbarian" tribes. These converts received minimal instruction before or after baptism.

Infant baptism became the norm. The instruction of children was the role of parents and godparents, who were expected to teach their children the Our Father and the Creed. Some Bishops and priests gave some catechetical instruction, mostly on Christian morality.

Priests as well as laity were generally uneducated. What catechetical tools there were tended to center on memory devices based on numbers like the 7 sacraments, 7 capital sins, 7 works of mercy.

The main focus of catechesis during these long centuries were the Christian culture of Europe, and the arts. Mystery and morality plays grew out of the now unintelligible liturgy. Bible stories and lives of saints were learned through plays, song, verse and pictures. Devotional practices brought Christ, Mary, and saints very close to the people. Shrines, feast days, patron saints filled the day to day lives of Europe's peasant population.

The rise of the mendicant orders like the Franciscans and Dominicans led to a renewal of preaching as a source of instruction in the faith. Priests were encouraged to explain the Catholic faith on Sundays.

St. Thomas Aquinas preached several series of influential catechetical sermons based on the creed, Our Father (to which he added the sacraments and the Hail Mary), and commandments (centering on Jesus' law of love).

Devotional piety often degenerated into what was in fact more superstition than faith. In practice catechesis became progressively disconnected from its major traditional sources of Bible, liturgy, and the central doctrines of the church.

3. Modern Catechesis (16th to 19th Centuries)

Martin Luther was very aware of the need for a more traditional and systematic catechesis. Making use of the recent invention of printing, he prepared a catechism book for children in 1529. For the first time in the church's long history of catechesis a book became its primary source. Classroom catechesis using a book seemed natural in an era marked by the invention of the printing press and the rise of schools for children, particularly of the upper classes.

Luther used the ancient elements of creed, Lord's Prayer, and commandments, but placed the commandments first. He required children and uneducated peasants to memorize the catechism's content in the form of questions and answers.

Catholics reacted swiftly with the publication of their own catechisms. Between 1555 and 1558, Peter Canisius, S.J., published three very popular catechisms—a large one for priests, a very small one for children, and a small one for youth. Similar catechisms soon appeared in France, Spain, and England.

In 1566 the Roman Catechism called for by the Council of Trent was published. It was primarily for priests and had four parts: creed, sacraments, commandments, and prayer (especially the Our Father). The text was strongly biblical and drew heavily on early Christian writers.

The most influential of the Post-Reformation catechisms was that of Robert Bellarmine, S.J. In 1597 he published a short catechism, and the following year a larger one for priests and teachers. He structured the text according to Augustine's arrangement of what is to be believed (faith), hoped for (hope), and loved (charity).

It is the small, simple versions of these catechisms that became the model for the hundreds of catechisms down to our own *Baltimore Catechism* which appeared in 1885. These short texts tended toward more abstract, theological questions and answers, reflecting the prevailing theology of the times. Their content most often reflected the by now common arrangement of creed, commandments, sacraments, and prayer.

The methodology since Luther's time rested on memorization of the questions and answers, followed by an explanation of the text. Since the language of the catechism was typically abstract and philosophical, catechists attempted to illustrate its meaning with analogies and metaphors. The small catechism, memorized and explained, remained the primary approach to catechesis until the twentieth century. Particularly since universal school attendance became compulsory in the 18th and 19th centuries in Europe, the setting for catechesis became primarily schools for children.

4. Twentieth-Century Catechesis

What came to be known as the "Catechetical Movement" originated in Europe at the turn of the century and steadily spread throughout the Catholic world.

(a) 1900: Methods of catechetical renewal. The first focus of catechetical renewal was on *methodology*. Catechists looked at the customary method of memorization of abstract questions and answers and asked a critical question: *Is this, in fact, how children learn best?*

They were led to this now obvious question by the then novel scientific research into how children actually learn. Educational psychologists in Munich and Innsbruck discovered that children learn best by doing (including seeing, feeling, tasting, smelling, as well as hearing). They also found that children learn best what relates to their experience.

Drawing on these discoveries in the psychology of learning, German and Austrian catechists devised a methodology based on creative activities close to the children's daily experience. Using the catechism as the basic text, these catechists developed a practical approach to planning lessons that would ensure contact with the children's experience. They included creative activities that involved more than memorizing questions and answers.

Sr. M. Rosalia Walsh, M.H.S.H., adapted this approach for the United States in her program called the "Adaptive Way."

(b) 1936: Content. The catechetical renewal took another major leap forward in the mid-thirties when the Austrian theologian Josef A. Jungmann, S.J., looked at the catechism and asked a basic question: *Is this what we should be teaching?*

Jungmann pointed out that the original catechesis was a proclamation of the good news of Jesus Christ, rather than a dry analysis of doctrinal truths. He saw the catechist as a joyful herald of the good news as well as a teacher of truths. From the Greek words for "herald" and the herald's "message" Jungmann developed the term "kerygmatic" catechesis.

The content of the good news was the record of God's great deeds of love—salvation history as recorded in the Bible. Jesus Christ is the center of salvation history, the focal point of the good news. All doctrines, all prayers, all moral commands need to be seen in relationship to Jesus Christ. Catechesis, then, must be *Christocentric*, and all parts of the content of catechesis must clearly relate to Jesus Christ. Creed, prayer and sacraments, and commandments need to be seen in their dynamic interrelationships and in relationship with Christ, rather than as three isolated elements of catechetical content.

The Bible is the record of God's great deeds of love. The liturgy is our celebration and reenactment of these saving deeds. Doctrine interprets and explains the meaning of what God has done. Christian living as a response to God's loving actions gives witness to our faith in God's loving deeds.

The content of catechesis, therefore, could not just include Catholic doctrines. It must also embrace the Bible, liturgy, and Christian living. These *four signs* or *sources* of catechesis became known as Bible, liturgy, doctrine, and witness.

Exemplified in the 1955 German Catechism for youth, this became the dominant approach to catechesis in the United States in the late 1950s and early 1960s. Sr. Maria de la Cruz Aymes, H.H.S., created the *On Our Way* series (Sadlier) for grade-school children, the first of a wave of American textbooks based on kerygmatic, salvation history catechesis.

(c) 1960s–1970s: Process. Enthusiasm for the kerygmatic-salvation history catechesis slowly gave way in the 1960s to a serious question: *If God did such great saving deeds in the past, what about today?*

This question led to the realization that God is present and active, saving and revealing in contemporary experience and culture, much as God was present and active in the great saving revelatory deeds recorded in the Bible. Salvation history, then, is not just past history recorded in the Bible and reenacted in the liturgy. Salvation history and revelation continue today. Today's world is graced by the presence of the risen Lord and filled with his holy Spirit.

There are then not just four signs or sources of catechesis: Bible, liturgy, doctrine, witness. There is a fifth, namely, life (or experience). The key to effective catechesis is the process of relating this contemporary, experiential fifth sign with the four traditional signs.

The development of this experiential, discovery, or

process catechesis took place primarily in the United States and in Holland. The Dutch church put out a new catechism for adults in 1966, beginning not with the creed, but with the mystery of existence and contemporary questions about life's meaning and purpose. In 1968, Janaan Manternach and Carl J. Pfeifer authored the *Life, Love, Joy* series (Silver Burdett), the first curriculum for children based on the new process of integrating life and Catholic tradition. Other texts soon followed.

Unlike the earlier catechetical lesson plans, which began with an experience of the students to arouse interest, this new approach viewed the opening experience as part of the actual content of catechesis. The validity of this model of catechesis was affirmed by the Vatican's *General Catechetical Directory* of 1971, and also in the American *National Catechetical Directory* of 1979. By the beginning of the 1980s, this model of catechesis was at the core of mainstream Catholic catechesis.

(d) 1980s–1990s: Context. Up to 1980, all of the developments of the twentieth century catechetical movement assumed a school or classroom setting. Now the question arose: Is the classroom the best context for catechesis? The shifts from concern about method, to content, to process were important growth stages. The gradual shift of emphasis from catechesis of children to the inclusion of youth catechesis, to the present priority concern for adult catechesis, has been necessary and healthy.

Recent catechetical developments do not question these valid developments but focus on the context in which catechesis has been taking place, namely the educational setting of a classroom, be it in school or in homes, whether in parochial school or CCD.

The NCD clearly set catechesis within the ministries of the church, as a form of the pastoral ministry of the Word (30). The ministry of the Word is one part of the church's mission, intimately linked with the ministries of community building, worship, and service. So, while catechesis has an educational, instructional orientation, its home should be less in the school than in the broader world of home, parish, and church. The natural *context* for it is not so much the classroom as the family and parish community. All catechesis needs to be oriented to and integrated with the community and its ministries.

The restoration of the catechumenate, the Rite of Christian Initiation of Adults (RCIA), has become a model for all catechesis. It is a pastoral model of community initiation and growth. The life of the community and its diverse individuals now are seen as both the primary curriculum or catechism and the primary catechist.

In Latin America, the church has come to vibrant new life in small communities of people, most often the poorest and least educated. These small Christian communities are composed of perhaps 20 individuals or families. Their leaders are normally elected by the community. Catechesis takes place as an integral part of the community life and meetings, and is clearly marked by concern for the larger community which the church serves. Such catechesis has therefore a strong dimension of concern for justice and peace. In the United States there is a similar increase in concern among catechists about justice and peace.

When we acknowledge that families and small Christian communities within the parish are the normal context for catechesis, spirituality becomes an important focus. Believers within community are not primarily students, but people struggling to live good Christian lives, sometimes in very difficult and hostile conditions. What they believe needs to find expression in how they live. This is the realm of spirituality, the living out of one's faith. Learning about Catholic beliefs (orthodoxy) needs always to be related to learning how to live that faith (orthopraxis).

Such concerns have led catechists to rediscover the ancient catechetical conviction of the importance of imagination and feeling. People cling together in communities less because of abstract intellectual definitions than for deeply felt convictions and values. Symbols, pictures, poems, songs touch these heart-felt values and convictions, and give moving expression to them. Identity, stability, security, courage, faith, hope, love are communicated through symbol and feelings as well as through ideas and theories.

Interestingly these current developments are fashioning a catechesis that draws on the best catechetical approaches of the Early, Medieval, Modern, and Contemporary periods as we face the new challenges of the 21st century.

Questions for Reflection and Discussion

1. In which period of catechetical history did you receive your own religious education? What do you remember most about it?
2. What dominant threads seem to weave their way through the changing fabric of catechesis over the centuries?

HISTORY OF CATECHESIS

Period	Context	Content

Early Christian (1st–5th centuries)	Home
	Church
	   Sunday Liturgy
	   Catechumenate
		Two Ways
		   Life-Light
		   Death-Darkness
		(Faith) Apostles' Creed
		(Hope) Our Father
		(Love) Law of Love/Ten
		   Commandments
		Biblical Stories
		Liturgical Rites

Medieval (6th–15th centuries)	Home
	Church
	   Popular Devotions
	   Arts
	Catholic Culture
		(Faith) Apostles' Creed
		(Hope) Our Father/Sacraments
		(Love) Law of Love/Ten
		   Commandments
		Stories/Arts
		   Biblical
		   Christian Heroes/Heroines

Modern (16th–19th centuries)	School Classroom	(Faith) Apostles' Creed (Love) Law of Love/Ten Commandments (Hope) Our Father/Sacraments/ Prayer

Contemporary (20th century)
  1900
	School
	Classroom
		(Faith) Apostles' Creed
		(Hope) Our Father/Sacraments/
		   Prayer
		(Love) Law of Love/Ten
		Commandments

1936–1960s	School
	Classroom
	Church
	   Liturgy
		Kerygma/Salvation History
		   Christocentric
		Four Sources: Bible, Liturgy,
		   Doctrine, Witness

1960–1970s	School
	Classroom
	Home/Family
	Church
	   Liturgy
		One Source: God's Word
		   Christocentric
		Four Signs: Natural (Experience)
		   Biblical (Bible)
		   Liturgical (Liturgy)
		   Ecclesial (Doctrine,
		     Creed, Witness)

1980s–1990s	Community of Faith
	Home/Family
	Church
	   Liturgy (RCIA)
	   Service/Action
	School/Classroom
	comunidades eclesiales de base
	World Community
		One Source: God's Word
		   Christocentric
		Four Signs: Natural (Experience)
		   Biblical (Bible)
		   Liturgical (Liturgy)
		   Ecclesial (Doctrine,
		     Creed, Witness)

Process/Method	Catechist's Role	Period

Preaching
Liturgical/Experience,
    Then Explanation
Salvation History
    Biblical Narrative
	Witness to Faith
	Herald of Good News
	Teacher
		Early Christian
		(1st–5th centuries)

Informal Socialization Devotional Practices Cultural Absorption Arts (Architecture, Painting, Sculpture, Music, Drama) Mnemonics (List of "7s")	Witness to Faith Teacher	Medieval (6th–15th centuries)
Catechism Book Memorization of Questions and Answers Explanation	Teacher	Modern (16th–19th centuries)
Catechism Book Lesson Plans Active Methodology	Teacher	Contemporary (20th century) 1900
Biblical Narrative Liturgical Rites Munich Method Active Methodology	Witness to Faith Herald of Good News Teacher	1936–1960s

Integrating Life and
Tradition
Experimental/Discovery
Learning
Active Methodology
	Minister of the Word
	    Prophet
	    Discerning God's Word
	    Witness to Faith
	    Herald of Good News
	    Teacher
		1960–1970s

Integrating Life and
Tradition
Experimental/Discovery
Learning
Active Methodology
 	
Communal Discernment
	Community and Catechists
	Minister of the Word
	    Prophet
	      Discerning God's Word
	      Working to Change the
	      World
	Witness to Faith
	Herald of Good News
	Teacher
		1980s–1990s
		
		This chart is adapted with
		permission from *This Is Our Faith*
		(Silver Burdett & Ginn).

3. Why do you think the church's catechesis has changed so much over the centuries?

4. What previous periods of catechesis seem to find greater resonance in current catechetical trends?

5. What did you learn from the survey of history that you feel would help you be a better catechist?

Ways to Respond

1. Share memories. In many parishes and schools catechists may span a broad number of years, perhaps even generations. It can be very interesting and helpful to gather together to share memories of your own early religious education experiences. Compare the strengths and weaknesses of the catechetical approaches you each experienced as children, youth, and adults. Then talk together about what you have learned that can be helpful to you in your present-day teaching.

2. Study the chart. Take some time to study the chart of catechetical history on pages 24-25. Circle items on the chart that are part of what and how you teach. Put a square around those items that are not part of your teaching style and content. Consider the results. Weigh both sets in the light of the period in which they were strong, and the contemporary situation. Decide which of these many historical items to introduce into or stress more in your teaching, or remove from or stress less.

3. Compare texts. If at all possible, locate one or more religious education text from the past. Many parish or school libraries have copies of the *Baltimore Catechism* and subsequent texts. If you cannot find old texts, gather several different textbooks currently in use. In any case, examine them carefully, comparing their various features. Notice "content," "methodology," "process," and "context" of each. Then try to pinpoint what historical period each most reflects, and what you can learn from each for your own teaching.

PART II

CONTENT OF CATECHESIS:

GOD'S WORD AND ITS SIGNS

5

Content Source: God's Word

> The source of catechesis, which is also its content, is one: God's word, fully revealed in Jesus Christ and at work in the lives of people exercising their faith under the guidance of the magisterium, which alone teaches authentically. God's word deposited in scripture and tradition is manifested and celebrated in many ways: in the liturgy and "in the life of the church, especially in the just and in the saints"; moreover, "in some way it is known, too, from those genuine moral values which, by divine providence, are found in human society." Indeed, potentially at least, every instance of God's presence in the world is a source of catechesis."
>
> *National Catechetical Directory*, 31, 41

"Sticks and stones may break my bones, but words shall never hurt me."

This popular childhood taunt reveals our contemporary Western view of words as harmless and ineffectual, even though we all experience in our young years how hurtful angry, mocking words can be.

Eliza Doolittle in *My Fair Lady* gives classic expression to our need to test and prove our words by corresponding deeds as she challenges her infatuated suitor:

"Words, words, words!...I'm so sick of words....If you're in love...show me!"

Our modern Western tendency to separate words from actions makes it a bit difficult to grasp what is meant by "God's word" in the Bible and in church documents.

Since the *National Catechetical Directory* says catechesis is part of the "ministry of the word" (31-32), and that the source and content of catechesis is "God's word" (31, 41), it is vital for our teaching that we explore the meaning of "God's word."

A Dynamic Word

Coming out of a verbal rather than a print or electronic culture, the biblical writers believed words were powerfully effective. A blessing *made* someone blessed—so much so that Isaac, realizing he had blessed the wrong son, could not retract his blessing of Jacob (Genesis 27). Nor could Jacob revoke his word to marry Leah whom he mistakenly thought to be Rachel (Genesis 29).

In the Semitic world of the ancient Near East, words were considered *dynamic*, flowing from the energy of the person speaking them. Words accomplished what they expressed. They did what they meant. The Hebrew term for "word," *dabar*, means both "action" or "deed," as well as what we normally mean by "word."

What is true of human words is even more evident of God's word. The creation narratives dramatically reveal the creative, dynamic quality of God's word. "Then God *said*, 'Let there be light,' and there *was* light" (Genesis 1:3).

The prophet Isaiah sums up the Hebrew view of God's dynamic word. Included in a beautiful offer of life and love, God says: "So shall my word be that goes forth from my mouth. It shall not return to me void, but shall do my will, achieving the end for which I sent it" (Isaiah 55:11).

The Bible sees God's word as active, concrete, creative, and dynamic. The word *does* something, *effects* something, *brings* something *to be*.

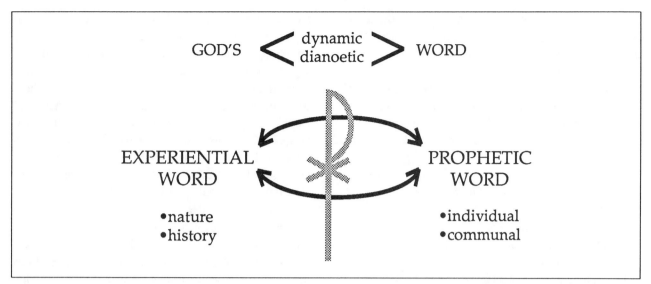

A Revelatory Word

At the same time, a word, whether God's or our own, *says* something, *reveals* something. A word expresses the speaker's inner self. The word, and the word concretized in what it has accomplished, reveals the thoughts and intent of the speaker of the word. For the Semite, a word is both dynamic and *dianoetic* (revelatory).

So, what God's word accomplishes reveals God's mind and heart. The whole of creation is a living parable revealing God's love while making that love present as sacrament. "The heavens declare the glory of God, and the firmament proclaims his handiwork...; Through all the earth their voice resounds, and to the ends of the world, their message (Psalm 19:1-5).

God's dynamic word reveals God's plans, God's innermost thoughts, God's "heart" (see Psalm 33:11). Through what God's word accomplishes, God's word reveals who God is, what God is like, who we are and what we are like. God's word is revelatory (*dianoetic*) as well as dynamic, effective.

Where then does one go to hear God's word? Where is God speaking to us?

An Experiential Word

Because of their understanding of "word," the biblical peoples do not turn first to their "Bibles" or liturgies to hear God's word. They tend to hear God's word in places where we may not at first tend to look—the world around us, social and political events, our daily experiences, our hearts and our history.

The Hebrew slaves in Egypt recognized God's liberating yet binding word in their dramatic escape from Pharaoh's brick factories. The Jewish people have never forgotten that momentous word of freedom and love. In its light they learned to listen for God's word in victories and defeats, in joyful and painful times. Crossing the Jordan, founding a kingdom, experiencing defeat and exile followed by restoration—all these were seen as effective expressions of God's word to them, for them.

As time went on they reflected on new experiences in the light of the past to hear God's word accurately in the present. And in the process they heard more deeply God's past word in the light of what they heard God saying in the present. Contemporary and historical experience, in creative dialogue, revealed God's word more sensitively in both, fusing them into one comforting, challenging word. What God's word accomplished and revealed centuries ago at the Red Sea, God's word continues to do and say today.

Looking back beyond those historical events, the biblical peoples also came to recognize God speaking in events that predated recorded history, like the fall, the flood, and the alienation of peoples from God and one another at Babylon's proud tower.

Within the people's *shared historical experiences*, individuals also recognized God's word in their *personal experiences*, in their very hearts. Abraham amidst success in ancient Ur, Joseph dreaming in Egypt's dungeons, Moses hiding out in the desert, David tending his father's sheep, Ruth choosing to go with her mother-in-law, Naomi, Hosea grappling with his wife's infidelity, Deborah settling disputes as a judge, Rachel meeting Jacob at a well, Rahab entertaining Joshua's spies: these and the rest of the key biblical figures heard God's voice in their experiences and in their hearts.

"It is something very near to you, already in your mouths and in your hearts; you have only to carry it out" (Deuteronomy 30:14/Romans 10:8).

In addition to the people's communal experience of God's word in historical events and personal experiences, the Bible also looks to the *created world* in which we live for echoes of God's word. Biblical writers encounter God's life-giving word in the things around them: women and men, children and the elderly, a kiss, a touch, an embrace, trees and mountains, sun, stars and moon, flower-filled fields and dry deserts, birds and cattle, bread and wine.

> He sends forth his command to the earth;
> swiftly runs his word!
> He spreads snow like wool;
> frost he strews like ashes.
> He scatters his hail like crumbs;
> before his cold the waters freeze.
> He sends his word and melts them;
> he lets his breeze blow and the
> waters run (Psalm 147:15-18).

A Prophetic Word

But how can God's word be recognized in life's ordinary and extraordinary experiences? How know it is God speaking in the escape of slaves from captivity, the infidelity of a spouse, the beauty of a sunset, the power of storm, a lover's kiss, or in a dream or persistent desire?

In the history of God's people it seems that God selects individuals and gifts them with special sensitivity to God's word. Miriam, for example, sang out in the first moments of freedom from Pharaoh's slave-masters that it was God who set them free (Exodus 15:20-21). Moses heard the same divine word of freedom in God's liberating action (Exodus 15:1-18). Somehow God's Spirit attuned them to hear God's freeing word in what others saw simply as a clever escape from oppression.

These gifted individuals are the *prophets*. One of them, Amos, affirms their importance as discerners and speakers of God's word: "Indeed, the Lord God does nothing without revealing his plan to his servants, the prophets" (Amos 3:7-8).

Individual Prophets

The prophets become the chosen interpreters of God's experiential word. They are the privileged hearers of God's word in the world around them. They then share with the people the meaning revealed in their experiences and in world events. God speaks through them. "Thus says the Lord," is the constant refrain of the prophets.

As Miriam and Moses recognized God's word in their escape from Egypt, Moses discerned God's word repeatedly in the desert wanderings despite the people's grumbling incomprehension. Elijah heard God's voice in a gentle breeze on the same mountain where Moses recognized God's word in the midst of lightning and thunder. Samuel read God's word in the face and stature of David, a shepherd boy, to whom the prophet Nathan later spoke God's word of condemnation and promise in view of David's sinfulness. Amos and Hosea spoke God's word of justice in the midst of greed and luxury. Jeremiah heard God's word in the advancing armies of Sennacherib and in the pain of exile in Babylon. And so on until the full revelation of God's word in Jesus. "In times past, God spoke in partial and various ways through the prophets; in these last days, he spoke to us through a son...who sustains all things by his mighty word" (Hebrews 1:1-3).

A Prophetic Community

Over the years the people remembered the more striking words of the prophets. Groups of disciples normally grew up around the prophets themselves or after their deaths. They often gathered together in written form the words of the prophets. Sacred Scriptures developed.

The people heard the Scriptures read in liturgical celebrations. As a result the worshiping community tended to be formed on the words of these inspired spokespersons of the Lord. Slowly the prophetic words of individual prophets became woven into the tradition of the people as a whole.

God's people became a *prophetic people,* learning to hear God's word in their experiences and the world at large in the light of their Scriptures and its traditions of interpretation, and in their family and liturgical worship.

As a people they became better able to discern God's word amidst the mixed words of their world, which in turn opened up new nuances to God's word in their Scriptures. The Psalms remain as a living witness to this process.

A Demanding Word

Finally, the word of God, wherever heard or through whomever spoken, always cuts to the heart, calling for a response. "Indeed, the word of God is living and effective, sharper than any two-edged sword, penetrating even between soul and spirit, joints and marrow, and able to discern reflections and thoughts of the heart" (Hebrews 4:12).

God's word is a word that needs to be heard. It is a word of comfort and grace, an invitation, a challenge, a command. God's word calls for a response. How one responds has serious consequences: life or death. "Choose life, then, that you and your descendants may live, by loving the Lord, your God, heeding his voice, and holding fast to him" (Deuteronomy 30:19-20).

That response ultimately is faith, a personal surrender to and acceptance of the word, leading to appropriate changes of heart and lifestyle—that is, to on-going conversion. Hearing the word of God and doing it is at the core of the covenant and the heart of discipleship.

The New Testament praises the great women and men of faith from Abel up to Jesus (Hebrews 11). Jesus himself lived perfectly that faith response to God's word in his own life (4:1-11; 26:36-39), and pointed it out as the characteristic of his disciples (Luke 8:21). The New Testament singles out Mary as the first and model disciple because of her faithful response to God's word (Luke 1:45; 11:27-28).

A Personal Word

A final nuance in the biblical understanding of God's word is its gradual personification. The personification culminates in the New Testament identification of Jesus Christ as the word of God.

"In the beginning was the Word, and the Word was with God, and the Word was God.... And the Word became flesh and made his dwelling among us, and we saw his glory, the glory of the Father's only Son, full of grace and truth" (John 1:1, 14). For the Christian, then, the response to God's word is ultimately a commitment to Jesus Christ and his way. Jesus *is* God's word.

Ministry of the Word

This brief overview of Judaeo-Christian tradition suggests the richness and centrality of God's word in our lives. It provides also a grounding for catechesis as a "ministry of the word," and for a catechetical spirituality.

If God's dynamic, revelatory word may be heard in the 1) material world of creation, 2) the large and small events of history, 3) personal experiences, and 4) the depths of the human heart, then all those realities are part of the source and content of catechesis and fit within the ministry of God's word. Catechesis then needs to be experiential.

If God's revelatory, dynamic word may be heard as well in the 5) words of individual prophets, perhaps gifted with sensitivity to hearing and interpreting God's word, and 6) in the prophetic sense of the people of God, then catechesis needs to draw upon the prophetic word found in the community's written Scriptures, creeds, doctrines and teachings, as well as in the example and words of prophetic members of the community.

If God's imperative word calls for a response of 7) faith, surrender, commitment, and conversion, then catechesis needs to aim at an ever growing, maturing faith, a continuing conversion.

And if God's dynamic and revelatory word may be heard uniquely in 8) Jesus Christ, the word of God incarnate, then catechesis must center in Jesus Christ and foster a personal relationship with Christ.

It is just such a "theology of the word,"—so briefly and partially summarized here—that is the key to understanding contemporary catechesis and to becoming an effective, creative catechist, a *minister of the word*. The biblical theology of the word provides a rich overview of all that makes up the source and content of catechesis.

Questions for Reflection and Discussion

1. Where do you most readily turn to hear God's word in your own life?

2. What strikes you most in the above summary of the rich meanings of God's word?

3. Why do we tend to think of God's word chiefly in relation to the Bible or church teachings?

4. If all of life is a parable spoken by God, why is it so hard to hear God's word in the confusing voices of our experience?

5. What kinds of challenges do you find for your own teaching in this broad view of God's word as the content of catechesis?

Ways to Respond

1. Look at your textbook. Go quickly but carefully through the catechetical textbook you are using. Compare its content with the rich content suggested by the biblical understanding of God's word. How experiential is it? How attuned is it to contemporary life, students' experiences, as well as the Bible, the church's worship and social action, its doctrines, history and saints? How well does it relate biblical, liturgical, doctrinal teachings with contemporary issues and experiences?

2. Start a journal. Try becoming more sensitive to God's word in your own life and in the world around you by daily jotting in a journal or diary what is happening and how you are thinking, feeling, and acting. Perhaps read a few moments from the Bible after completing your journal entry each day.

3. Check biblical resources. You may wish to trace the riches of this one word in the Bible by looking up "word" or "word of God" in a biblical concordance or Bible dictionary. See Chapter 7, p. 44, for references.

Take your time to savor the meanings of this key biblical term by looking up and reading at least some of the many references to God's word listed in the resource books.

6

Natural Signs: Life and Culture

Its prophetic mission requires that the church, in communion with all people of good will, examine the signs of the times and interpret them in light of the Gospel. Catechesis seeks to teach the faithful to test and interpret all things, including natural signs, in a wholly Christian spirit.

Central human values are expressed in the arts, science, and technology; in family, culture, economic, and social life; in politics and international relations. Catechesis for adults should therefore teach them to evaluate correctly, in light of faith, contemporary cultural and sociological developments, new questions of a religious and moral nature, and the interplay between temporal responsibilities and the church's mission to the world. It must give an intellectually satisfying demonstration of the Gospel's relevance to life. In short, it has the task of examining at the most profound level the meaning and value of everything created, including the products of human effort, in order to show how all creation sheds light on the mystery of God's saving power and is in turn illuminated by it.

National Catechetical Directory, 46

It was missing a piece.
And it was not happy.
So it set off in search
of its missing piece.
And as it rolled
it sang this song—
"Oh I'm lookin' for my missin' piece
I'm lookin' for my missin' piece
Hi-dee-ho, here I go,
Lookin' for my missin' piece."

So begins one of our favorite books written for childlike persons of all ages. *The Missing Piece* is by Shel Silverstein, who wrote the classic book *The Giving Tree*. Both books are profound in their captivating simplicity.

The Missing Piece is about a happy circular being that has a jagged triangular gap in its otherwise circular whole. It senses its incompleteness and sets out in search of the missing piece. Along the way, hampered by its awkward gap, it rolls slowly enough to appreciate such things as sun and snow, rain, worms, flowers, and butterflies. After a long frustrating search over land and sea, valleys, forests, and mountains, it finds its missing piece. At last it is whole, a perfect circle!

But now it finds that it rolls so fast it can no longer enjoy the worms or flowers or butterflies. It cannot even sing anymore. So it gently sets its missing piece down and slowly rolls on, singing once again and noticing the marvelous world around it, continually looking for its missing piece.

Life's Missing Piece

What Shel Silverstein had in mind in creating this beautiful story we can only guess. But his story speaks to what we feel is at the center of our lives, of everyone's life. We are aware, in times of great happiness and satisfaction, as well as in times of frustration and sadness, that there is more to life than those experiences encompass. There is something more to life than the sum total of all its obvious pieces. There is a missing piece for which we are constantly searching. This is what motivates real religion and faith growth—a beguiling experience of God's absent presence.

True religious experience is the constant quest for the missing piece that gives ultimate meaning to life, that brings total peace and joy. Religion—with its doctrines, moral codes, and ritual—can express and stimulate the search, or it can give the illusion of being the missing piece.

Jesus called our awareness of missing something "poverty of spirit" (Matthew 5:3). People who have this gift, he said, are "blest" or "happy." Theirs is God's kingdom. For they are like little children (Matthew 18:1-3; 19:13-14). The "poor in spirit" are those who sense their need of God and other people, who are open, searching, close to other searchers. The only persons Jesus condemned were those who had lost any sense of need, any loving, any desire, any search. In the Book of Revelation Jesus says the "rich" are those who are satisfied that they have all the pieces together (Revelation 3:20).

For Zacchaeus, the little man growing wealthy through graft, who climbed a tree to see Jesus; for the Samaritan woman, living unwed with seven successive men, yet searching for living water; for Nicodemus, whose expert knowledge of religious law never stifled his longing for truth—for all these Jesus found words and gestures of acceptance. All of them found in Jesus the missing dimension of their lives. Only those whose inner quest had been quelled, who no longer felt the pain of a missing piece, who were self-contained and self-satisfied—only these failed to recognize Jesus as their light and life.

Personal Story

We'll never forget a man we met some years ago in a train station. We were waiting for the same train and began chatting as the waiting time got longer and longer. As we talked, he recalled how he had won a gold medal for religion when he graduated from parochial school and had stopped going to church for years afterwards because of the meaninglessness of that gold medal. He explained, "I had a lot of questions. Most of them rose out of my life, which was not easy. While a child, there were always problems at home. So I asked questions out of what was happening to me as they surfaced in my consciousness during catechism class. I believed there had to be some answers there. Sister, seemingly too concerned about covering what was in the catechism, consistently avoided my questions with what was a real answer for her. 'Jimmy,' she'd say, 'that's a very good question, but now we have to deal with the assigned material.' I knew that material and gradually lost all interest. What was happening in our religion classes glossed over my pain and my search. I found myself growing angry and disbelieving. The medal was the final ironic touch and I left the church."

He had learned all the answers, but they had not answered his questions. It is an unusual story, but an in-

structive one. Separated from the real experiences of life and the honest questions that arise from life, correct biblical, liturgical, or doctrinal "answers" may actually thwart the deep inner quest for the missing piece that is the source of true religious growth.

This is not to say that knowing the answers the church has to share from its rich tradition is not important. It is to caution against thinking such knowledge is *of itself* conducive to believing. The genuine doctrinal and moral teachings of the church—which arose out of years of searching by the Christian community in past ages—do not stifle the religious search of faith if they are taught in relation to life. The church's doctrines or "faith" are an accurate but limited naming of an unnameable reality that always opens out to mystery. Every biblical story or church doctrine, while providing insight into life's deepest questions, inevitably opens up new questions.

The real danger is that religious knowledge or practice becomes the missing piece that closes us off to the wonders of God in other people, in the sun and clouds, the rain, worms, flowers, and butterflies—to the mystery of life in all that surrounds us. Then the song dies, the search ends, and God is closed out.

Catechesis and Life

The basic call to those of us who are religious educators is to share our faith tradition in such a way that it opens people rather than closes them to life's mystery. The teachings of the church need to be learned in relation to the questions of life—to the actual experiences of the adults, youth, and children we teach. Life experiences, contemporary issues, basic values, significant questions, personal and social happenings—all of these must be seen as an important integral part of catechesis. For faith will be alive only to the extent that it arises out of and speaks meaningfully to people's growing experience. Catechesis is an engagement in the faith-process of looking at life in the light of one's tradition and exploring that tradition in the light of one's experience. Catechesis relates our stories with the great Story that is cherished by the Christian community.

For example, we believe in "creation." We teach "creation" as a doctrine of the church, and find creation running as a thread through the whole Bible. We believe that the creator is acting and sharing with us in the world around us and within us. If we really believe in creation, however, we will foster a growing appreciation of all that exists, a deepening sense of wonder at life's beauties and tragedies, a profound questioning of life's puzzles and probing of its mysteries. In other words, life

EXPERIENTIAL CATECHESIS

NATURAL
SIGNS

BIBLICAL SIGNS
LITURGICAL SIGNS
ECCLESIAL SIGNS

Life & Culture

Catholic Tradition

itself—if we take seriously the doctrine of creation (and even more so that of the incarnation)—is in a real sense sacramental. Human experience can reveal God's hidden presence and allow us to come into closer contact with the risen Christ.

Teilhard de Chardin, a Jesuit archaeologist, simply reminded us in his writings of what Saint Paul long before had written to the Roman Christians (Romans 1:19-20), namely, that life is a "divine milieu," that the invisible God may be caught sight of in the visible world, that human experience participates in the mystery of God. The world is full of significant experiences that open out to the mystery of God: joy and sorrow, birth and death, good and evil.

Pope John XXIII did much to remind theologians and religious educators of the religious importance of daily experience and contemporary culture. He spoke frequently of learning to read the "signs of the times." By this he meant that we need to look closely at what is happening in our world as well as in our personal lives to discern or discover the presence of the Lord and the guidance of the Spirit.

Jesus himself, long before John XXIII, used the same term. He challenged a group of religious leaders looking for a sign with the question, "Can you not read the signs of the times?" (Matthew 16:3).

Vatican Council II took up Pope John's terminology. The Bishops point to God's presence in the "signs of the times," which includes all the "happenings, needs, and desires" of people of our age (*Church in the Modern World*, 11). They teach that the "Church has always had the duty of scrutinizing the signs of the times and of interpreting them in the light of the Gospels" (4).

Using a similar expression the Council urges all

members of the church "to hear, distinguish, and interpret the many voices of our age, and to judge them in the light of the divine Word" (44).

What these terms refer to is the full realm of contemporary experience, personal and cultural. *"Signs of the times"* and *"voices of our age"* embrace all that is of human and secular value in our individual and social lives. Our individual, personal "signs" and "voices" are recognizable in the mystery of our own experiences: joys, sorrows, questions, loves, successes, failures, work, vacations, relationships, dreams, frustrations, and opportunities. In our contemporary world, the Council points to such experiences and values as the dignity of the human person, the community of all human beings, science and technology, family, economic and social life, the arts, business, politics, and international relations.

Looking for Seeds

Another related term used by the Council is *"seeds of the Word."* The Council indicates that the church in missionary countries must closely identify itself with the social and cultural conditions of the people among whom it exists (*Missions*, 10). Such identification is grounded in Catholic belief in the incarnation. Using language from the ancient Fathers of the Church, the council speaks of discovering "seeds of the Word" in varied national and religious traditions (*Missions*, 11). The Word, of course, is Jesus Christ. The implication is that signs of his presence are already in the native culture even before missionary activity begins. The first task of the missionary is to discover these signs, to lay bare these seeds. That means approaching another culture with deep respect.

The suggestive term "seeds of the Word" dates back to

the time when the very young, mostly Hebrew church grappled with how the Gospel message could be expressed in the dominant Greek culture of the Roman Empire. Bishops and laity alike struggled to discover in the art, literature, philosophy, and religious traditions of Athens and Rome indications of God's presence because they found much truth, goodness, and beauty in the Graeco-Roman culture. They spoke of those cultural values as "seeds of the Word" that would come to full flower in the knowledge and love of Jesus Christ, the Word Incarnate.

The Second Vatican Council recaptures these early insights—often lost in later church history. Any expression of truth, goodness, or beauty in human culture is "a sort of secret presence of God" (Missions, 9). The task for all of us is to search out this hidden presence and lay bare these fruitful seeds.

Catechesis and Culture

Appreciation of human culture does not apply just to missionary situations. In other documents, the Council broadens its awareness to include the appreciation of beauty, truth, and goodness in one's own culture. An entire chapter of the document on the Church in the Modern World is devoted to the interaction of church and culture. Laity and clergy alike are repeatedly urged to respond to all that is of genuine value in their contemporary world and in their own particular cultural traditions. In them they are to work at discerning or discovering the presence of God. The catechist's task is to help in this process of discernment.

To lay bare the seeds of the Word lying hidden in our own cultural values and patterns is one of the major challenges of the catechist. Catechesis is a catalyst bringing faith and culture into creative dialogue. The catechist—whether a parent, religion teacher, priest, or bishop—has a responsibility to foster a positive appreciation of all that is good, beautiful, and true in one's own culture, as well as in other cultures.

Such positive appreciation, of course, needs to be joined with critical judgment. Not every aspect of our own or of foreign cultures is necessarily good. Some aspects of every culture are expressions of human sinfulness rather than "seeds of the Word." Every culture reveals the hidden power of evil as well as the secret presence of God. It is important that catechesis involve a critique of cultural values in the light of the Gospel—as well as an appreciation of them.

Challenge to Catechists

Catechists face the challenging task of helping children, youth, and adults fill in the missing pieces of life, to discover the one who alone gives wholeness and meaning. Catechists want to help people find answers from Catholic tradition to the questions of life. This involves an understanding of the church's rich tradition: doctrines, liturgy, scripture, and inspiring witness. As Catholics, we believe that within the living tradition of the church lies the key to making sense out of life's ambiguity.

But we also believe that daily life, with its ambiguity as well as its clarity, speaks of God and speaks to the church with its rich tradition. Our task, therefore, is to encourage wonder at the whole of life—its ugliness as well as its beauty, to support an open, questioning attitude, to share the vision that God's presence in life makes it sacramental. Life's mysteries, no less than the mysteries of the church (which developed in response to coping with human experience) can never be fully defined or solved. Life and doctrine are always open to deeper insight and development through their conscious interaction.

As catechists—at home or in school—we are called to look with interest and excitement at what all the doctrines and rituals are really about, a marvelous, mysterious God who never tires of surprising us through the joys and jolts of daily living. The *National Catechetical Directory* calls life's experiences and values "natural signs" of God's presence. God's presence, as well as his absence, can be sensed through photos and fairy tales as well as through stained glass windows and Gospel stories; through a warm shower as well as through the waters of Baptism; through the pain of suffering as well as the oil of anointing; through the struggle to love as well as the sacrament of Matrimony; through family dinners as well as through the Eucharistic meal; through the questions of life as well as the answers of doctrine.

"Natural signs" are necessarily clothed in particular cultures. So Pope John Paul II urges catechists to become more sensitive to the culture in which they live and the cultures of those with whom they work. Referring to the importance of "acculturation" or "inculturation" in catechesis, the Pope writes in his 1979 *Apostolic Exhortation on Catechesis:* "Catechesis will seek to know these cultures and their essential components; it will learn their most significant expressions; it will respect their particular values and riches. In this manner it will be able to offer these cultures the knowledge of the hidden mystery and help them to bring forth from their own living tradition original expressions of Christian life, celebration and thought." (53)

Our task is to help people find life's missing pieces through the living tradition of the church—while never giving the illusion that the church or its tradition is the ultimate missing piece. Only God is that, whose presence also creates a sense of absence. "Unless you had already found me, you would not be looking for me." Security in God's love stimulates a song-filled search for our ultimate missing piece.

Oh, I'm lookin' for my missin' piece
I'm lookin' for my missin' piece
Hi-dee-ho, here I go,
Lookin' for my missin' piece.

Questions for Reflection and Discussion

1. How and where do you most experience God in your life?

2. What do you feel opens a person to the mystery of life? What tends to close a person?

3. How can religion stifle our quest for God? How can religion stimulate that search?

4. What biblical or church teachings really speak to your life? What teachings of the church seem unrelated to your life? What seems to make the difference?

5. What do you most look for in the church and its teachings: a sense of security, encouragement in your search, answers, or good questions? Why?

6. What aspects of American culture do you feel most reveal the presence of God in our midst and most open us to the mystery of God's hidden presence? What aspects of our culture do you find doing just the opposite?

Ways to Respond

1. Study your textbook. Take the student's edition of the textbook series you are using. Look through it for every sign of ordinary experience: photos, poems, stories, etc. Try to get a feel for why your text makes the use it does of these life experiences. Notice if and how the life experiences are related to the doctrinal teaching. Focus on one unit or one lesson to see more clearly how daily life and church teaching are interrelated. Study the structure of a lesson plan. Compare your findings with those expressed in the chapter. This may be more interesting if done in teams.

2. Consider graced moments. Reflect on your own life experience. What are some recent moments in which you felt God's presence or action in your life? What was the occasion? What happened? Who was involved? Expand your reflection to the span of your lifetime. What were critical turning points, peak experiences, significant moments? Think about them.

How do you experience God's presence and action, caring and guidance, in your life? Jot down your reflections. If possible, do this with other catechists, sharing the fruits of your reflection. Compare your experiences and try to come up with a group listing of your own "signals of transcendence."

3. Discuss signs of the times. Pope John popularized the term "signs of the times," used by Jesus in the Gospels (Matthew 16:4). Vatican Council II took up the term, and since the Council it has been used frequently to describe indications of God's presence and guidance in the happenings, trends, and developments in the contemporary world. (See *Church in World,* 4 and 11, and "voices of our age" in 44, 53, and 62. See also "seeds of the word," in the *Decree on Missionary Activity,* 11.)

Individually or in small teams list modern developments that you feel might be "signs of the times" in the positive sense that Pope John and the Council used it.

To make your search more realistic, work with assorted newspapers and magazines as resources. To make your lists more attractive and meaningful, create collages or posters entitled "signs of the times." Instead of newspapers and magazines, collections of slides might be the resource for creating a slide-sound collage with the same title.

In the process of the work, look up the texts cited above from the Gospel and the Council documents. Parts of these texts could be incorporated in the creative lists.

4. Look at American culture. Adapt the previous activity so that you focus on typical expressions of our North American culture. Look especially for strongly positive aspects of our way of life, values, and national beliefs, our social, economic, political, and artistic expressions. Likewise look for the shadow side of our country's present-day culture. Create some form of media expression of these two sides of contemporary North American culture.

Compare what you find with positive and negative aspects of other cultures represented in your own family or in others in your parish.

BIBLICAL SIGNS: SCRIPTURE

> Catechesis studies Scripture as a source inseparable from the Christian message. It seeks ways to make the biblical signs better understood, so that people may more fully live the message of the Bible.
>
> Catechesis encourages people to use the Bible as a source and inspiration for prayer. It fosters informed participation in the liturgy by helping people recognize biblical themes and language which are part of the readings and sacramental rites. It reflects constantly on the biblical signs in order to penetrate their meaning more deeply.
>
> *National Catechetical Directory,* 43

Jim is a good friend. He recently told us about a very difficult personal decision he is facing. He is torn between two attractive possibilities for his future and has been in an agony of indecision.

Not long ago, he began keeping a journal, thinking this might help him discern the more prudent choice. Each evening, he spends 15 minutes writing whatever seems most significant of that day's happenings and feelings. At the end of each week, he reviews his journal to discern any patterns or clues.

On a recent visit, Jim shared his journal with us. It was a fascinating mixture of entries. Very ordinary happenings, like trouble with the car, were noted. So too were a wide range of feelings—anger at a friend, longing for affection, anxiety about his decision, and frustration. Some were descriptions; others were prayers. Bible texts were sprinkled throughout the journal entries.

We asked Jim about the surprising incidence of Scripture texts. He explained that along with keeping a journal, he had been reading a prayer book that was made up largely of biblical texts. He said that the biblical passages really spoke to him in his painful situation. He used them for prayer as he tried to arrive at his pending decision. He found that he would remember the biblical words during the day. It was perfectly natural then at night to weave them into his journal.

We talked about that at some length. He was finding that the Bible spoke to his situation. Biblical texts at times expressed his anxiety and anger, at other times his longing for peace, or his yearning for light and guidance. He found in the Bible a source of meaning and hope. He was discovering new meaning in some of the familiar texts he had heard often before. The scriptures seemed to touch a deep chord in his own heart. He sensed a harmony between his experience and the biblical words.

A New Experience

For Jim, this harmony between his life and the Bible was something of a new experience. He had been familiar with Bible stories learned as a child along with the catechism. He knew the more common Gospel stories heard year after year at Sunday Mass. He had picked up some facts about the Bible in college courses. But up till now the Bible had held little meaning for his everyday life.

Jim's experience is no longer as exceptional as when he first shared with us his journal. Thousands of Catholics in our country have been finding new meaning for their lives in the Bible. Some have discovered the wisdom and power of the Scriptures much as Jim did through personal reflection, reading, and writing. Others have found new meaning in the Bible through participation in study groups or prayer groups of various kinds. In Third World countries hundreds of thousands of often impoverished peasants discover their personal dignity and social responsibilities by reflecting on their harsh lives in the light of the Bible. In the process they find their Catholic faith deepened, enriched, and challenged to mature.

The way Jim and millions more Catholics are approaching the Bible—whether explored individually or in a group—suggests a helpful model for the use of the Bible in catechesis. Their experience focuses attention on what is at the heart of an effective biblical catechesis: a prayerful search for meaning in one's life. Catechesis at times seems overly occupied with facts about the Bible—literary forms, historical origins, authorship of various books, types of biblical criticism. All such background is valuable and at times essential for understanding scriptural texts. But in terms of catechesis, such factual knowledge remains an aid to something more basic: the search for life's meaning through the Bible. Our more vital objective is to help people come to know the Bible as a source for meaning for their lives. Jim and others had taken courses, but now they had come to experience the Bible itself.

Why? What clues can we find in their experience to guide us as catechists and parents? We think there are at least three very helpful principles suggested by recent experience:

1. There needs to be *direct contact* with the Bible itself in relation to one's own life. Jim's approach was not speculative but practical and experiential. His journal immediately related the biblical insights with his daily experience.

2. The Bible and people's own life search are best joined in a context of *prayer*.

3. While individual exploration of the Bible and one's life experience is desirable, and in Jim's case very fruitful, a shared exploration in a small learning, praying *community* can enrich each one's personal reflection and prayer with the experiences and insights of others.

If the Bible is to become a meaningful guide, it needs to be approached in close relation to real life experiences. The most practical and basic approach to its use individually or in a group is one that allows for firsthand experience with it through personal readings, study, and prayer on the part of the catechist. The Scriptures—as

Jesus himself reminds us (Luke 24:44)—are an irreplaceable way of getting to know Jesus himself. And Christ is the heart of the matter for the teacher of religion.

With that realization in mind, we might take a moment to ask ourselves some honest questions:

• What should our personal attitude toward Scripture be?

• Do we read the Bible at all? Regularly?

• Do we honestly believe that without Scripture we are seriously hindered in coming to know Jesus better? In coming to know better the meaning of our lives?

• To what extent can we honestly say that the Bible nourishes our faith, is a source of prayer, or helps us better grasp and grapple with the mysteries of life?

• Do we ever turn to the Bible for encouragement, guidance, illumination, or comfort?

Questions like these might be the place to begin in an attempt to improve our relationship with God's Word. Unless the Bible is a functional part of our lives, we will be hard put to convince our students that the Bible can be an important part of theirs. Therefore, our first suggestion for better use of the Bible is for the catechist to explore God's book firsthand by reading parts of it regularly and trying to relate it to daily life.

It may be helpful, and at times necessary, to turn to guide books to grasp the meaning of some of the texts. A warning though: Resist the temptation to replace actual reading of the Bible with reading about it from other sources.

Use Textbooks and Lectionary

Another way of making Scripture more a part of life and catechesis is to use religion textbooks and the Lectionary as guides. Going through and charting, lesson by lesson, and/or Sunday by Sunday, the scriptural passages suggested for use throughout the year is very helpful. The chart makes it possible to see the primary focus at a glance.

Then study, alone or with others, and pray over each passage or story during the time preceding the teaching of the lesson. You may soon notice that the scriptural texts find a growing place in your consciousness and also in your own daily life. You may begin to notice that the Scriptures touch down on everyday living. In this way, your preparation for teaching becomes an integral part of your own growth and personal appreciation of the Bible as a source of meaning and hope in ordinary living.

A friend of ours shared with us a helpful approach that you might use with the particular passage(s) you are reading and will be teaching. Her approach has five steps, each beginning with a P: Prepare, Picture, Ponder, Pray, Promise.

Here's how it works if a lesson uses the story of the Prodigal Son, for example. First *prepare* by putting work and worries aside to become still and quiet.

Next, read the passage and *picture* the scene visually. Project in imagination the people involved, seeing what each is doing, hearing what each is saying, perhaps finding an art masterpiece that depicts the event and looking at it for a long time.

Next *ponder* or mull over the event, noticing what feelings the story evokes and questioning what it means in terms of daily life. Part of pondering may be to consult a guide or commentary or any background provided in the textbook.

Now *pray* about the things read, pictured, and pondered. Allow thoughts and affections to bring you into communion with a loving and caring God and then be silent so God can communicate with you.

In the final step, *promise* to do something about what you have seen and heard through the story. You make God's Word yours by translating it into a concrete attitude or action.

A Context of Prayer

The suggestion above, like Jim's journal approach and group methods, encourage catechists to approach the Bible as a source of insight into life's meaning within a context of prayer. We believe the Bible is the Word of God expressed in human words. We believe that God continues to speak to us through the Bible if we approach it with open minds and hearts and read it in an honest search for insight into the mystery of life. The natural environment for reading it is a prayerful environment.

When you use the Bible actively in your own life, you are ready to think more practically of how to guide your students to a similar engagement. The better textbook programs provide a sound structure for relating the Bible to everyday life in a way that is faithful to the text itself and faithful to contemporary life.

For example, the story of Abraham is not just a fascinating saga of an ancient desert nomad seeking a more settled existence. It is the story of every human being struggling to trust, to let go, to move from the security of the known into the fearful unknown. Over and over again the theme of trust is orchestrated in the Bible in new situations.

So, too, with Moses. The story of his leading the Hebrews from slavery to freedom finds echoes in every struggle for freedom—in each heart, in every home, in every community, in all areas of socio-political life. Throughout the Bible the exodus becomes reinterpreted as it is tested against new experiences in people's lives. It becomes a key theme woven like a thread through the entire biblical fabric, providing rich insights into the meaning of freedom.

Goals and Priorities

As we engage our students and ourselves in this process of integrating Bible and daily experience, it helps to establish certain goals and priorities. It is too tempting to remain on a superficial level of curious facts and details. Among important goals are the following:

1. Foster reverence and acquire skills. Vital in approaching the Bible is a sense of reverence for it as a medium of God's Word. The Bible is a special book. We foster this in our children by how we hold it, carry it in procession, enthrone it, kiss it, read from it. Reverence is critical if we have any expectation of approaching the more important goals of biblical catechesis.

Also necessary are certain basic skills. These vary with age and education. Basic skills include listening and reading, locating texts, using the notes and helps printed in good Bibles. Again, this goal is critical for achieving the more important goals.

2. Experience content. Given the proper reverence and necessary skills, we engage ourselves and our students with a biblical story, quotation, or prayer. We need to experience it as well as just know it, feel it, enter into it, imagine it. Gradually we want ourselves and those we teach to become familiar with the basic content of the Scriptures—the key events, themes, stories, and prayers.

3. Absorb the background. To understand the biblical content often requires accurate knowledge of back-

ground. For example, when did the Exodus happen, where are Nazareth and Jerusalem, who were the Pharisees or publicans, when, why, and for whom was each Gospel written? Such knowledge may be necessary to get into the biblical text, but it is itself quite secondary to more important goals.

4. Discover meaning. Much more important is the meaning of the biblical text in relation to the meaning of one's life. The meaning of the story of Ruth, for example, is fully grasped only when her story speaks to my story, our story. The deeper meanings of the Bible are all about life's meaning.

5. Find a way of life. The Bible not only sheds light on our life, but can help us learn to live happily in response to God's Word. From encountering the Bible we can learn a lifestyle grounded in God's values and Jesus' example.

6. Develop a relationship. Ultimately the goal of biblical catechesis is to help us grow in our relationship with God who speaks to us through Jesus in fellowship with the Spirit. The innermost core of the Bible has to do with God's Word, personally addressed to each of us, inviting each to respond with faith and love.

Helps and Hints

With these goals in mind, and trusting in the sound structure of textbook programs, with their careful rela-

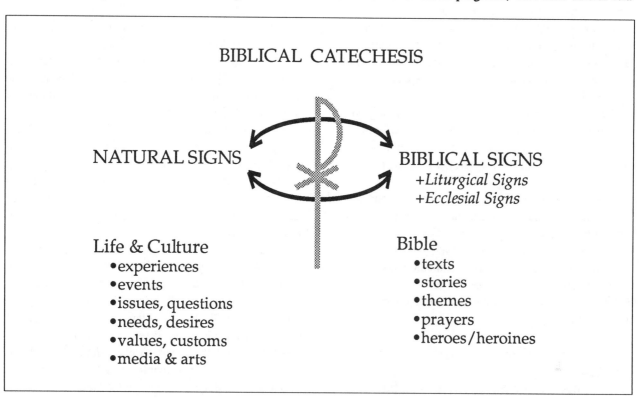

BIBLICAL CATECHESIS

NATURAL SIGNS

BIBLICAL SIGNS
+Liturgical Signs
+Ecclesial Signs

Life & Culture
• experiences
• events
• issues, questions
• needs, desires
• values, customs
• media & arts

Bible
• texts
• stories
• themes
• prayers
• heroes/heroines

tion of life themes and biblical themes, you can find many practical ways of fostering a more meaningful, prayerful engagement with the Scriptures. We would like to share here a few that appeal to us (in addition to the five-part plan already discussed).

1. A reverent attitude Just the way people handle the Bible and read from it is significant. A genuine reverence conveys without words a sense of its importance and value. Enthroning the Bible before or during class may further symbolize the Bible's reality as God's Word to us. Lighting a candle before or beside the Bible (where this is not forbidden by fire laws) may add further to a sense of reverence as well as symbolize our belief that it is Jesus who speaks to us through it.

2. Sacred art One of the most helpful approaches to drawing youngsters and adults into Bible stories is the use of good sacred art. Since Christian art spans 20 centuries and the entire globe, its use helps us to realize how meaningful it has been in people's lives in every age and place. The variety of artistic depictions reveals how various people understood and responded to the Bible. Good reproductions of professional art may be found in many libraries and art museums, in art books, in magazines, and in many churches (stained glass windows, paintings, sculpture). A fine source by mail is the National Gallery of Art in Washington, D.C., which has reproductions of great art at very reasonable prices.

3. Photographs The intimate link between life and the Bible can be fostered with photographs. Students can be challenged to find biblical texts that provide appropriate captions for photographs. Or Bible passages may be selected with the challenge to find photographs that meaningfully relate to them. Or a Gospel parable could be selected and the students challenged to create a contemporary counterpart using photos and their own words.

4. Dramatization Students could be encouraged to dramatize a Bible story or the meaning of a biblical text. They might create a contemporary version conveying the same message as the story.

5. Visualization Many creative forms of visualization can prove very helpful: simply drawing the Bible story or its meaning; creating a collage to bring out its meaning; a slide-sound presentation; a simulated TV show, using long paper pulled through a box with a "screen" cut in its front; staging a biblical scene or its present day counterpart; photographing a scene to make a slide of it; making filmstrips, films, or videotapes.

6. Music A rich resource is music. Not only are there hymns based on psalms and other biblical prayers, but there are dozens of songs and hymns based on biblical texts and Bible stories, like the black spirituals and Protestant Gospel hymns. Some contemporary rock and rap echo biblical themes and stories.

7. Newspapers and magazines The news media provide a steady source of materials related to biblical places, archeology, and contemporary events taking place in biblical lands.

8. Journal Perhaps we can conclude by recommending the approach we noted at the beginning, namely journal keeping. Just as Jim kept a journal and learned to relate the Bible to his life, so, too, our students should be encouraged to keep a daily journal to record their reflections on God's Word in relation to their own life experiences.

As catechists, we face the challenge of turning to the Bible ourselves in a prayerful search for life's meaning and then of guiding our students in a similar search. Jim's experience and that of millions of Catholics in the First and Third World suggest how fruitful such a search can be.

Questions for Reflection and Discussion

1. Have you ever found the kind of resonance with the Bible and your life that Jim experienced through his journal? What was it like? What were the circumstances?

2. To what extent do you agree or disagree that biblical catechesis is effective within a prayerful search for meaning in one's life?

3. What obstacles do you find to greater involvement on your part with the Bible?

4. What do you think of the way the Bible is used in your textbook or religion program? Why?

5. What methods have you found most effective in helping your students appreciate the Bible in relation to their lives?

6. What would you like most or feel you need most as a help to more effective use of the Bible in your religious education work?

Helps in Using the Bible

1. To study the biblical texts:

"Study editions" of good translations provide a wealth of helps. One of these may meet your needs. *The Catholic Study Bible* [New American Bible] (Oxford University Press, 1990); *The New Oxford Annotated Bible with the Apocrypha* [New Revised Standard Version] (Oxford University Press, 1991); *The New Jerusalem Bible* (Doubleday, 1985). For a Third World flavor see: *Christian Community Bible* (Claretian Publications, 1988).

2. To find a particular story or quotation when you remember only a word:

Nelson's Complete Concordance of the New American Bible, ed. Fr. Stephen J. Hartdegen (Liturgical Press, 1977). *QuickVerse 2.0* [computer software concordance in your choice of translations] (Parsons Technology, 1990).

3. To find the meaning of a name, place, symbol, object, word, or theme:

The Dictionary of the Bible by John L. McKenzie, S.J. (Macmillan, 1967) or *Dictionary of Biblical Theology* by Xavier Leon-Dufour (Seabury, 1977).

4. To compare Gospel stories:

Gospel Parallels: A Synopsis of the First Three Gospels by Burton H. Throckmorton, Jr. (Thomas A. Nelson, 1979). *Let Each Gospel Speak for Itself* by Rhys Williams (Twenty-Third Publicatons, 1989).

5. To find background information and interpretation of biblical texts:

The Collegeville Bible Commentary (Liturgical Press, 1989). *The New Jerome Biblical Commentary* (Prentice-Hall, 1990). *How to Read the Old Testament* by Etienne Charpentier (Crossroad, 1982), and his *How to Read the New Testament* (Crossroad, 1984).

6. To find the location of a biblical place:

Collegeville Bible Study Atlas (Liturgical Press, 1990) or the *Atlas of the Bible Lands* (Hammond, 1984).

Ways to Respond

1. Study your textbook. After carefully studying the principles in this chapter, examine your textbook or program, and consider the use of the Bible in it.

Begin with the student's book. Examine the way the Bible is presented—in words and in art. Consider how the biblical material is related to the life experiences under consideration. Are you happy with the biblical presentation? Why? Why not?

Then look at the teacher's manual, particularly the lesson plans. Again examine how the Bible is used in relation to the experience, the aim, and the activities of the lesson. Evaluate to what extent it is used in accord with the principles sketched in this article. Question yourself as to how realistic its use seems to be, how appropriate and motivating the biblical materials are to the capacities of those you are teaching. Consider, too, to what extent the Bible is suggested for use in prayer.

This examination of the program being used may be done individually or in small working teams.

2. Use photo language. An interesting way to explore the relation between the Bible and daily life is through photographs. Many variations of the following two approaches may be worked out.

• Begin with a biblical text, preferably a brief one of just a few lines. Then search for one or more photographs (in magazines, newspapers, etc.) that illustrate the biblical quote. The photo might then be mounted on cardboard and the biblical text written below it in the form of a caption.

• Begin with photographs. They may be symbolic or realistic, or a mixture of the two. Search for the most appropriate biblical text you can find to interpret the photo. Then mount the two together. After the photos and biblical texts have been found, they may be shared and discussed with other catechists. The discussion should focus on the relation of the Bible to significant life experiences. A display of the photos and their biblical captions could be created and displayed in the church or school so that the entire parish might share it.

3. Pray and meditate. Several biblical texts on God's Word can provide fruitful material for an extended period of group prayer and meditation. For example, among many others you may wish to use are 2 Timothy 3:15-17 and Romans 15:1-6. Read the texts in silence. Then read them aloud. More silence. Follow the silent meditation with sharing of reflections. Close with spontaneous prayer and/or a hymn.

LITURGICAL SIGNS: WORSHIP

The liturgy and sacraments are the supreme celebration of the paschal mystery. They express the sanctification of human life. As efficacious signs which mediate God's saving, loving power, they accomplish the saving acts which they symbolize. In and through the sacramental rites above all, Christ communicates the Holy Spirit to the church.

There is a close relationship between catechesis and liturgy. Both are rooted in the church's faith, and both strengthen faith and summon Christians to conversion, although they do so in different ways. In the liturgy the church is at prayer, offering adoration, praise, and thanksgiving to God, and seeking and celebrating reconciliation. As for catechesis, it prepares people for full and active participation in liturgy (by helping them understand its nature, rituals, and symbols) and at the same time flows from liturgy, inasmuch as, reflecting upon the community's experiences of worship, it seeks to relate them to daily life and to growth in faith.

National Catechetical Directory, 44, 113

Janine and her family had moved into the neighborhood just a few weeks earlier. She was still getting adjusted to her new fifth-grade classmates. Then one day Janine excitedly told the class that she had a new baby brother. Everyone became interested. Talking about her baby brother made her feel much more at home.

Someone asked about the baby's baptism. That question sparked further interest. The youngsters wanted to be involved. They began thinking up all kinds of plans for celebrating little Joel's baptism.

With Janine's parents' consent and with their teacher's guidance, the youngsters worked hard at preparing the baptismal celebration. They planned a procession with altar servers in white robes, carrying candles. Hymns were selected and practiced. The youngsters worked in teams, each team taking responsibility for one aspect of the celebration. They gave periodic progress reports in which they shared not only what they were doing, but what it meant to them. When plans were complete, they made a booklet to be used at the baptism and then kept as a souvenir.

Saturday afternoon finally arrived, the day of Joel's baptism. The fifth-graders were intimately involved in every part of the rite. They sang. They processed. They responded to the ritual questions. They professed their faith, renewing their own baptismal promises. Afterwards, they shared in a party with the parents and friends who had participated in the baptism. Janine's parents let each of her classmates hold Joel, something they did with reverent care. "It was a very happy day—a day to remember," wrote the youngster's catechist, Sr. Mary Adele Shea, S.S.N.D.

We were impressed with Sr. Shea's description as we recently reread it. It suggests a helpful model for liturgical catechesis. What we like about it is that it shows such a clear relationship between catechesis, liturgy, and life. In some respects, the experience of those fifth-graders seemed made to order for the study of baptism with the arrival of Janine's baby brother. On the other hand, it was the catechist's sensitivity that allowed the happy event to enter into the realm of her catechesis. Catechesis, liturgy, and life blended into a meaningful, memorable experience because of Sr. Shea's sensitivity to the relationship among all three.

Careful Blending

The key to good liturgical catechesis lies precisely in the careful blending of these three elements of *catechesis,*

liturgy, and *life.* Of the three, the most important is life. As Catholic Christians, we believe all of life is graced by the presence and activity of Jesus Christ and his Spirit. The whole of life, therefore, is a more basic "sacrament" than all the liturgical sacraments. Nature, happenings, experiences—and especially people—all are signs or sacraments revealing the gracious presence of Jesus Christ. Openness to the sacramentality of daily life underlies meaningful appreciation of the church's liturgy. The profoundest of all liturgy is that of faithful living. "The fact is," writes Saint Paul, "that whether you eat or drink—whatever you do—you should do all for the glory of God" (1 Corinthians 10:31).

Liturgy is meaningful insofar as it celebrates what is experienced in daily life. In celebrating Christ's presence in the eucharist, for example, we are really celebrating his presence with us always. The eucharistic community finds its roots in the experience of community that precedes and follows the liturgical celebration. The sacrament of reconciliation celebrates the ever-available forgiveness of an always-merciful parent who forgives through friends and neighbors as well as through the priest. Anointing the sick recalls and celebrates the fact that the healing Christ is with us in our daily grappling with diminishment and death.

Liturgy is not its own focal point; it is a prism revealing the rich but hidden colors of daily experience. Good liturgy always arises out of and flows back into the day to day experiences of life, which are themselves sacramental. Janine and her classmates' experience reflects this healthy realism. They were encouraged to experience some of the wonder and joy of new life, and the discomfort of being an outsider. Both aspects of life lie behind the baptismal initiation into new life and a new community. The party and the holding of the infant insured that the liturgical experience culminated in a return to the mystery and joy of everyday living.

Just as meaningful liturgy rests on growing appreciation of life as liturgy, so effective liturgical catechesis depends on experiencing good liturgies. In earlier centuries of the church's life, catechesis took place not in classrooms but in the context of the liturgical celebration itself. The Christians did not have catechisms or textbooks about the sacraments. They experienced the Eucharist and other sacraments, during and after which catechesis took place. The catechesis interpreted and explained what the people had experienced in the liturgy as a celebration of life's mystery. Worship was the norm not only of doctrine *(lex orandi lex credendi:* as you pray, so you believe) but of catechesis as well.

In more recent times, catechesis has sometimes become separated from liturgy. Catechesis has tended to center more on catechetical books, programs, and media within instructional settings. There is a built-in hazard to such an approach, namely that catechesis will remain on a verbal, conceptual, academic, abstract level, cut off from its vital and direct links with liturgy and life. There is often a wide gap between catechetical language, liturgical experience, and daily life. Fortunately, the restoration of both the Rite of Christian Initiation for Adults

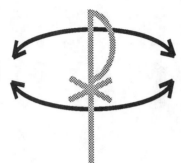

LITURGICAL CATECHESIS

NATURAL SIGNS

LITURGICAL SIGNS
+Biblical Signs
+Ecclesial Signs

Life & Culture

- experiences
- sense of mystery
- sensitivity to symbolism
- poetic sense
- imagination
- creativity
- sense of community

Liturgy/Worship

- sacraments
- liturgy of hours
- sacramentals
- symbols
- rituals
- devotions
- feasts and seasons

and lectionary-catechesis have restored essential links between catechesis, liturgy, and life.

Again, the experience of Janine and her classmates is instructive. Not only did their baptismal involvement keep them in touch with basic life experiences, but their catechesis about life's mystery and about baptism was intimately involved with the liturgical celebration itself.

The vital blending of catechesis, liturgy, and life would seem to be best accomplished in three important moments or stages: *before, during,* and *after* the liturgical celebration.

Before Liturgy

Prior to the actual experience of sacramental liturgy, whether it is the eucharist, penance, confirmation, marriage, holy orders, or anointing of the sick or baptism, catechesis has an important part to play. But its role in preparation for the sacraments is much broader than may at first be thought.

Catechetical preparation for intelligent liturgical participation is not just a matter of understanding the gestures, actions, and words, although the liturgical texts are a primary source of insight into Catholic beliefs. Since the sacramental celebration celebrates the mysteries of life, which are themselves sacramental, liturgical catechesis needs to look first at life. Perhaps the most important aspect is an enriching, probing, creative exploration of those basic experiences of life that liturgy

celebrates: birth and death, love and sin, health and sickness, freedom and slavery, togetherness and loneliness, service and selfishness, peace and anxiety, joy and sorrow, growth and diminishment, creativity and destructiveness. A sound liturgical catechesis must range broadly and dig deeply into significant human experiences that in their depths open out to mystery.

Catechesis and liturgy are profoundly related. Both have their roots in the mystery of life touched by a gracious God. The best preparation for liturgy is not narrow rubrical analysis, or even rich biblical background—although such understanding of the actual ritual and its biblical background is also needed. The best preparation for liturgy is the creative appreciation of life's mysteries. Liturgical catechesis must be grounded here.

Sensitivity to Symbols

Along with encouraging a growing appreciation of life, liturgical catechesis needs to foster an increased sensitivity to symbols. Again, preparation for the liturgy is not first of all a matter of learning the symbolism of this or that specific liturgical rite or gesture—although obviously this is important. Rather, it is much broader. Catechesis needs to open up imaginatively and explore the whole realm of symbolism. After all, sacraments are signs, or better still, symbols.

Contemporary life tends to be scientific, quantitative, measurable. Education often reflects the same preoccupation with facts, information, statistics, and data. Catechesis often shares this leaning toward the conceptual and measurable. But life and liturgy escape the neat categories of science or philosophy. Life is rich, vibrant, mysterious, ambiguous. Liturgy celebrates life's richest, most vibrant, and profound mysteries. The avenue to insight into both life and liturgy is therefore the poetic, symbolic, and imaginative. Symbol touches deeper depths of life than do statistics or scientific definition. A sense of the symbolic and poetic is a vital part of understanding and entering into the liturgy.

Liturgical Catechesis

Liturgical catechesis should be characterized by a creative openness to the richness of natural, cultural, and biblical symbolism. Such catechesis will tend to be much more imaginative, expressive, and poetic than conceptual and analytic. Poetry, film, art, literature, photography, gesture, music, story are all important helps toward developing a sensitivity to the symbolic. Since the liturgy is made up of signs or symbols, appreciation of the symbolic is an important part of preparation for liturgy.

The meaning of baptism, for example, is conveyed not just through the words of the priest and community, but through the rich symbolism of water as a life-giving, death-dealing, cleansing, nourishing, liberating, and refreshing power. The extensive biblical symbolism of water grows out of water's natural symbolism. One who does not appreciate all that water symbolically reveals about life will miss much of the meaning of the baptismal ritual and the biblical readings that interpret its signs and gestures. The same is true of the liturgical use of material things like light, oil, bread, wine, rings, hands, and communal actions like gathering, sharing food and drink, laying on of hands, and anointing.

Liturgical catechesis encourages all that is creative, poetic, imaginative. Within this broad context, the appreciation for specific liturgical symbols and their biblical overtones is important. But the successful appreciation of particular liturgical symbols depends on an openness to the symbolic in general. The catechist needs to be more poet perhaps than scientist, more creative artist than historian or philosopher.

The *immediate preparation* for the liturgical celebration will build upon the general attitudes to life and to symbol, focusing them more sharply on the particular sacrament to be celebrated. As with Janine and her class-

mates, the direct preparation can be one of excitement and fun and therefore highly educational. Selecting appropriate hymns, practicing them, preparing visual materials like banners, posters, or slides, studying the actual ritual and its meaning, writing brief commentaries and prayers, preparing the biblical readings: all such activities will be understood and remembered because they are clearly related to real people about to celebrate an event important to all involved.

During Liturgy

Once all the preparations have been made, the key to effective liturgical catechesis is the quality of the actual celebration. It is obviously essential that the liturgical event not contradict or negate the prior catechesis. Meaningful homilies or observations by the celebrant can provide further catechesis during the celebration itself.

The whole experience of a community at worship, of joy and peace, of mutual collaboration and concern, all of this can lead to greater understanding of the liturgy and of the mystery of life with Christ that it celebrates. Good liturgy incorporates a built-in catechesis. Poor liturgy makes even the finest liturgical catechesis problematic. The major factor is the genuine community expression of honest faith and love through good ritual.

After Liturgy

The third moment of liturgical catechesis comes after the celebration. It is valuable, sometime after the liturgical experience, to help people reflect on and share their insights and feelings about that experience and its meaning. Honest, critical reflection and conversation about what was experienced can be very valuable. Such an approach helps close the gap between catechetical language and actual liturgical experience. It can lead to fresh insights into liturgy and life because it is a reflection of what was actually experienced, what thoughts surfaced, what feelings emerged. Because the reflection is grounded in actual experience, it is more likely to touch one's life more deeply.

In simple, practical, creative approaches along these lines, a sensitive catechist can do much to help people— children, adolescents, or adults—better integrate 1) what they are learning, 2) with how they are celebrating it, and 3) how they are living it out day by day. The key to liturgical catechesis, as Janine and her friends exemplify, is in the careful creative blending of catechesis, liturgy, and life.

Questions for Reflection and Discussion

1. What are your impressions of the experience described by Sister Shea at the beginning of this chapter? Explain.

2. Have you ever experienced God's presence and love in an ordinary daily happening? In a relationship? In nature? In what ways?

3. How realistic do you think it is to speak of "life as a sacrament" or "living as the most basic liturgy"?

4. In your opinion, what are the greatest strengths in your own liturgical experience and education? What are the greatest weaknesses?

5. Why is it important to foster sensitivity to the symbolic as part of learning to understand and appreciate the liturgy?

6. Of the three catechetical moments—before, during, and after the liturgical celebration—which do you feel is most important? Why?

Ways to Respond

1. Explore a symbol. Following up on the suggestion in this chapter about exploring symbolism, engage in as rich an experience of one selected symbol as can be arranged. For example, water is an important natural and sacramental symbol.

Experience water: pour it, feel it, drink it. Creatively express water's symbolism: enjoy photos or slides of streams, oceans, dew; listen to water music; draw or paint water; make a collage about water; photograph water; look up Bible passages about water; check the rite of baptism for water symbolism.

In other words, really get involved with water. Sense its life-giving capacity, its destructive, death-dealing power, its cooling, soothing, refreshing, nourishing, cleansing abilities. Then explore how the Bible and liturgy draw upon this symbolism. The same approach can be taken with sacramental symbols like fire, light, oil, laying on of hands, etc.

2. Share successes. This chapter recounts a successful experience in liturgy and liturgical catechesis. Invite members of your team to share successful experiences they have had or heard about. Consider the good experiences that are shared, trying to discover what common factors there might be in the various experiences that account for their success. Attempt to make up a list of basic principles for successful sacramental catechesis based on the success stories that were shared.

After considering positive experiences and principles, look at less successful experiences. Again the purpose would be to examine the failures to discover what went wrong. Any new principles discovered by looking at poor liturgies or ineffective liturgical catechesis could then be added to your list.

3. Pray together. Gather with a group of co-catechists and after reading this chapter, invite everyone to select a symbol that is personally meaningful. It may be a symbol from an ad or commercial, a movie, or from biblical or liturgical sources. When all have made their symbol selections, ask them to spend a few moments thinking quietly about what the symbol suggests to them. Next invite participants to write prayers based on their reflections about their symbols.

If possible, darken the room and light a candle. Allow time for silent reflection. Invite each person to approach the candle and read his or her prayer. Reflective music might be played softly in the background. Appropriate slides could be shown. When all have finished with their personal prayers, sum up the prayer experience with a general prayer. End the experience with an appropriate song or hymn.

ECCLESIAL SIGNS: CREEDS AND DOCTRINES

Other aspects of the church's life besides liturgy are important for catechesis. In general, these ecclesial signs are grouped under two headings: doctrine or creedal formulations, and the witness of Christian living.

Creeds and formulas which state the church's belief are expressions of the living tradition which, from the time of the apostles, has developed "in the Church with the help of the Holy Spirit."

Human language is limited, however, especially when it comes to expressing transcendent mysteries. Therefore it is valid to distinguish between the truth itself and the language or words in which it is expressed. One and the same truth may be expressed in a variety of ways. Catechesis must nevertheless recognize creedal statements and doctrinal formulas as indispensable instruments for handing on the faith.

National Catechetical Directory, 45

"They walked back to the hogan together, Annie and the Old One.

Annie picked up the old weaving stick.

'I am ready to weave,' she said to her mother. 'I will use the stick that my grandmother has given me.' She knelt at the loom.

She separated the warp strings and slipped the weaving stick in place, as her mother had done, as her grandmother had done.

She picked up a strand of gray wool and started to weave."

So ends the beautiful child's book, *Annie and the Old One*, by Miska Miles. It is a charming story of a young Navajo girl struggling to understand the approaching death of her grandmother. Annie tries desperately to hold back the death of this one she loves so much. Finally one morning, Annie and the Old One walk out through the cornfield together and sit quietly on the small open mesa.

Looking off toward the rim of the desert, the Old One shares her personal wisdom drawn from her Navajo heritage and years of living. She speaks of life and death, sun and earth, of cactus petals drying up and falling to the earth. Annie listens breathlessly and is filled with wonder. Then they walk back to the hogan together and Annie picks up her grandmother's weaving stick and begins to weave as her grandmother and mother have done before her.

We love this book, and have read it again and again. It is a classic piece of literature, one that speaks to adults as well as children. Sensitive illustrations add to the story's appeal.

We like it for another reason, too. We think it speaks to one of the major issues in catechetical work today, the place of doctrine and tradition. *Annie and the Old One* helps us see the vital role of tradition and doctrine in catechesis. This role is at least threefold: It *interprets;* it leads to *insight;* and it offers *identity.* These three "I"-words occur in the dialogue between Annie and her beloved Old One.

Doctrine Interprets Life

The Old One interprets for Annie the meaning of death in the ceaseless cycle of life. The interpretation comes from Navajo tradition, from generations of Navajos who have grappled with the mystery of death as Annie is now grappling. Over the generations the Navajos gradually formulated a traditional interpretation of the mysterious reality of death. It was this tradition, this "doctrine," that the Old One passed on to Annie as they sat together on the mesa.

For us Christians doctrine is essentially an interpretation of life's mysteries. Doctrine is the community's tested "official" interpretation of life graced by God's mysterious presence. As such, doctrines "arose from experience" before being "handed down by authority." Doctrines originated out of questions before they became "answers."

For example, the friends and disciples of Jesus knew him from daily observation and interaction with him. They walked with him. They listened to him. They ate and drank with him. They were drawn to him because of his humanness, his sensitivity, intelligence, wisdom, compassion, and courage. They found him extremely attractive. They also found themselves continually puzzled by him. He was not like the other rabbis. He spoke and acted with authority and power. They found themselves asking one another, "What sort of man is this?" (Matthew 8:2).

Their attachment to Jesus was challenged when they saw him die as a condemned criminal. Then the disciples experienced the presence of the risen Christ, a joyful but disconcerting experience.

All of these experiences gave rise to questions. Interpretations of their experience, answers to their questions, were found by turning to the Hebrew Scriptures.

So the early Christians interpreted Jesus in biblical categories: messiah, lord, priest, savior, servant, king, shepherd. Such interpretations made great sense to those steeped in the Hebrew Scriptures. These biblical interpretations helped Jesus' followers grasp just who he was—so attractively human yet so awesomely divinely unique. These observations are the first "doctrines," and they are part of the New Testament.

But people who were not Jewish, who knew little or nothing of the Hebrew sacred books, also came to experience Jesus Christ. These Greek-speaking followers of Jesus had new questions about him. Their questions arose from their experience and culture. They wondered how God could be a man, and how a man could be God. Was Jesus a divine person living within a human body? Did Jesus have two wills, one human and one divine? How can a human nature and a divine nature be united in a divine person? These were not the questions of the disciples in Judaea and Galilee. These questions arose in the minds and hearts of people more familiar with Homer, Plato, and Aristotle than with Isaiah, Jeremiah, and Ezekiel. Their experience surfaced new questions. To find interpretations of their experience and answers to their questions, these second and third generation Christians in the Greek world turned to the Gospels, to the Hebrew Scriptures, but also to Plato and the Greek philosophers.

In this process, different interpretations were expressed by various Christians. Some felt Jesus was God and just appeared to be a man. Others taught that Jesus was only a man in whom God acted. There was great confusion among Christians. There was also heated debate among laypeople, theologians, and bishops. Eventu-

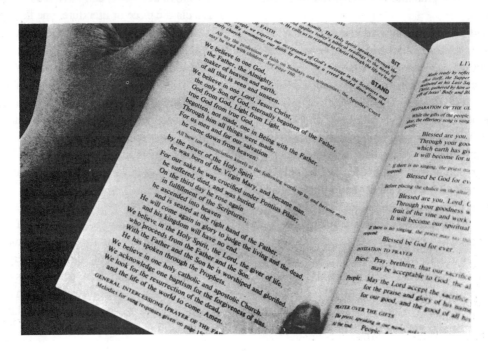

ally the church of the time felt a need for a shared interpretation of who Jesus really is. Worldwide (or ecumenical) councils were convened in Nicea (A.D. 325), Ephesus (A.D. 431), and Chalcedon (A.D. 451). These councils arrived at what were to be taken as "official" agreed upon statements about the nature of Jesus Christ. They formulated what we still affirm in the Nicene Creed which expresses the church's faith in Jesus, using Greek terminology drawn from Greek philosophy.

Doctrine is just this kind of interpretation, agreed upon by the church as a whole as an orthodox and authentic expression of what we believe. Doctrines evidently arise out of experience, are often called forth by questions and controversies, and eventually are agreed upon by believing Christians.

Evident from the very brief example we just considered is that doctrine develops within the church as life experiences change, as new questions arise, as new tools for interpretation are discovered. In each generation the "faith experience" needs to be interpreted by believers. Authentic reinterpretation requires openness to the experience and continuity with previous interpretation. In this way Catholic doctrine continually develops.

Doctrine Gives Insight

Doctrine as interpretation of experience is meant to lead Christians to insight, to make sense out of their experiences. Once the Old One shared her Navajo interpretation of death and life with Annie, in relation to her own grappling with those mysteries, Annie saw life and death in a new way.

The church's doctrinal teachings are meant to help us see life in a new way. They are not just official statements to be obeyed. Rather they are interpretations that have come from centuries of experience and reflection, sharing and prayer. They are interpretations of life graced by God that help us penetrate the mysteries of life. Interpretation is for insight.

"Creation," for example, is a doctrine about our own creativity as well as God's, since we share God's creative power in shaping a better world for humanity. "Grace" is not just a doctrine about God's graciousness, but about our lovableness and dignity. The "Incarnation," God taking flesh in Jesus, also refers to our share in divinity through Jesus. "Resurrection" happened to Jesus, but it will also happen to us. It happens to us in every experience of new life.

These and all our doctrines are expressions of insight not only into God's reality in our lives, but into the meaning of our lives in the light of God's involvement in them. The church's doctrines ultimately are about life as it is graced by the presence and activity of God.

As catechists, we are interested in sharing with others the church's rich doctrinal heritage. But we need to ask ourselves what place the church's doctrines have in helping us make sense out of our everyday lives and coping with its challenges. This is really a key question in trying to understand the role of doctrine in catechesis.

Insight through doctrinal interpretation is evidently a *communal* reality. The interpretations of life that have become doctrines have been formulated through an intense community process. They are treasured and passed on by a community through a living tradition. They are normally learned within a Christian community, a Catholic parish. Most basically they are learned in the primary Christian community, the family—the domestic church.

Doctrine Fosters Identity

The communal nature of doctrine suggests that traditional formulations of belief play an important role in the identity of Catholic Christians. We are Catholics. Our doctrinal heritage helps us identify ourselves, our worldwide community today, and our centuries-old heritage. Knowing the church's doctrinal teachings is an important means of developing and preserving our identity as Catholic Christians. We conclude our profession of faith at our Confirmation with the proclamation: "This is our faith. This is the faith of the church. We are proud to profess it in Christ Jesus our Lord."

Doctrine, then, is vital in catechesis for the church's interpretation of life, leading to insight, and fostering identity. As the Vatican's *General Catechetical Directory* points out, the "ministry of the word is not a mere repetition of ancient doctrine, but rather it is a faithful reproduction of it, with adaptation to new problems and with a growing understanding of it" (13).

Principle Elements of the Christian Message

A. The Mystery of the One God

B. Creation

C. Jesus Christ

D. The Holy Spirit

E. The Church

F. The Sacraments

G. The Life of Grace

H. The Moral Life

I. Mary and the Saints

J. Death, Judgment, Eternity

(National Catechetical Directory, 82-111)

DOCTRINAL CATECHESIS

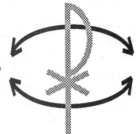

NATURAL SIGNS   ECCLESIAL SIGNS
                                              +*Biblical Signs*
                                              +*Liturgical Signs*

Life & Culture   Creeds & Doctrines
                                 +Christian witness, saints

- experiences
- events
- questions   • creeds
- issues   • dogmas
- language   • doctrines
- media/arts   • teachings

However, traditional formulas and definitions do need to be taught. As members of a church community and institution with a heritage of 20 centuries, our Catholic adults, youth, and children have a right to learn the classic expressions of that tradition. Key catechetical documents of the past two decades carefully spell out the basic doctrinal content of catechesis and provide helpful criteria for its teaching—for example, *General Catechetical Directory* (Vatican, 1972), *To Teach as Jesus Did* (NCCB, 1972), *Basic Teachings for Catholic Education* (NCCB, 1973), *National Catechetical Directory* (NCCB, 1979), and *Guidelines on Doctrine for Catechetical Materials* (NCCB, 1990).

Unless people find in the classic formulations of Catholic belief some value for their lives, the doctrinal learning tends to remain merely academic. It is vital then that doctrines be learned in relation to the deep experiences of life. That is the only way they can be understood for what they are. Doctrines are the gradually developed expressions of Catholic faith. They arose over the centuries out of ongoing dialogue with new experiences and questions as believers worked out the implications of their lives and their faith.

Doctrine and Life

The impact of this basic principle of doctrinal catechesis is evident in a simple comparison of the Baltimore Catechism and any of the more modern texts. The Baltimore Catechism presents doctrines abstractly, academically. Where illustrations have been added, they are usually art representations of Jesus, Mary, saints, and angels, or vis-

ual analogies attempting to make the abstract language more understandable. The newer programs in contrast are filled with photographs of ordinary experiences as well as religious art. Abstract language—at least in the earlier grades—is replaced by concrete, personal expressions drawn more immediately from daily life. There is an immediate impression of an organic relationship between the church's teachings and contemporary experience.

A closer look at individual textbooks confirms this impression. For example, a book on the Eucharist will teach about it in relation to common experiences of community, meals, and celebrations. A book on Catholic morality or conscience will present the teachings of Jesus and the ten commandments in relation to experiences of honesty and dishonesty, justice and injustice, poverty, hunger, and failure. A book on the seven sacraments will present the church's doctrinal teachings about the sacraments in the context of experiences of birth, death, love, sickness, sorrow, and community as well as the symbolism of fire and water, oil and candles, laying on of hands, and signing with the sign of the cross.

The structure of individual lessons reveals the same pattern. The dynamic of the typical lesson moves from some significant experience into a doctrinal teaching and back again to the experience. Although various texts designate the steps in the process with differing names, the process tends to be similar since it reflects a widespread consensus among religious educators. It also reflects the very process by which Catholic doctrines came into existence and developed over the centuries.

The key then to doctrinal teaching is that it be both traditional and relevant to daily life. It is beautifully modeled by Annie and her grandmother. Such catechesis does not happen in books, whether the Baltimore Catechism or more modern texts. It happens through sharing, dialogue, mutual growing—walking along a road, sitting reflectively on a mesa, conversing in a classroom, or sharing around a dinner table. It occurs as believers share common experiences and questions to which the doctrinal tradition of the Catholic Church brings centuries of accumulated wisdom.

To be able to encourage this kind of dialogue, you need to be living that process in your own life on a more conscious level. The Old One could bring light and peace to Annie because she had integrated her Navajo heritage so personally into her own life. She had herself faced the same questioning, the same anxiety.

So it is with us. If the great doctrines of the church remain for us classic but abstract, traditional formulations, we won't be able to guide our learners to a more meaningful awareness of what those doctrines say about life. Today we catechists need, perhaps more than in earlier days, to exercise the process of doctrinal development in our own lives. It is a process of thinking about life in the light of the church's teachings, and reflecting on those teachings in the light of personal experience. The process leads naturally to prayer, arising out of experience and being nourished by the church's spiritual heritage. It also leads to action motivated by the present needs or desires as interpreted in the light of Christ's call. For that reason Latin American Christians insist on the need for orthopraxis (faith-filled living) as well as orthodoxy (faithful belief).

No responsible catechists, and certainly none of the widely used catechetical programs and texts, question the need to share with adults, youth, and children the church's basic doctrinal and moral teachings. The question is not "doctrine or no doctrine," "basic truths or no basic truths." The real concern is to share authentic church teachings in such a way that they are related to everyday life.

Annie grasped the traditional Navajo wisdom because the Old One sensitively shared that wisdom in terms of Annie's anxiety about death. Her traditional teachings took on new meaning because the Old One helped her deal with a very real challenge in her life.

Criteria for Teaching Doctrine

1. *Authentic:* in harmony with Catholic tradition and magisterium
2. *Complete:* gradual, balanced presentation of interrelated parts of the whole of doctrine
3. *Incarnate and dynamic:* related to experiences of life, "signs of the times," biblical, liturgical, and ecclesial signs
4. *Holistic and progressive:* moves toward maturity of faith and life-long conversion
5. *Respectful of hierarchy of truths:* recognizes some teachings as more central and important than others
6. *Respectful of the learner's situation:* sensitive to the learner's developmental stages and to the circumstances of the local church community
7. *Incarnated in cultures:* appreciates the diversity and cultural dimensions of the Catholic faith experience
8. *Fosters unity and community:* provides common experiences and a shared language of faith
9. *Fosters Catholic identity:* so that believers will hear, live, and share the Gospel message as Catholics (adapted from the U.S. Bishops' *Guidelines on Doctrine for Catechetical Materials,* 1990)

Questions for Reflection and Discussion

1. What do you view as the role of doctrine in catechesis?

2. What are some issues or questions in your life that Catholic doctrine most speaks to? Fails to speak to? What questions and issues in our culture cry out for "doctrinal" interpretations?

3. Why did Jesus' first followers turn to the Hebrew Scriptures to help them interpret their experiences? To what sources can we similarly turn to interpret our experiences?

4. Why did Greek Christians have different questions than Jewish Christians? Why were their answers in different words than those of the Gospels?

5. What Catholic doctrine means the most to you at your present stage of life? Why?

6. How does your text relate traditional Catholic doctrines to contemporary life? What clues do you find for this in the structure of the lesson plans? In the students' book?

Ways to Respond

1. **Make a list.** Take five minutes to write down a personal list of "basic truths" or "essential doctrines" that you think every Catholic should know. Share your list with other catechists and create a composite list that the entire group can agree upon as "basic" or "essential." Then prioritize your doctrines, listing the most essential first, and so on.

Next look at the doctrine ranked as the most important. Think about and write down your own answers to these two questions: 1) What is the meaning of that doctrine? 2) What difference does knowing it make in my life?

Again share your answers. Through discussion, become more aware of your own knowledge or ignorance of the church's doctrinal teachings. Then evaluate your approach to teaching doctrines to your students in the light of your own findings and in terms of this chapter.

2. **Translate doctrines.** Ponder any basic doctrinal teaching of the church, for example, creation, grace, incarnation, resurrection. What does it mean to you? Then try to describe its meaning without using any religious language. If you can do this with others, talk about what the doctrine means to you and then attempt to describe it in non-theological, non-religious language. In this way you are forced to get at the real meaning of the doctrine in terms of daily life without hiding behind any religious terms.

3. **Pray the Apostles' Creed.** After each phrase of this ancient prayer, pause for 30 seconds to allow yourself to comprehend and savor the words. Jot down your thoughts, feelings, and insights as you reflect.

4. **Write your own creed.** In your own words write down what you most deeply believe as a human being and a Catholic Christian.

10

Ecclesial Signs:
Witness of Christian Living

> The church also gives witness to its faith through its way of life, its manner of worship, and the service it renders. The lives of heroic Christians, the saints of past and present, show how people are transformed when they come to know Jesus Christ and the Spirit. The forgiveness and reconciliation experienced by repentant sinners are signs of the church as a healing community. Concern for and ministry to the poor, disadvantaged, helpless, and hopeless are signs that the church is a servant. Uniting in love and mutual respect people from every corner of the earth, every racial and ethnic background, all socio-economic strata, the church is a sign of our union with God and one another effected in Jesus Christ. Every Christian community, characterized by its stewardship, is meant to be a sign of that assembly of believers which will reach fulfillment in the heavenly kingdom. Such a community catechizes its members by its very life and work, giving witness in a multitude of ways to God's love as revealed and communicated to us in Christ.
>
> *National Catechetical Directory*, 45

...to laugh often and much;
to win the respect of intelligent people
and the affection of children;
to earn the appreciation of honest critics
and endure the betrayal of false friends;
to appreciate beauty;
to find the best in others;
to leave the world a bit better
whether by a healthy child,
a redeemed social condition
or a job well done;
to know even one other life has breathed easier
because you lived—
this is to have succeeded.

—Ralph Waldo Emerson

This, perhaps, is to be a saint! This is to have taken the gift of life and shaped it so that there was something to laugh about often and molded it so that others were better off.

The stuff that saints are made of is the stuff that everyone has at his/her disposal, both within and without. The stuff within is a complex mixture of personal strengths, weaknesses, and talent coupled with data that is continually absorbed out of experience. The stuff without is environment and other people. To sanctify, by effectively utilizing what is within and without, is the challenge of life. Each one of us is called by God to be equal to that challenge. There are many who are and have been equal to it. We call them saints. Some are canonized. Many others are not.

Models and Guides
While the New Testament calls all the followers of Jesus "saints," the church very early singled out women and men as models of what it means to be a Christian. First there were the martyrs who gave their lives for their faith during the Roman persecutions. After the persecutions, Christians looked also to others who lived their faith in attractive and challenging ways.

A medieval saint, Hugh the Great, an 11th-century Abbot of Cluny, gave a still valid description of saints as persons who "loved in their due order—God above all, their neighbor equally with themselves, and the world beneath their feet." In our own time, Romano Guardini echoes Hugh's words in even briefer form by describing a saint as someone "who takes the great commandment of love seriously."

Through the centuries the church has looked to saints as models of how to live as followers of Jesus, although at times devotion centered more on them as miracle workers and intercessors. Today, Catholics continue to pray to favorite saints, turning to them for help, but they also look to them as models and guides.

The greatest of all the saints for Catholics is Mary, the mother of Jesus. The Vatican Council II, recapturing New Testament images of Mary, drew attention to Mary's role as mother and model of the church, as well as mother of God.

The Gospels portray Mary as *the* woman of faith, the first disciple of Jesus and model of Christian discipleship. She not only hears God's Word to her, but lives it out faithfully. We are meant to do the same in our own lives. So is the church as a whole.

We Catholics continue to honor Mary as the virgin mother of God and our mother, immaculately conceived and assumed into heaven, but we also look to her as our sister—in solidarity with us, especially with the poor—a model disciple and model of faith, a liberated liberator and prophetess of justice. Mary exemplifies what is at the heart of discipleship: total openness to God's will in all life's ups and downs. She is the woman for all seasons, the first of all saints.

Our Brothers and Sisters

To deal with Mary and the saints is to deal with family, in our case the Christian family. That's probably the most important reason for an interest in these people. It's good to know that we come from holy stock, that the blood of saints runs through our veins.

Our children need to know that they have "ancestors in the faith" to look up to. They also need to sense that they themselves have an individual and personal call to be holy. However, in introducing children to Mary and the saints, it is of utmost importance for catechists to point out that each saint is unique. We are not asked to consider their lives as rigid blueprints. Saints are creative models. Their example contains a call to create something unique with the gift of life.

Children need to meet saints simply as people who did their thing—who lived out God's personal call in a uniquely creative way. No one saint can be a total pattern, although one great Christian may have a special appeal and relevance to an individual. Getting to know a variety of different saints helps us recognize the gracious action of Christ—healing, helping, encouraging, comforting—as incarnated in many models. If his Spirit has transformed such diverse people into Christ's image, then why not still others? Why not us?

We believe that children need to know Mary and as many of the saints as they can—some better than others, of course. That saints come from every walk of life is important; that they are young, middle-aged, and old, lay and clerical. Sanctity didn't just happen to them; with God's grace they helped it happen.

Knowing Mary and the saints can help children get in touch with the potential in themselves. Knowledge of Christian saints puts the children in contact with people who can give them the deepest kind of roots.

things very well, who accomplish great things for others in spite of tremendous odds against them, who overcome obstacles with love, who do it all for Jesus. We also have an undying desire to be this way ourselves. If our parents and teachers had not told us stories about people who exemplified these qualities, we probably would not have acquired a taste for this kind of living, nor would we be sure that such a life is possible.

1. Focus on Mary. Mary deserves a special place in our teaching. Place a beautiful painting or statue of

CATECHESIS OF CHRISTIAN WITNESS

NATURAL SIGNS

Life & Culture

- experiences
- desires, dreams
- opportunities
- challenges
- needs
- values
- life-style

ECCLESIAL SIGNS
+*Biblical Signs*
+*Liturgical Signs*

Christian Witness, Saints
+Creeds & Doctrines

- models
- mentors
- guides
- ideals
- inspiration
- intercessions

Getting Acquainted

Let's consider some simple, practical, common sense ways of introducing children to important persons in the Christian tradition. No matter what age children are, they respond to saints who are believable, who make them feel comfortable, and who inspire them. Determine who their favorites are. Some favorites of ours are: Ignatious Loyola; Therese, the Little Flower; Francis of Assisi; Elizabeth Anne Seton; Bernadette; Patrick; Catherine of Siena; Mother Teresa; and Oscar Romero. We know from experience that the stories of these saints are remembered by children we've told them to. On a moment's notice—months or even years later—they can write short stories about them.

Children have a right to be shown what is the noble way, what is the saving, the loving, the Christian way to live. We adults are impressed by people who are courageous in the face of adversity, who try to do even little

Mary in the room where you teach. Involve the children in keeping a fresh flower, lighted candle, or other sign of honor by Mary's statue or picture. Perhaps change it each month to expose the children to various images of Mary. Keep May and October as times of special focus on Mary. Celebrate her feasts during the year with brief prayer experiences. Occasionally pray together the Hail Mary or other Marian prayers, such as part of the Rosary. Invite children to explore and share any Marian feasts and shrines special to their family's national or ethnic heritage.

2. Saint a month. We encourage catechists not to let a single month go by without taking time to tell children about one of the saints. Our advice to catechists is to select one particular saint for each teaching month. Try to create as thorough and as delightful a "getting-to-know-you" experience as possible. Search out art masterpieces, coats-of-arms, symbols, statues, stained-glass windows, films, filmstrips, biographies, and encyclopedias. These will help both you and the children discover who the saints were, what motivated them, what they did, why they turned out that way. The children can also do the searching out.

3. Celebrate all saints. Begin with the festival of All Saints, which is celebrated on November 1. Because it is a day given to no one saint in particular, but to all who deserve to be called "saint," this feast is a teachable moment for discovering what children know about saints.

This is how we used November 1 as a teachable moment with a mixed group of first and eighth grade youngsters. The tools we used were posters. The idea came from Good Apple (Box 299, Carthage, IL 62321), that prepares creative materials for "teachers and their kids." They sell posters such as, "My Very Own Poster All About Me," and" My Very Own Poster About My Community." Inspired by them, we came up with two posters of our own: One for the eighth graders:"My Very Own Poster About Saints"; and one for the first graders: "I Am Like a Saint When I Do This and This." The children filled in the posters with drawings, stories, and examples.

4. Look for saints today. Saints who have lived in the past are important people to know. But people who are showing signs of sanctity now are also very important people to note. For example, the news media reports frequently on great contemporary Christians like Mother Teresa, Dom Helder Camara, Jean Vanier, Oscar Romero and the other martyrs in El Salvador, as well as on less famous women and men whose lives of quiet heroism break unexpectedly into the news. Hardly a week goes by without some kind of striking example of more than average goodness being described in the news. For example, this story about "David Sutton, Crime-Fighter" appeared in *The Washington Post*:

> If we were in the business of handing out good-citizenship awards, one would certainly go to David Sutton, a seven-year-old apartment-dweller in Silver Spring, Maryland who was largely responsible for convicting a robber.
>
> As recounted by staff writer Felicity Barringer, David was sweeping off his family's balcony when he saw two men "walking very suspiciously" nearby. He ran in, got his father's binoculars and watched from a window as the two accosted an elderly neighbor and took $137.
>
> Three months later David identified one of the robbers from a police mug shot. Recently he showed up in county court to testify, but the defendant decided to plead guilty to a robbery charge instead of standing trial with David as the state's star witness.

Some people may be less impressed by David's alertness and good memory than by the fact that he was sweeping the balcony in the first place. We were impressed by both. Even more commendable is David's clear understanding of how the system of justice is supposed to work. While waiting in court, he asked the prosecutor if he would "have to sit in the truth chair—that chair there next to the judge where you have to tell the truth?" We can't think of a better description of the witness chair, or for that matter a better example of how a conscientious witness can help fight crime. We wonder where he learned so much; no doubt from his parents, and perhaps a bit from television too. What matters is that he's learned.

"I'm proud of myself," David said. He should be.

You might start to collect stories and news reports of this kind. Any class day can be a day of commemorating someone who reveals goodness, generosity, and the courage to do the loving thing. This is the kind of thing that people who are saints do over and over and over. Their actions flow out of an attitude that they have toward themselves, toward other people, and toward God.

5. Notice saints close at hand. Finally, the children themselves are key resources for coming to grips with the business of being "saints." But children need witnesses like their catechists to show them by example the Christian way to live. They also have to sense in themselves the potential for "sanctity"—for courage, patience, kindness, concern.

You will often see signs of sanctity, for example, when a child is courageous and compassionate, or generous and loyal, reverent and thoughtful, industrious and good humored, honest and open, or sensitive and prayerful. One benefit of being a catechist is the opportunity to affirm and support, encourage and rejoice in these signs.

A further challenge of being a catechist is to be for your students one of the most important and influential models or mentors in their young lives. *Washington Post* editorialist put it well in a column on "People Children Can Admire." He suggested that if you ask adults about their childhood role models, "they'll nearly always name a parent or other adult who spent time with them and paid attention to them and nudged them toward better behavior." We are called to be such adults in the lives of those we teach.

Questions for Reflection and Discussion

1. What place does Mary have in your life? How do you feel about her? How would you describe your relationship with her? How has it changed over the years?

2. What are your favorite images of Mary? What are your favorite prayers to her? What questions do you have about Mary?

3. Who are some persons you consider role models for your own life? What is it you admire and are drawn to imitate?

4. Who are some of your favorite saints? Why are they special to you?

5. Why is it that the life of a saint—past or present—can have such a strong impact on our lives?

6. Who in your family, neighborhood, town or city has recently acted in a saintly way?

7. How would you define a saint in your own words?

Ways to Respond

1. Learn about Mary: Look up and reflect prayerfully on New Testament texts about Mary, for example: Mark 3:31-35; 6:1-3; Matthew 1-2; Luke 1-2; 4:16-30; 8:19-21; 11:27-28; John 2:1-12; 19:25-29; Acts 1:12-2:4; Revelation 12:1-6. Read a good book about Mary.

2. Attend to your personal relationship with Mary. Reflect on your own feelings about Mary and how you relate to her. Select one or two ways you think might help you give Mary a more vital place in your heart and life.

3. Learn about saints. Most Catholics are named after saints. Besides our baptismal names, we also select the name of a saint as a Confirmation name. Take some time to learn more about the saint after whom you were named. Consider what there is about him or her that most appeals to you. See if there is something in his or her life that can be a practical inspiration or guide to you in your present life. Write your own prayer to your patron saint, and try to pray it daily.

4. Research names. Consider the many streets, towns, cities, and rivers in your area that are named after Mary and other Christian saints. You and your co-catechists might enjoy researching some of these place names. Who actually named the places? Why were saint names used? How do these names reflect the religious history of the places? Use what you discover as a guide to further investigation of the saints and share your findings with your classes.

5. Make a saint book. You might find it interesting to make your own book of Mary or other saints. Start with your patron saint(s). Then involve your family and friends by adding their patron saints. Expand by putting in other saints that have special meaning for you and your family. Include any examples from your experience or from the news media about people who show saintly qualities. Use pictures, your own reflections and prayers, news clippings, etc. Make your own the kind of acquaintance with and love for the saints that will be encouraging to those you teach.

PART III

KEYS TO CREATIVE CATECHESIS

When I hear, I forget.
When I see, I remember.
When I do, I learn.
—Chinese Proverb

CHILDREN REMEMBER:
20% of what they HEAR
30% of what they SEE
50% of what they SEE AND HEAR
70% of what they SAY
90% of what they DO

11

BEING CREATIVE

> Catechesis is not limited to one methodology. Although certain norms or criteria apply to all catechesis, they do not determine a fixed methodology, nor even an order for presenting the truths of faith. For instance, catechesis can begin with God and proceed to Christ, or do the reverse; it can proceed from God to humanity, or from humanity to God; and so on.
>
> Whatever the method, catechists are responsible for choosing and creating conditions which will encourage people to seek and accept the Christian message and integrate it more fully in their living out of the faith.
>
> Although even the best preparation for catechetical ministry will have little effect without the action of the Holy Spirit in the hearts of catechists and those being catechized, catechists should certainly seek to acquire the knowledge, skills, and abilities needed to communicate the Gospel message effectively. They must have a solid grasp of Catholic doctrine and worship; familiarity with Scripture; communication skills; the ability to use various methodologies; understanding of how people grow and mature and of how persons of different ages and circumstances learn.
>
> *National Catechetical Directory,* 176, 211

At one of our catechist workshops, a teacher told us a sad story about a little boy who was very creative—until he went to school. There he learned to "conform," and ultimately his creativity was crushed. Before he went to school, the author says,

> he always wanted to say things: He always wanted to explain things: So he drew. Sometimes he would just draw and it wasn't anything. He wanted to carve it in stone or write it in the sky. He would lie out on the grass and look up in the sky and it would be only him and the sky and the things inside that needed saying.
>
> When he started school, he sat in a square, brown desk like all the other square, brown desks. It was tight and close. And stiff.
>
> One day they drew. And he drew all yellow and it was the way he felt about morning. And it was beautiful.
>
> The teacher came and smiled at him. "What's this?" she said. "Why don't you draw something like Ken's drawing? Isn't that beautiful?"
>
> After that he always drew airplanes and rocket ships like everyone else. And he threw the old picture away. And when he lay outside looking at the sky, it was big and blue and all of everything, but he wasn't anymore.
>
> He was square inside and brown, and his hands were stiff, and he was like anyone else. And the thing inside him that needed saying didn't need saying anymore. It had stopped pushing. It was crushed. Stiff. Like everything else.

We don't know who wrote this sad story, and we don't know who published it. But the crushing of that child's creativity remains a stimulus to us to want to grow as catechists, more and more able to give life to unsuspected, untapped creative powers. If it is important for teachers of other subjects to foster creativity, it is even more vital for catechists to do so. After all, we believe that we share the creative power of the Spirit of the risen Lord who is with us to make all things new (Revelation 21:5). One of the best things that has happened in catechetics over the past 40 years is that we have rediscovered how traditionally Catholic it is to be creative in the ministry of catechizing.

"But I'm Not Creative"

The initial reaction of many catechists is to pull back, professing a lack of creativity. Bill Moyers did a 17-part series for PBS on creativity. His conclusion is reassuring. "Not for a minute am I suggesting," he said, "that you be the next Picasso, Bach, Shakespeare, or Einstein (although I am willing to be surprised). But after completing a television series about creativity in America, I am convinced that each of us is innately creative and, with effort and discipline, can open that private reservoir of creativity to improve our daily lives."

We didn't always believe this either, but we do now. We'd like to share an important experience in a teacher's life, one in which she discovered that she and the children she taught were much more creative than they ever suspected.

Creativity Discovered

Several years ago this teacher accepted a teaching position in Chicago in a depressed part of the city. The walls of her classroom had not been painted for years and were black with soot and dust. At first she wasn't aware of the walls, so preoccupied was she with the 45 fourth and fifth graders in her class. It didn't take long to build a relationship with the children and she remembered thinking to herself, "This is going to be a good year."

But everything inside her started going downhill after that one happy thought. She found herself gradually hating to go into the classroom, and she would leave it as soon after school as she could. Something was affecting her negatively but she was not consciously in touch with what it was.

To cheer herself up, one morning she arranged a bouquet of fall flowers and sat the vase on her desk. During that day her eyes traveled to the flowers often and she found herself feeling a bit more lighthearted. And while conducting a reading class with the fifth graders, she noticed some of the fourth graders not working but absorbed in her vase of flowers. She quickly put an end to their "beauty gathering" by telling them in no uncertain terms to "get back to work."

But that evening she wondered why she felt better and dismissed the possibility that the flowers had done it. The flowers died as flowers will, and she missed them. To her surprise, the children missed them, too. This became evident one morning when a few of them were chatting together before the first bell. One of the boys said, almost angrily, "This place needs flowers. It's so ugly in here." The moment he said it something that was the beginning and continuing of a creative time exploded within the teacher. She hugged the little guy, to his utter amazement, and announced with unrestrained joy, "You're right, Zachary, you're absolutely right!"

The room was incredibly dingy and depressing and she knew instantaneously that she needed to do something about it.

It took a few days to size up the situation. One of the first things she looked into was painting the walls. This was a dodge because she was trying to get someone else to do something creative about the place. In any case, she was told that painting would not be done. As she was dealing with that, an idea came: "Rearrange the desks so the children will be facing each other rather than looking at the walls." They did this and it was a gracious beginning.

In art class that week the children painted still lives of a bowl of fruit or a vase of flowers. They framed them with construction paper and tacked them, exhibition style, on a strip of bulletin board that ran above the blackboards covering two walls of the room. The paintings made an exciting difference. A friend of the teachers made a huge banner. It was hung from the ceiling to the floor in the darkest corner of the room. Splashed across its cream colored cloth were the words, "God said, 'Let there be light' and the whole world became bright."

Each new thing they did awakened them to another creative possibility. That's how the teacher continually experienced the power of creativity—as a burst or shoot from something creative that she'd started to do. The power was often called forth from a need, the need to transform, the need to change something it might be but hasn't yet become.

Gradually they transformed and kept transforming that classroom into a place that the children and the teacher loved being in. What took place in that classroom began to catch on throughout the whole school. The final part of the story is that the principal decided at the end of the year to have all the classrooms painted!

Creativity Is Personal

We've reflected on this experience often because the teacher was actually one of us. What happened was not the result of a huge creative gift or an exceeding amount of talent in those 10 and 11 year olds.

What happened was very personal (a quality that we believe is common to all that's really creative). The teacher's spirit was hungering for something that was lacking. Her psyche and emotions, demanding something that was absent, were pushing at her sensibilities and disturbing them. Her depression was arising from a subconscious sense, an awareness, very vague at first, that she had a gift to do something to make the place more beautiful, more human. It was a time when she, because of who she was, had to introduce light into what was dark, make beautiful what was environmentally ugly, unleash not only the creative power in herself, but the powers that were in the children and in the place itself.

One of the most mysterious things that we feel in the creative process is this: once we give ourselves over to it, everything around us begins to contribute to what is happening. And from all that power, the creative thing takes on its own personality and begins to dictate the direction it will and should go. As soon as we feel that, we know we've got it and it's wonderful.

Creativity Draws Out

We learned from that experience not only that creativity is personal, but also that the power to be creative rests in a capacity to sense—to have an idea—that something can be done to a place, to a thing, or with persons to make it or them more beautiful.

It's very much like the story that's told about the great painter and sculptor Michelangelo. One day, it seems, he was pushing a huge piece of rock down a street. A curious neighbor sitting lazily on the porch of his house called to him and inquired why he labored so over an old piece of stone. Michelangelo is reported to have answered, "Because there is an angel in this rock that wants to come out." What happened to Michelangelo's rock is what creative catechizing is all about. Our task is to create the conditions for faith to grow and at the signs of its growth, to nourish it still more.

Jesus did this over and over again. Think of him with the blind man who pleaded that he wanted to see. Think of him with Zacchaeus, whose faith drove him up a tree. Think of him with the leper whose faith made him courageous enough to flaunt serious social taboos and approach Jesus.

Remember Zachary, the child who said, "This place needs flowers. It's so ugly in here." The remarkable and creative thing about that moment is not only that Zachary sensed what was needed and voiced it to his teacher, but she heard what he was feeling. The creativity that each of us possesses is often given a boost by another who is graciously affected by one stroke of our brush and tells us that he or she needs more of what we can do.

This is a significant moment for the "creator." He or she has to make a choice, at this point—to accept the challenge to continue creating, or to ignore and deny it.

Creativity Is Chosen

We personally feel that very few people are actually creative because they don't trust the power in themselves, or because they don't trust the wisdom of the "another" who suggests that they are creative. Beyond our own feelings about creativity there are statistics and observations that support this from people who have studied creativity. Finley Eversole, the author of the article "The Politics of Creativity," says this:

In our society, at the age of five, 90 percent of the

population measures "high creativity." By the age of seven, the figure has dropped to ten percent! And the percentage of adults with high creativity is only two percent! Our creativity is destroyed not through the use of outside force, but through criticism, innuendo, and subtle psychological means that the "well-trained" child learns to use upon himself!

Eversole continues his observations. "But if Freud was right that nothing is lost to the unconscious, then the creativity of early childhood must still be present in all of us—latent, repressed, crippled—but present!"

We also feel that many people are apparently noncreative because they have long stopped listening to their own needs, long stopped discovering what is genuinely satisfying in the world around them, long stopped really listening to others, so busy are they with the struggle to be heard and to survive. The power, process, and experience of creativity is personal—a response to a need that everyone individually feels. Great painters, great musicians, great poets, great writers, great dancers, great teachers are compelled by the need to forge, to shape, to make, and to express. Creativity often happens out of a tension, a pull from without against a pull from within. Everybody experiences this because everyone possesses a secret that is uniquely beautiful and special.

Creativity Is for Others

We have an essential understanding of creativity when we consciously and purposely create not only to satisfy a need in ourselves—for our own joy—but also for the joy and well-being of others. Leonard Bernstein, the great musical composer and conductor, said: "I would like to be remembered as someone who made music for his fellow human beings. Not just as someone who made music, not how well or badly, but that I made music for my fellow human beings."

From our own experience we have come to agree with Bill Moyer's conviction that people are more creative than they imagine. If that is true, we as catechists need to continually foster our own creative potential. As we trust our own creativity more, as we dare to risk a bit, experiment a bit, grow a bit, we can become more creative in drawing out the creativity of our students. Our success in fostering creativity is both a matter of attitude and of constructing learning activities that are genuinely creative.

Research suggests several very practical ways of fostering creativity in others. Some of these ways may at first seem contrary to common practices in many classrooms. Our culture and our educational system in America tend to reward action, accomplishment, and success more than creativity. And many catechists focus more on the learning of truths than on fostering creative religious insight. Yet, as Arnold Toynbee writes: "To give a fair chance to potential creativity is a matter of life and death for any society." One might say the same of the vital importance of creativity for the contemporary church.

E. Paul Torrance, noted researcher on creativity, suggests five principles by which teachers can reward—and thereby foster creativity: 1) treat unusual questions with respect, 2) treat unusual ideas with respect, 3) show children that their ideas have value, 4) provide opportunities for self-initiated learning and give credit for it, and 5) provide periods of nonevaluated practice or learning.

Notice that Torrance's principles seem to reward divergent thinking rather than conformity. He and others have discovered a close connection between divergent and creative thinking. One reason creativity declines as children pass through school is—as our opening story exemplified—such thinking is not readily encouraged.

Creative Activities

We encourage creativity in our students first of all by our own creativity. Next in importance are our attitudes of acceptance and encouragement of each child's uniqueness and unique contributions. We further foster their creativity by involving them in activities that are creative.

The fact that we learn by doing is commonly accepted and understood. Yet, the doing we learn by is an activity that is often couched in mystery requiring both an active and a contemplative involvement.

Catechists instinctively know when an activity is a learning as well as a doing one. They feel good and exhilarated when it is both. They feel bad and frustrated when it is merely a doing kind of experience. Frustration is heightened when as much preparation has gone into an activity that fails as into one that succeeds.

We use six criteria against which activities for learning and creativity can and should be measured. They are:

1. Purposeful The general purpose of an activity within a lesson is to enable the learner to experience and feel something in a new and fresh way or to understand and see what, up until then, was hidden or unknown. Specifically, an activity's purpose rests in the stated aim of a lesson. Activities should be a means to achieve a lesson's aim.

In most lessons, the aim's purpose is not totally dependent upon a single activity. However, each activity should either set the stage, focus the issue or introduce the problem, or provide the solution.

2. In proportion The time an activity takes must first of all fit the amount of time available. It should also be geared to achieving the stated aim of the lesson. Some activities are more important than others in a given lesson. The amount of time should normally be proportionate to the particular activity's importance in that lesson.

The time an activity takes will also depend on the students. Some children need time to "sit and wonder" before anything creative will happen for and to them. Others need to plunge right in. For them, "doing" is a primary stimulator for entering in and carrying through. Some children consistently take longer than others; some are consistently quicker.

A good rule of thumb is to expect an activity to take more rather than less time. Another good rule to follow in terms of determining the time an activity will reasonably take is to do the activity ahead of time yourself and time it.

3. Personal A class activity will be personal only if the catechist doing it feels eager about it in terms of results. Is it something she can adapt and shape so that it fits her teaching style? Is it something he is fairly sure will work for him because he has done it before and wants to do it again?

In terms of the children, most of the activities in the teacher's manual will be generally geared to the average psychological age and pedagogical needs of a particular group. However, in every group, personal dimensions need to be considered, such as ethnic backgrounds, the experiential largeness or smallness of their everyday worlds, and the overriding positive or negative attitudes present in the group toward God and religion, themselves, and others. Some of the same questions asked above need also to be asked from their point of view. For example: Will an activity be a "turn on" or "turn off" experience for most in the group? Will the results of their involvement be satisfying and rewarding, informing and provocative, challenging and healing?

Catechists will find that many activities are fairly easy to personalize once they are convinced that nearly all require some touching up, some tailoring. Activities that we find easy to personalize are those that involve story, poetry, drawing, creative writing, singing, and the study of photos and art masterpieces. We are also successful with discussions if we can tailor them to enable children to surface their own thoughts and feelings in relation to the lesson.

4. Penetrating A story is heard or read, a picture is looked at or drawn, a song is listened to or sung, a question is responded to or asked, an idea is discussed or written about. Those involved should be drawn beneath the surface of what is seen, felt, heard, or recognized. The penetrating activity becomes a powerful tool, a perfect vehicle through which profound sharing and real discovery can take place. Essentially what a catechist is saying as he or she puts a penetrating activity into motion is "I believe that there is more to reality than we can ever examine, but with this activity we can go below the surface, reach toward mystery, open out to the transcendent."

When an activity is penetrating, it affects the inner vision, the spirit, and that's why it tends to be indefinable. There are signs, however. A child may simply say, "Oh!" or in amazement, come up with an incredible observation. We remember a third grader stopping dead during an activity and proclaiming out loud to no one but himself, "If God wouldn't-a-loved us, he never would-a-made us!" And a second grader once told us, "We say that God made everything out of nothing, but what we really mean is that God makes everything out of God."

A child may simply smile mysteriously or become peacefully quiet; may indicate an overwhelming eagerness to show-and-tell or reveal, without words, genuine wonderment at what he or she has created. All of us have seen these signs. They are, however, so special, so sacred, that we simply hold them in our hearts, sensing that, out of context, what has happened cannot be described. We know that we are and will always be mostly on the outside of what is mysteriously shaping, with God's help, in the person of another.

5. In continuity Continuity flows from something and leads to something else. Nothing transforming can be done in an active and productive way with children unless it hinges upon what they have already done or experienced.

Usually there is more than one activity in a lesson plan. Here, also, is where continuity comes into play. In preparing a lesson, the question to ask about continuity is "If we do this activity will it really prepare us for what is to happen in and through the next activity?" Activities within a lesson are like pieces of a jigsaw puzzle; they fit together.

A good rule of thumb is to read through a lesson and put it aside for a few hours or overnight. If continuity exists there is an immediate at-homeness with the plan. If catechists can easily remember the sequence of activities, that, too, is a good sign that a natural progression exists.

Looking for continuity is a sensible kind of experience. Anyone who has ever listened to a child practicing a piece on a piano, violin, or other instrument is acutely aware when the notes are being played in continuity, in harmony. Anyone who has teaching experience is capable of the same acuity with regard to how activities need to relate so that lessons have continuity.

6. Completing The real worth of an activity depends on how much it helps both the catechetists and learners get themselves more fully together. This may seem to place too great a burden on an activity, but, unless it has that potential, it will be a waste of time—pleasant perhaps—but still a waste of time.

An activity gives evidence of this potential if it pulls together for the children both knowns and unknowns, if participation in it is challenging, and if the outcome for each child is something of a surprise. If, when all is said and done, an activity generates life-giving surprises both in the children and in the catechist, it is indeed a completing one.

In Summary

Creativity is a vital dimension of catechesis. The principles and criteria we have looked at have been carved out of much teaching experience. They have been affirmed by the growing body of research into creativity. They spring from faith, from our Judaeo-Christian conviction that we are made in God's image. We as Christian religious educators are challenged to tap our own innate creative potential and to help our students discover and develop theirs. We hope none of our students will find their creative spirits crushed like the boy whose sad story we told at the beginning of this chapter. When they draw "yellow" because they feel that way about morning, we hope their creative catechists will say, "And it was beautiful."

Questions for Reflection and Discussion

1. How would you describe what happens to you in a creative experience?

2. How can feelings be a guide to becoming more creative?

3. How is a catechist's creative power comparable to that of a great artist like Michelangelo?

4. What examples can you think of that shows Jesus' creativity?

5. Why can we equate a "learning" activity with a "creative" activity? What is common about both words?

6. Why is it important in creative catechesis to work with activities that get below the surface of life, of a Bible story, liturgical symbol, doctrine, or saint's life?

Ways to Respond

1. Do something creative. We often ask those we teach to do creative activities, even though we may never have done these activities ourselves. Take the teacher's edition of your textbook and look over the activities suggested for the next few lessons. Try out several yourself—draw a picture, write a poem, take a photo. Do exactly what you will be asking those you teach to do.

As you do so, try to notice what happens inside you. How do you feel as the drawing takes shape? How do you feel as you discover just the right word for a poem or story?

Avoid criticism of yourself or your work. Notice things you enjoy doing, things you feel came off well. Build on your experience of satisfaction and success.

2. Explore your creative potential. Find a time and place where you will be assured of 30 uninterrupted minutes. Place yourself in a relaxed position. Put on some relaxing background music. Breathe in and out slowly, consciously, rhythmically. Feel the tension easing throughout your body. Start with your face muscles. Move down through your neck and shoulders, arms, hands, and fingers. Feel your whole body getting heavier, pressing down upon the chair or floor. Feel the tensions ease in your chest and stomach, your legs, feet, and toes.

As you become more fully relaxed, continue breathing deeply. Let your mind wander freely as you explore the most beautiful place in the world, or the farthest reaches of space, or the innermost part of your own being. See these things. Feel them. Smell them. Now take up a pencil, or crayons, paint, a musical instrument, or typewriter, and express what you experienced. Do not criticize or analyze your feelings at this point. Just express yourself freely in whatever medium you choose.

Later look at what you have created. Notice the positive feelings you experienced and the creative ways that you expressed them. Follow up along these positive, creative lines.

3. Break through your limits. Try one or more of these classic "creativity tests."

Make a list. Think of a subject and list as many things about it as you can. The subject itself is not important. What *is* important is that you stretch yourself to come up with as many examples as possible. Notice how many more items you come up with than you originally may have thought possible.

Brainstorm. At a gathering of catechists try this. Pick a random topic. Ask someone to record every idea that is expressed (on large newsprint so all can see). As a group, try to come up with as many possible ideas or examples as you can. Do not stop to criticize or evaluate any idea at this point. Go over the list and evaluate only when every possible idea has been expressed. Notice how many creative and workable ideas come from the group, probably more than any of you expected.

Count the squares. Look carefully at the squares pictured here. Count all the squares that you see. Look again, and again. Don't stop until you are convinced that you have discovered every possible square.

Join the dots. Look carefully at these nine dots. Connect all nine with four straight lines. Go through each dot only once. Do not lift your pencil from the paper. Keep trying.

Consider your hands. Look at your right hand. Look at your left hand. Look at them both. Move them. Touch them. Trace one or both hands on paper, or draw them. Then write down as many things about your hands as you can think of.

12

Knowing the Learners

The most important task of catechesis is to provide, through the witness of adults, an environment in which young people can grow in faith.

The following guidelines offer supplementary assistance to catechists.

1. In order to understand children and youth and communicate with them one must listen to them with respect, be sensitive to their circumstances, and be aware of their current values.

2. Both in the church and in human society, children and young people have a dignity of their own. They are important not only for what they will do in the future, but for what they are here and now—for their intrinsic value and their value in relation to the common good.

3. Through catechesis all should be encouraged to know and respect other cultural, racial, and ethnic groups. Catechetical materials should be adapted to accommodate cultural, racial, and ethnic pluralism, the concerns of particular groups, and persons with special needs.

4. Effective catechesis takes into account the fact that the child's comprehension and other powers develop gradually. Religious truths are presented in greater depth, and more mature challenges are proposed, as the capacity for understanding and growth in faith increases.

5. Catechesis also provides experiences to live faith and apply the message of salvation to real-life situations. It encourages the use of imagination, as well as intelligence and memory. It stimulates not only exterior but interior activity—a prayerful response from the heart. Fostering a sense of community is also an important part of education for social life.

National Catechetical Directory, 181

Our nephew Tim was critically injured in a motorcycle accident when he was 12 years old. Besides the initial injury, gas gangrene set in and the surgeons had to incise and lay open the wound still further. Tim accepted each assault on his body without whimpering, with surprising courage, even with good humor. His parents were amazed at his inner resources and good nature. At times they were overwhelmed! They discovered that the knowledge they had of this child had been somewhat superficial, even though they had lived with him for 12 years and had often spent quality time together.

What is true of our relatives is true of many parents and teachers. We don't get to know children as unique individuals who have stories that need to be told, heard, and helped to a happy ending. We act as though the content is consequential, but the children are inconsequential.

Children will meet time after time with a catechist and, if the catechist is not interested in who they are, they will reveal very little of themselves. From 80 to 90 percent of the time, children take their cues from adults and respond only with the data that is asked for and expected. Rarely do children consider themselves as the holders of critical data unless they are considered as such by their teachers. It took us many years of teaching children and some summers of teaching adults to realize this. As Eve Merriam says so insightfully in her poem "A Lazy Thought," "It takes a lot of slow to grow."

Knowing Self and God

In that slow growing process we realized that our efforts at getting to know the children were actually helping the children to get to know themselves. Their attempts to share something of themselves with an interested catechist (or parent or friend) allows them to discover more about themselves. Sometimes a surprised smile or an embarrassed glance reveals the discovery of a previously unknown talent, insight, or trait. It often happens to us all that we recognize something more about ourselves as we attempt to share with someone who, we sense, really cares about us. Helping children to search for and discover themselves is to give them an effective instrument for continually searching for and discovering God.

Centuries ago, Saint Augustine discovered God by learning to know himself more fully. Christian spirituality has repeatedly verified Augustine's experience. Self-knowledge is a key to knowing God, because we are made in God's image and likeness. That being true, it becomes clear how important a part of the content of catechesis is helping the children come to know themselves better. Catechists can do this by seriously attempting to get to know their students.

Taking Time

A very effective way of getting to know students on a personal level is simply to make ourselves available to them before and after class. Just being there early enough to have everything set up and arranged before the children arrive frees up time to chat with them in a relaxed manner. These can be precious moments for moving relationships with children to a more personal level of mutual trust and understanding. As the children sense the willingness to take time for them, they share more of their lives with us.

Making Posters

We normally have the children make a poster portrait of themselves at the beginning of the class year. In our experience with children of various ages, as well as with youth and adults (modifying the format to suit differing ages) the results are normally interesting, sometimes surprising, and occasionally quite revealing.

With children, we typically do something like this. We provide them with posterboard on which there are empty spaces of various shapes, with directions or questions indicating what we would like them to do with each space. For example:

• Draw your family.

• Write three wishes you have.

• Paste magazine pictures that show some of your favorite things.

• Write how tall you are, what color your hair and eyes are, how old you are, and your birthday.

We often take polaroid pictures of each child as the group works on their posters. We paste the picture in a space set aside for it on each one's poster. When the posters are completed, we enjoy an unrushed and well-planned sharing time with the children. We give each an opportunity to tell his or her story, with the posters as a guide. We seat them in a semi-circle facing a wall on which the posters are attached. One at a time, of the children tell their own stories to the listening audience. Sometimes a little coaching in good listening is necessary, and if the group is large, we use three successive classes so each of the children has a chance to talk.

Catechists might want to keep such posters for study and for follow-up use. We normally take slides of each, to keep them for future reference and viewing. We consider the posters one of the chapters in a story each child will tell about him or herself during the year.

Challenging Children

The purpose of the poster project and similar activities is

not simply to help children express what they readily know about themselves, but to help them discover what lies hidden and unknown. The activities that do this are those that challenge, those that bring children up against something they have never done before, something that they initially resist because they're sure they can't do the assigned task.

This places some demands on the catechist, particularly in terms of imagination, preparation, and attitude. Regarding imagination, it is necessary to challenge each child in the group, especially children who seem to be equal to every task. Keep creating and testing until you find worthwhile things to do that require stretching the imagination, even by the most able and willing. Regarding preparation, it is helpful to draw a profile of each child. These profiles can be shaped by consistently studying pieces of the children's work, by keeping a record of little and big things about them that reveal who they are.

Regarding attitude, it has to be one of expectancy, expectancy, expectancy! Once activities have been decided upon, expect each child to produce with it. Encourage, pray to the Holy Spirit, tease, cajole, listen, dialogue, be sympathetic, but, by all means, be expectant. Knowing that each child can meet the challenge will, in many instances, provide the children with the momentum they need to do the job.

An activity that is challenging is one that prompts children to reach into and draw upon their inner resources. It's an activity that forces them to go where they have never been. It's an activity that may cause them to bubble with excitement, that jolts them with the surprise of it all, and that may even bring forth the marvelous utterance, "Wow, I didn't know I could do that!" It's at these moments that catechists may feel like echoing Saint Irenaeus, "The glory of God is people fully alive."

Finishing Sentences

Writing something original is almost always challenging. From time to time, we have the children finish sentences such as: "For me happiness is…", or we ask them to make booklets that tell what happiness is for them. If this activity is done more than once during a year, each time as a probe for different "happiness things," the down deep things that make the children happy will surface.

We also have them finish the sentence, "Unhappiness is…." We did this once with a group of sixth graders. We especially remember one of the girls in the class—we'll call her Cheryl—because the first time around she insisted that she didn't have any happy things to write about. We searched with her until she came up with "a

room of her own," "getting a letter," and "having the dentist say, 'no cavities.'" Two months later we had the group do "Unhappiness is…." Cheryl sat for a time with a blank sheet of paper, but it was obvious that she wasn't asking for help. When the time was up, she handed hers in with the others. Cheryl had named only one thing but had also illustrated it. Her words were, "Unhappiness is being alone in a crowd." Her drawing showed an unhappy face surrounded by half moon-like symbols touching one another (her way of showing a crowd).

During the sharing time Cheryl chose not to elaborate but to just read what the words said. Others in the group interpreted what her drawing meant to them. Cheryl was not threatened by their observations, only silent.

Many things happened in the weeks that followed, but only one that really was important to Cheryl—she began to feel more accepted. During one of the last classes we again did "For me, happiness is…." Cheryl listed five things and then added a sixth, which she also illustrated: "Happiness is having a friend." Again, a face was in the center, this time a smiling one, and again, the touching half moons. Only this time two of them were touching the smiling face.

Writing and Drawing

Children can be challenged even more into self-knowledge by finishing open-ended stories which reveal a choice they would make in a given situation. They can also write the endings of stories, pretending they are the persons in the stories; for example, the rich young man (Mark 10:17-31). They might also rewrite parables in contemporary terms. Each of these writing activities, as well as numerous others found in teacher's manuals, has the potential for revealing to catechists and children what they have to say, what they can do, what responses are unique to them, how they see the consequences of acting responsibly or failing to.

Other types of writing that children do well are poems, prayers, songs, stories, and letters. Most of these activities show something of who a child is at the time they are written. An effective way of discerning and helping children discover how they are changing and growing is the keeping of a journal. Time may be set aside during class for writing in the journal. What is written may deal with how they feel, what they think, personal experiences, stories—anything that is important to the writer.

Children have more to reveal and to discover than they can say or write. Giving life to this is the challenge of various non-verbal activities. One of the easiest of these activities is drawing. What children feel but often can't express in words will often show up in their drawings. Feelings about themselves and others, the world, and God are somehow easier for children to express if they are given the tools and encouragement to picture them.

Drawing or painting are prime media for self-expression. Not "coloring" or "tracing" but original drawings—whatever their artistic merit or lack thereof. The choice of colors, the lines, the composition, as well as the obvious "story" can all reveal to catechists and to the children themselves clues about who they really are and what is going on in their worlds. Cheryl's drawing of unhappiness, for example, showed her feelings about loneliness as it revealed her experience of it.

Writing and drawing (or painting) are just two of many ways of getting to know children and helping them get to know themselves and God. Role-playing, photography, gesture and interpretive dance, discussion, interviews, and values clarification techniques are among the many others.

These are activities through which children can discover who they are while they are discovering who God is, and they can be found in every lesson plan. The desire to know children personally, however, must come from the catechist must know and love the children's personal stories before God's story can become for them a living, loving, and transforming one.

Questions for Reflection and Discussion

1. How much do you know about the lives of those you catechize?

2. Cite an experience from which you learned something about yourself through sharing with another?

3. When have you last felt the excitement of a new discovery about yourself through someone else's challenge?

4. Have you personally experienced growth because someone believed in you and genuinely expected you to grow?

5. Why is it important to give those you catechize a chance to do original rather than rote kinds of activities?

6. Name some of your attitudes that free your students to share something of themselves? What attitudes hinder them?

Ways to Respond

1. Check your knowledge. Sit down and list the names of those you teach. Beside each name jot down whatever you know about that person and his/her family. In this way you will easily get a picture of how well or how poorly you presently know your students. Decide how you can get to know better those whom you don't know well.

2. Keep a "memory line." Again list the names of those you teach. Next to the names draw a chart with horizontal lines stretching out from each name. Draw vertical lines to mark the dates you teach. Be sure to leave space between the lines so you can write. For example, you might note that on November 13 you noticed several things about one of your students. Write these things beside his or her name for that date. Each week you can add to your growing knowledge of those you teach.

3. Do an "About Me" poster. To get a sense of the value of this activity, create your own "About Me" poster as described in this chapter. Use your creativity much as you would want your students to use theirs. Afterwards hang the poster where you can look at it often. Feel free to add to it as time goes on. You might even want to share your poster with those you teach. You may also use it as a focus for prayer, asking the Lord to help you become more fully who you are.

4. Create journals. People of all ages can learn more about themselves—and let you get to know them better—by keeping informal, creative journals. Photos that express what they feel, think, or believe, drawings that express feelings or ideas, or written reflections, verses, and poems can all be included in journals. Or they may want to list questions they have about what you are teaching, note personal insights, or clip media items that speak to them in a particular way. The journal can be used to record their prayers, reflections, and meditations. Such journals can help people discover just how unique they are.

13

Maintaining Discipline

Emotional development at this age is mainly a matter of growing in the capacity for satisfactory relationships with a wider circle of children and adults. Self-acceptance, trust, and personal freedom undergo significant changes, with acceptance of self coming to involve an awareness of specific talents (or their absence), unqualified trust of others giving way to a qualified trust which excludes some people and situations, and the expression of personal freedom being modified by recognition that other people, too, have rights and freedom....The child's first experience of work, usually in school, is relevant to catechesis. It serves as an introduction to values important in both the secular and religious spheres of life: the joy of doing things well, cooperation with others, and discipline experienced as something understandable and reasonable.

National Catechetical Directory, 178

Long ago in China lived a boy named Ping, who loved flowers and could grow anything.

The Emperor was very old and decreed that the one who raised the most beautiful flowers that year would become his successor.

All the children of the land came to receive special seeds from the Emperor. Ping went right to work. He planted the seeds and tended them. But all year nothing grew. At year's end children from everywhere presented their colorful flowers to the Emperor. Ping sat sadly alone with his empty pot.

The Emperor frowned at the flower-bearing children but smiled as Ping showed him his empty pot. He named Ping his successor, pointing out that all the special seeds had been cooked and couldn't possibly grow into flowers. Only Ping had been faithful and honest.

The story of Ping, told in word and art by Demi in her beautiful book *The Empty Pot* (Henry Holt and Company, 1990), leads us into the heart of what discipline is all about.

Discipline is always one of the chief areas of concern voiced by catechists and religion teachers. Over the years, from experience and study, we have developed some basic convictions about discipline in catechesis

and have found some dos and don'ts that work. We feel it is important to begin with the convictions.

Basic Convictions

1. *Self-discipline* Ping's story exemplifies our first conviction about discipline. Ultimately discipline needs to become self-discipline. It comes from within. No one made Ping keep trying honestly to make the Emperor's special seeds grow. All the other children cheated, replacing the dead seeds with others. For a Christian, discipline needs to be part of a growing faith-response to God's call or will.

Sr. Carleen Reck, S.S.N.D., suggests that effective discipline in a Catholic setting helps students move from externally imposed *discipline* to *self-discipline* to *discipleship*. It is a process of helping youngsters make their own the basic principles and values of a thoroughly human and Christian way of life.

Our goal is not just to stay in control and keep a modicum of order, but to help those we teach to grow as more responsible, self-directing individuals. We can guide them to discover in themselves inner powers they never knew they had.

2. *Motivation* Our second conviction flows from the

first. Discipline becomes self-discipline through motivation. It is a matter of ideals, desires, models, and images more than of rules and regulations. As catechists we need somehow to touch on the deeper yearnings of those we teach. We believe—despite much seeming evidence to the contrary—that children like order and peace, enjoy learning, developing new skills, and want to become more responsible, cooperative, and courageous. Part of our task as catechists is to tap into those powerfully motivating values and ideals.

External discipline may make it possible for young people to experience what they may otherwise rarely experience—quiet, orderliness, predictable responses, the joy of self-discovery, beauty, the satisfaction of giving, and collaborating. This external structure allows for the growth of inner self-discipline.

3. *Models and mentors* A third conviction is suggested almost in passing by the role of Ping's father in *The Empty Pot*. He was a quiet, supporting presence and guide during the year Ping labored so hard and honestly. The old Emperor, too, a powerful authority figure, exemplifies honesty and trust.

The most effective help toward discipline in children and youth is the example of significant adults in their lives. We catechists foster discipline best through our own way of being with those we teach. As Barbara Vasiloff and Paula Lenz—authors of *Discipline With Purpose* and friends from whom we have learned much

about discipline—put it, "Children need adults to demonstrate there is power in being self-disciplined."

By observing us and how we treat them and others, our students can learn what self-discipline may look and feel like. In addition to being with us they need contact with others who live lives based on the values of Jesus. Ideally children are to find this at home, but in many homes parents do not provide the needed example. Children and youth also need exposure to the values and ideals of great women and men, heroes and heroines, particularly Mary and some of the saints. Part of our catechetical task is to expose them to such models.

4. *Respect* Our fourth conviction hinges on our Catholic belief in the dignity of every human person as imaging God. Every human being deserves our respect. We also believe that as catechists those we normally teach share a special dignity as baptized Christians. The very Spirit of Jesus Christ lives in them. So every approach to discipline needs to flow from and foster respect—for self, others, and God.

Such respect begins with our attitude toward ourselves and our ministry. We catechists need to respect ourselves and our ministry. We are made in God's image and likeness. We are called by Christ and his church to participate in the vital ministry of helping those we teach develop as human persons and grow in faith as Catholics. Ours is a ministry and career deserving respect—especially from ourselves.

Respect also means that we show constant respect for each individual we teach—no matter how troublesome or different some may be. Discipline may never be used to put down or demean anyone. Rather discipline is meant to build up, to make possible greater self-esteem.

5. *Positive attitude* A fifth conviction is that genuine respect for each person requires and fosters a positive attitude toward ourselves and our ministry, toward those we teach, and toward the role of discipline. Few things are as destructive of good discipline as negativism. We need to think the best of ourselves and of each student—while being realistically aware of weaknesses and the reality of evil in the world and in the human heart.

Discipline needs to be a win-win opportunity, with no losers—even when there needs to be confrontation of inappropriate behavior. Efforts at positive discipline can help our students experience success and personal achievement. Good discipline also empowers those we teach to develop morally, grow in their sense of community, and sense genuine freedom and responsibility. A positive attitude keeps our focus on the good and the growth of all rather than on our own convenience as teacher.

6. *Develop skills* We are convinced that good discipline recognizes that, as children grow, they need to learn certain life-skills. Too often we assume mastery of basic skills rather than help our students develop them. Children are not born with skills like listening, following instructions, asking questions, sharing, cooperating, communicating, organizing time, distinguishing fact from feeling, and sacrificing (and more and more do not come to catechetical situations with them). Children normally need help and direction in learning and growing in these skills that are keys to self-discipline.

Skill-building is a developmental task. Mastering important skills for living and learning together happily must take account of age, readiness, and learning styles. We cannot expect first graders to learn skills appropriate to the learning readiness of a sixth grader. The most helpful program we have found for relating discipline to basic skills is *Discipline With Purpose* by our friends Barbara Vasiloff, Paula Lenz, and Christine Przybocki.

7. *Good teaching* Seventh is one of our deepest held convictions: good discipline hinges to a large extent on good teaching—which itself implies good planning. The very word "discipline" derives from the Latin *discilina*, which means "learning," "instruction," "disciple."

We have found that when we are well prepared and teach well, discipline problems tend to be at a minimum because we and our students are creatively engaged in learning. Discipline is intimately related to the quality of teaching. The very purpose of discipline is to make possible both learning and teaching.

8. *A caring environment* Finally, an eighth conviction of ours regarding discipline has to do with genuine care for those we teach. It is not just that we care, but that the students *experience* us as caring—for them as a group, for each individual, and for what we are teaching. Our caring fosters their caring, which leads to openness, mutual understanding, and trust—an environment or atmosphere conducive to self-discipline and learning.

These are our convictions or beliefs about discipline in catechesis. Given your understanding and acceptance of these convictions, the following practical dos and don'ts may prove helpful. They are simply ways of translating these convictions into appropriate disciplinary behaviors.

Some Things to Do

• *Be consistent.* Consistency allows youngsters to gradually make their own the values and ideals they come to expect and rely on. Inconsistency hinders self-discipline.

• *Be fair.* Children and youth, as well as adults, are extremely sensitive to fairness. Rules, rewards, punishments must be observed with great sensitivity to fairness.

• *Praise good behavior.* Make a point of praising individuals or the whole group for their good behavior. Praise is creative of a good self-image and positive self-esteem.

• *Confront bad behavior.* Do not readily allow inappropriate behavior to pass unnoticed. Turn such occasions into learning opportunities. Confront the child or group—firmly, directly, but without threatening, focusing on the reason for a rule. Explore together alternative, more appropriate, ways of acting.

In confronting negative behavior be sure always to criticize or condemn the behavior rather than the individual or group engaging in the behavior.

• *Have as few rules as possible but as many as necessary.* We normally invite the class at the beginning of the year to decide on four or five rules—like: Raise your hand to ask a question or make a comment. No talking while another is speaking. All are to be quiet while working on individual activities. Groups working together may not disturb other groups. Once all agree on a few basic rules, we insist on their observance.

• *Negotiate contracts.* We encourage self-discipline and responsibility through contracts. The terms of the contract are open to negotiation, but once there is agreement, the students are held to their contracts.

• *Use "I" messages.* Instead of saying, "You kids are being so disruptive!"—which puts down the students, try "I am beginning to feel angry and frustrated by what is happening"—which conveys how you feel, and invites student response.

• *Focus on inner strengths.* Often young people have little idea of what they can do. Just as often no one consciously helps them discover their gifts and learn ways of allowing fuller expression to their better selves. Work at helping them discover and exercise their inner capabilities. They have the inner power, for example, to be quiet—even though most children in our culture become almost addicted to noise. They also have within them the power to listen carefully, ask questions, speak correctly, be polite, respect others, work hard, work together, and sacrifice for others. As catechists we can consciously empower those we teach to exercise their inner powers, which often remain hidden even to themselves.

• *Know names.* Calling students by name conveys your respect and care. It also invites a sense of personal responsibility on the part of each individual.

• *Keep students actively engaged.* Boredom is often at the root of misbehavior in class. Good planning and creative teaching are the best preventive. Have the first few moments of class well prepared so as to engage the youngsters immediately. We often have worksheets on their tables or desks as they arrive so they can begin working immediately, even before the session formally begins and others may still be getting settled.

• *Work with parents.* Parents can be our best allies, particularly when we have problems with one or another child. Inform parents and invite their collaboration in resolving the problem.

• *Give opportunities for responsibility.* We occasionally walk out of the room while the students are engaged in an activity, leaving them alone to act responsibly.

• *Care for the physical environment.* Surprisingly discipline can be improved in a class at times by rearranging the seating, making the room more comfortable and attractive, having resources and materials readily accessible. Who sits by whom can sometimes make or break our best efforts at discipline.

• *Ask for help if needed.* Sometimes all of us encounter situations or individual children that seem beyond our ability to deal with constructively. Any group of children or youth may have several individuals who need professional help. Situations arise at times in any group that may benefit from the wisdom and skills of a more experienced catechist. In all these cases it is important that we reach out for help and also share what may be important information on the behavior of individuals or whole groups.

Some Things Not to Do

In addition to these positive techniques, there are some negative ones to avoid if we hold the convictions we shared above. Here are a few "don'ts" we have learned from experience.

• *Don't shout or yell.* Raising your voice angrily reveals your own lack of self-discipline. The louder and more frequently you shout the less effect you will have on your students.

• *Don't make threats you won't carry out.* It is good to be firm and convey a sense that you are in charge and that actions have consequences. But idle threats undercut your credibility and the students' appreciation of the need for discipline.

• *Don't make anyone the loser.* Handling discipline from anger, anxiety, or from a perceived threat to your power forces you into a power play that results in you or the students becoming losers. This undermines mutual respect and everyone's self-esteem. Never make negative remarks about any student; rather criticize his or her behavior. You thereby avoid suggesting to any child that she or he is bad or is a problem child. Avoid words that imply negative judgments of any child. Never put down any student, especially in public.

• *Don't be inflexible.* Again, be firm in exercising your responsibility, but don't be rigidly inflexible. Sometimes unforeseen situations or individual circumstances suggest changes or exceptions in agreed upon rules. But avoid being wishy-washy or inconsistent.

• *Don't think badly of the students.* At times it is easy to think the worst of an individual or group. Such negative thoughts and attitudes are death to true discipline, tending rather to vindictiveness and power plays that hurt everyone involved.

These are some practical dos and don'ts that flow from and foster the convictions we have about discipline. We hope to help our students develop the inner-directed self-discipline that Ping exemplified in his efforts to make the Emperor's special seeds grow into the most beautiful flowers in the kingdom.

Questions for Reflection and Discussion

1. How do you feel about discipline in catechesis and religion classes? How would you define or describe "discipline"?

2. What has been your personal experience with discipline? As a student and as a catechist or religion teacher?

3. What have you found to be the most effective ways to ensure positive discipline in your sessions?

4. What do you see as the greatest obstacles or challenges to maintaining discipline?

5. What do you think would most help you develop a more positive, purposeful approach to discipline as a catechist?

Ways to Respond

1. **Personal convictions.** By yourself or with other catechists, draw up a statement expressing what you really believe about discipline in religious education. Make it as meaningful and motivational to yourself as possible.

2. **Cardinal Virtues and Capital Sins.** Draw up a list of your own dos and don'ts. Title them "Cardinal Virtues" and "Capital Sins." Do them in your own words and out of your own experience. Write or type them on two cards, which you may insert in your religion textbook to help keep your mind full of your own rules for improving discipline in your classes.

3. **Interviews.** Plan several interviews of catechists or other adults, or of children or youth, or of administrators on what makes for good discipline and what tends to undermine it. Sometimes the students' comments can be extremely effective because they tend to respond directly out of their experience and perspective on the receiving side of disciplinary strategies. Note down helpful observations. Put together a booklet of tips for better discipline.

4. **Meet with more experienced catechists.** A meeting for catechists and DREs is well warranted each year on the important topic of discipline. Perhaps invite in an expert on the subject. Share experiences, convictions, and approaches among the catechists or religion teachers—learning from one another. Try to agree upon and write out a small presentation booklet outlining the consensus of the whole group.

United Nations: The Rights of a Child

Children have the right to:

- affection, love, and understanding
- adequate nutrition and medical care
- free education
- full opportunity for play and recreation
- a name and nationality
- special care, if handicapped
- be among the first to receive relief in times of disaster
- learn to be a useful member of society and to develop individual abilities
- be brought up in a spirit of peace and universal brotherhood
- enjoy these rights, regardless of race, color, sex, religion, national or social origin.

14

Using All Resources

> The quality of catechists is more important than the quality of their tools. But good tools in the hands of skilled catechists can do much to foster growth in faith. Catechetical "tools" are many and varied. They include human and organizational resources, the communications media, textbooks, and audio-visual materials.
>
> There are many organizational resources which provide catechetical information and services. A partial list includes the national Catholic organizations; colleges and universities, catechetical institutes and schools; publishers; diocesan offices; professional organizations associated with other churches; the educational components of local, state, and federal agencies; libraries and data banks; religious orders; and retreat houses.
>
> *National Catechetical Directory*, 249, 250

We were working quietly in our office one afternoon when a young woman walked in with two large boxes. "Be right back," she said after placing the boxes on the floor. We wondered who she was and what she wanted.

She soon reappeared with two more boxes, set them down, and introduced herself.

"Hi!" she said, "My name is Chris. I'm a catechist. I thought you might use these things I've collected for my classes. Or maybe you could use me." She began emptying the boxes. We were amazed. She had a marvelous collection of photos and an equally wonderful collection of religious art—all organized around common catechetical themes. She had games and puzzles, stories and poems, songs and plays.

Most amazing of all she had found all these great resources in magazines and newspapers her family subscribed to regularly!

Unfortunately we could not hire Chris, but we became friends and learned much from her.

Often catechists think of resources chiefly in terms of textbooks and other published materials. While these are valuable, sometimes indispensable, they are neither the most important nor the only resources for catechists. Catechesis deals with all of life, and just about everyone and everything can become a valuable catechetical resource.

We believe that there is a whole world of helpful resources for those who have the sensitivity to notice and appreciate them. Here are some of the more important catechetical resources we normally use.

People Resources

The most important resources for catechesis are persons, not books, media, or machines. Since catechesis is basically a dialogue between people about life and faith, the primary resources for catechesis are the following persons.

1. The Spirit It is not just a pious thought to suggest that the most vital of all the personal resources at hand is the Holy Spirit. It is only through the Spirit of Jesus that anyone can grow in faith in Jesus (1 Corinthians 12:13). The Acts of the Apostles record the dramatic role of the Spirit in the earliest ministry of Jesus' disciples after the Resurrection and Pentecost.

We catechists, then, need to be aware of the presence and activity of the Holy Spirit at the heart of the catechetical process. We need to try to become more con-

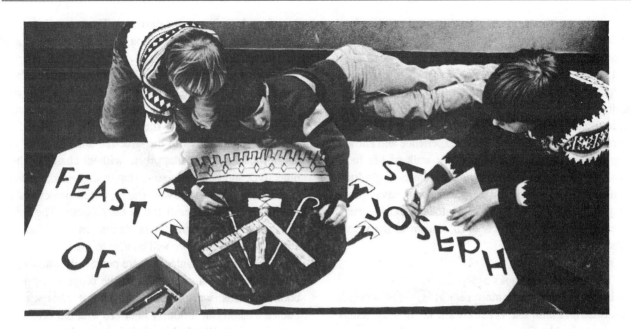

scious of the Spirit's presence and more sensitive to the guidance and more open to the action of the Spirit. This is done through prayer.

2. The learner   After the Spirit, the richest resource for creative catechesis is the learner. Learners have a wealth of human experience, knowledge, and creative talents. They also have experience and knowledge of God and Jesus Christ. Naturally, the degree of knowledge and experience will differ vastly in terms of age and other circumstances.

Then, too, the Spirit is at work in their lives. God speaks to them. God speaks to us through them. The Word of God may be heard not just through the church and the Bible, but through ordinary and extraordinary people or events as well. So it is imperative in catechesis to take seriously the experience, knowledge, abilities, and questions of those being taught.

As catechists, we need to believe in the giftedness of those we teach and open our minds and hearts to learn from them. Our students are one of our most valuable personal resources for more effective catechesis. We can tap this rich resource in four ways.

Respect them.   Respect is the key attitude that can unlock people's creativity and enable them to share their insights into life with God. Honest sharing is not the result of gimmicks. It arises only when there is mutual respect, trust, honesty. Respect implies taking students seriously and expecting much from them.

Question them.   Good questioning is one of the most important skills for the catechist. Good questions chal-

lenge thought, stimulate deeper reflection, invite personal and group discovery. Good questions touch on what is basic and significant in ordinary experiences. They rarely can be answered by a simple yes or no. They usually begin with words like Who? what, when, where, how, and why. Questions like "What do you think that means?" "How do you feel about that?" "What difference does that make?" encourage reaction. "Why?" is a useful and powerful question, but needs to be used with care and sensitivity, especially when referring to personal feelings or actions.

Don't be satisfied with superficial responses. Word your questions in such a way that you invite and enable learners to go deeper into their experience and their Catholic faith tradition.

Listen to them.   Listening is one of the rarest forms of respect and love. We all want others to listen to us, and we have to listen to others with hearts as well as ears.

Let them create.   Young and old express their inner ideas and feelings not only through words but through creative expressions of many kinds. Engaging learners in creative activities is not just a way of keeping them quiet or filling up time. Creative activities are important ways of allowing the students to deepen and express their insights and emotions. They are vital parts of the dialogue between catechist and student.

3. The catechist   A third often overlooked resource for creative catechesis is we catechists ourselves. We have so much valuable personal experience, so much untapped creativity, so much to share about life and Catholic faith. We may not be theologians or scripture scholars, nor even trained teachers. But we have lived as Catholics and are trying to grow as human beings and as believers.

4. *Other people* Other people provide another rich human resource. Every parish or community has people of diverse talents who would be delighted to be of assistance in catechetical work. Retired people, for example, represent a vast neglected pool of experience and knowledge for catechesis. People in every walk of life have something valuable to contribute. Catechists might look around their communities for people who have something unique to share with their students. Using such personal resources adds a note of realism to the whole catechetical project.

Textbooks as Resources

While people are the primary resources in the dialogue about life and faith that is catechesis, many other things are also valuable. One very valuable "thing" resource is the textbooks that catechists use. But any prepackaged, published program must be used creatively. It must be adapted to greatly differing situations and a wide variety of persons. Used creatively a textbook can be a marvelous tool. Used slavishly, it stifles honest dialogue and genuine discovery.

These five suggestions may be of help in getting the most out of a textbook.

1. *Realize its purpose.* A textbook can never replace people resources. It is designed to enable people to enter more effectively into a meaningful sharing about faith. It provides a carefully planned and tested structure for facilitating personal dialogue about life and faith. Few catechists have the necessary background in theology, scripture, and the social sciences to design a balanced, traditional, yet creative curriculum. Our textbook gives us a reliable structure.

The manual normally includes a great deal of theological, biblical, and methodological background to assist us in better understanding our faith, the capabilities of our students, and ways of facilitating creative dialogue.

Most manuals provide a wealth of practical suggestions for lesson plans, activities, and resources, and they often suggest which Bible stories, talks, or prayers to use.

2. *Read the introduction.* Most introductions give catechists a complete explanation of the program. Most important, they present the theological and educational principles upon which the entire program is built. It is vital that we become familiar with these principles. Otherwise,we may be attempting to use a particular text in a way for which it was not designed. There are also other helpful items in the introduction regarding activities and resources.

3. *Become familiar with all its components.* Catechists should take time to study the entire program with all its components, noticing how they are interrelated, when they are used, how they are meant to be used. If we become familiar with the structure and design of the lesson plans, we can adapt them without changing their objectives and grasp *why* each step is suggested, *how* the activities fit the objectives, and how the objectives of each lesson fit the overall aim of the program. The better we know the program—its faults as well as its strengths—the better we will be able to use it.

4. *Believe in it.* Unless we are personally sold—or at least open to becoming sold—on the program the textbook forwards, we will constantly be at odds with it. Such a tension can seriously interfere with our effectiveness. So we should deal honestly and quickly with serious questions or doubts we may have about it, and work with DREs and co-catechists in an effort to resolve our concerns.

5. *Don't be enslaved by it.* Textbooks should be adapted and used creatively. No textbook is worth more than the honest sharing that catechists and their students engage in. In fact, the textbook's worth is best measured in terms of how well it helps facilitate such dialogue.

Textbooks can help us draw upon and organize a whole world of readily available people and resources like these often overlooked ones.

See more about textbooks and lesson planning in Chapter 15.

Household Resources

1. *Family members* With a little imagination, courage, and patience catechists may find that their families can be valuable resources in their catechetical work. Bouncing ideas and questions off spouses, brothers or sisters, children, parents, or grandparents is very worthwhile. Experimenting with them to test out ideas and projects, and inviting them to help prepare creative materials adds a new dimension to the catechetical task.

2. *Family photos* Many families have numerous photos and travel pictures from weddings, anniversaries, birthdays, meals, picnics, and historic places. These may not be great masterpieces of photographic art, but they can be very useful in religion classes. At times they are more meaningful then other pictures because of their immediacy to catechists and those they are teaching.

3. *Family camera* Almost every family has a cam-

era of some kind. It can be useful in catechesis for taking pictures of people or scenes that relate to what catechists are teaching. A catechist's pictures of a baptism in the parish, for example, can have more impact on students than perhaps better photos of the baptism of strangers. Since so many families have inexpensive simple cameras, we should invite children more often to take their own pictures to use with current lesson topics.

4. Newspapers and magazines Daily newspapers and weekly or monthly magazines are invaluable resources for catechists. They provide a wealth of good visual materials—photos, cartoons, ads, maps, charts, drawings, sketches—as well as stories, news items, statistics, poems, essays, reports, and analyses. All of these materials can be used to enrich teaching, but only if we plan ahead. The news media can also be used by students in creating collages, posters, banners, or doing research.

5. Records and tapes Music, both instrumental and vocal, is an important medium in catechesis for all ages, but particularly for adolescents. Instrumental music should be used often to create atmosphere or provide background. Popular songs can be used to provide provocative messages that touch deep into life experience.

6. Television If we plan ahead and try to incorporate what we teach into our own thinking and living, we may notice many things on TV that will be useful in our teaching. News items, personal interviews, dramatic sequences, stories, ads—all of these can at times relate beautifully to what we are teaching and may also have been seen by many of our students.

7. Junk It is amazing how much of what one might consider junk can be used creatively in catechesis. Bags of all kinds can be used for making masks or puppets. Boxes can be useful in creating environments, for making modules and dioramas, for building models of biblical towns, for hanging or pasting pictures, for multi-sided "posters" or "collages," for dramatic props in plays or role-playing, for building a simulated TV set (through which a long sheet of paper with drawings is pulled), etc. Cardboard of all sizes can be used for mobiles, tag-board banners, posters, collages, drawings, paintings, symbols, etc. Cloth remnants make fine puppets, flannel board figures, costumes for plays and role-playing, banners, etc. Paper is useful for drawing, painting, making models or puppets, simulated stained-glass windows, and for free expression activities. Old sheets make marvelous costumes for dramas and role-playing, for silhouette dramas, for substitute projection screens, and for banners. Popsickle sticks can be used to make mini-signs, mobiles, picture frames, and symbols. Pipe cleaners are excellent for making "people" in various attitudes, actions, and relationships; for making symbols and mobiles. Paper cups may hold paints, become faces, or be torn, cut, or crumpled to express feelings, impressions, and ideas.

Neighborhood Resources

Rich as our families and homes are in useful catechetical resources, other riches may be found in the broader realm of the neighborhood. Some of the resources available in neighborhoods, towns, or cities are the following.

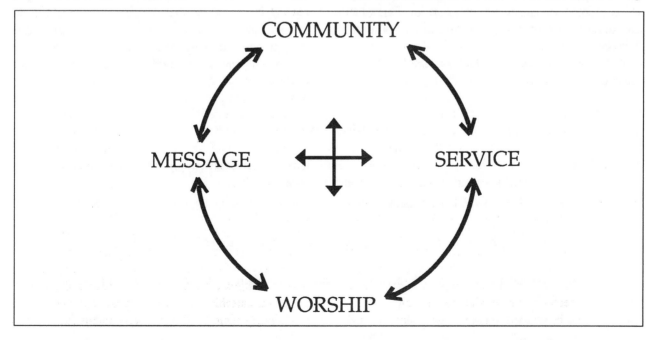

1. People Many people in the neighborhood have unique experiences, talents, or skills that might be drawn upon for catechesis. Elderly or retired persons may particularly be pleased to share their gifts with catechists and their students. A valuable person to cultivate is a skilled photographer. Others with artistic gifts like painting, sculpture, dancing, and music can be very helpful.

2. Libraries Libraries are great resources for children's literature and art books which are less readily available in homes or parishes. But libraries also have a variety of other materials: reproductions of sacred art, photos, slides, records, magazines, films and filmstrips—depending, of course, on the size and location of the library. Every catechist should become friends with their local librarian.

3. Museums Museums and their staffs can be a rich resource for catechists because they contain art treasures that illustrate human history and Christian tradition. They also frequently make available excellent reproductions of sacred and other art at reasonable prices. For example, a great selection is available by mail from the National Gallery of Art in Washington, D.C.

4. Schools Many public, private, and religious schools and colleges have a wide variety of useful resources available, including both people and media. In some situations, public resources may not be used for religious education. Normally, however, reasonable requests made in ample time are generously answered.

5. Book, art, and craft stores Such stores generally employ creative and knowledgeable people who can obtain materials that may be difficult to locate. When catechists become acquainted with the staff, they are often able to obtain good bargains or even free gifts of useful materials.

6. Churches, synagogues, mosques, temples Larger cities often have a wide variety of religious buildings.

Not only are the buildings useful for catechesis, but the ministers or religious leaders may generously assist catechists in their work. Some religious institutions have extensive educational programs with many materials that catechists might be able to use quite well.

7. Local business and professions Most valuable to catechists will be the people involved, with their experience, skills, judgment, and creativity. Many business and professional organizations, for example, airlines, ship, bus, and train companies, often have attractive posters, brochures, and maps that may be useful resources. Many large corporations have high quality publication materials that touch on all aspects of life—besides their products—that are immediately useful in religious education.

8. Civic and religious organizations Organizations like Red Cross, B'nai B'rith, U.S. Catholic Conference, National Council of Churches, and the American Bible Society have many useful free or inexpensive materials. They also have qualified persons who may be willing to assist catechists.

9. Nature The created natural world is full of potential resources for catechesis. Rocks are an interesting texture to paint brief Bible verses on; egg shells make great Easter eggs for Easter trees; and branches can become crosses. Natural settings can be ideal for prayer sessions. Water, oil, bread, and wine can be used as symbols when teaching the sacraments.

Since catechesis embraces all of life, almost anything can become a useful catechetical resource. The key to tapping these resources is a creative attitude and a certain amount of advance planning. With guidance from the textbook and careful lesson planning, catechists will discover how to use a world of valuable and available resources.

Questions for Reflection and Discussion

1. How conscious are you of the role of the Holy Spirit in your catechizing? How confident are you in the Spirit's creative presence with you and your learners?

2. How deeply do you believe that those you teach are themselves an important resource for catechesis?

3. How seriously do you trust your own experience, feelings, insights, and gifts? Why or why not?

4. How many people can you think of in your area who have gifts that might be valuable for catechesis?

5. Have you considered using some of the household and/or neighborhood resources mentioned in this article? Which ones might be of most benefit to you?

Ways to Respond

1. List your gifts. Many catechists are unaware of how much talent, experience, and insight they have. You might take some quiet time and note down on paper things like:

- what you most enjoy
- what you most believe
- what really worthwhile experiences you've had
- what you've learned from life, from others, from books, from schooling
- what you do well and what you have accomplished
- what you've suffered
- what you feel are your most attractive, most useful gifts

When you finish, quietly rejoice in being you and say a prayer of thanks to the Holy Spirit.

2. Look carefully at those you teach. Take time to think about each of those you are catechizing. Note what you know of the talents, abilities, experiences, background, and family of each. In the light of what you are exploring with them in this year's lessons, what use can each of them be in bringing particular gifts to bear on the catechetical experience? Plan ways of drawing upon their gifts more creatively as the year goes on. Pray on a regular basis for each of your students.

3. Explore your neighborhood. During a period of quiet time think seriously of all the resources available in your neighborhood, town, or city. Use the list of possibilities found in this chapter to guide you in discovering some of the rich resources close at hand. Determine ways to draw upon some of these available resources in your next few lessons.

15

USING TEXTBOOKS AND PLANNING LESSONS

Textbooks are guides for learning, summary statements of course content, and ready instruments of review. They must present the authentic and complete message of Christ and his church, adapted to the capacity of the learners, with balanced emphasis proportionate to the importance of particular truths. Modern texts do more than present information. Their graphics, for example, can foster learning and stimulate—or discourage—interest. The graphics in catechetical texts must be in the best tradition of Christian art, chosen with sensitivity to the age, psychological development, intellectual capacity, and background of learners.

Teachers' manuals are essential components of any textbook series. They should contain "an explanation of the message of salvation (constant references must be made to the sources, and a clear distinction must be kept between those things which pertain to faith and to the doctrine that must be held, and those things which are mere opinions of theologians); psychological and pedagogical advice; suggestions about methods." Manuals or developed notes for parents should accompany any materials designed for children. Wherever possible, special manuals for use in catechesis of the handicapped should be developed by professionals in special education.

National Catechetical Directory, 264

One of us used to teach each Sunday at an Army base about a half-hour drive from Washington, D.C. Five catechists made the trip together every Sunday.

Each week three of the group regularly prepared their classes on the way out. They had not looked at their textbook since the previous Sunday's class.

Not surprisingly almost every Sunday morning one or other of the three would discover that she did not have something the lesson called for, or that she had in her room at home a picture or story that would have been perfect for their lesson.

This experience convinced us of the importance of careful planning. We believe that probably the most important practical step in working to become an effective catechist is careful planning of lessons. This is as true for adult religious education as for the catechesis of adolescents and children. Careful planning allows us to do the following:

1. Deepen our own awareness of the faith-reality we will be exploring and sharing with students.

2. Sensitize ourselves to the wealth of resources available in daily experience, the news media, and in our textbooks.

3. Collect materials for use in our teaching.

4. More closely weave our catechetical work with the rest of our lives.

To achieve those goals, three stages of planning will help maximize involvement and allow us to uncover otherwise hidden resources.

Long-Range Planning

As soon as you know what grades you will be teaching or what groups you will be working with and the topics and texts you will be using, set aside an hour or two to try to get an *overview* of the whole year's work. Look through the text and related materials (e.g., teacher's manual, parents' materials, additional components, media, etc.), and note the *general area* of content (e.g., sacraments, world religions), usually evident from the title of the text. Next focus on the *major themes*, which may be the basis of the units or chapters, and try to become familiar with the approach used. Read the entire introduction to your curriculum.

By doing these things, you will have already focused your consciousness on the general topic and the major

themes as well as the overall approach. You will be more sensitive to things you see in newspapers or magazines and on television, and to what happens in your own experience related to that topic or one of its themes. In this way, much of life can be drawn into your catechesis.

We recommend that you also create a *personal resource center*. It may simply be an empty box or drawer into which you put anything you discover that is relevant to your classes. Or make a simple file with a folder for each unit, chapter, or lesson. In this way, you are already beginning to gather resources for your classes—resources that are meaningful because you have found or created them.

Short-Range Planning

As the year progresses, always try to plan a month or six weeks ahead, perhaps according to units or other major divisions of the course. Do basically the same things as in the long-range planning, but now focus more sharply on the *next major segment* of the course. Setting aside an hour or two to go over the materials in your textbooks will be a great help.

By carefully studying the material for the students, you will become aware of the kinds of experiences, the various topics, and the overall themes of that block of material. You will notice how units relate to the whole, particularly to what you have already completed. Note any materials that you will need, any media or other resources

called for by the text, and read carefully anything in the teacher's manual that gives background or direction.

In this way, you will be sharpening your sensitivity to the many things in your experience that relate to what you will be teaching, things that would otherwise slip by unnoticed.

Immediate Planning

Now you are down to the actual lesson that you are about to teach. Immediate planning works best if you concentrate your planning in two moments.

First Moment Shortly after finishing a class, take some time to look over the *next lesson,* noting the same kinds of things as in the previous planning stages. Read the material in the student's text, the lesson plan, and any background information provided in the teacher's manual to help sharpen the sensitivity now focused on the specific theme of the lesson. Look carefully also at any supplementary materials included in your curriculum, like a "Teacher's Resource Package," "Home Program Guide," or "Music Program."

Second Moment This is shortly before teaching the lesson—the day, evening, or morning before. Go through the lesson plan carefully, making every effort to adapt it to your situation and needs. Draw from your personal resource centers, questioning the lesson plan and challenging it in terms of your students and your resources and your own personality and preferences: all will enhance your lessons.

```
┌─────────────────────────────────────────────────────────────────────┐
│        PERSONALIZED LESSON PLAN    Lesson _____   Pupil's Book, pages_____ │
│                                                                       │
│        Date_____                          Teacher's Book, pages_____ │
│                                                                       │
│        AIM _____        │
│            _____        │
│                                                                       │
│        REVIEW (if needed) _____           │
│                                                                       │
│                                                                       │
│              I. LEARNING ABOUT OUR LIVES          RESOURCES/MATERIALS │
│  Approximate                                              needed       │
│     time                                                              │
│  ____ mins.      A. _____              │
│                  B. _____              │
│                  C. _____              │
│                                                                       │
│              II. LEARNING ABOUT OUR FAITH                             │
│  ___ mins.       A._____               │
│                  B._____               │
│                  C._____               │
│                                                                       │
│              III. LEARNING HOW TO LIVE OUR FAITH                      │
│  ____mins.       A._____               │
│                  B._____               │
│                  C._____               │
│                                                                       │
│        AFTER-CLASS NOTES _____       │
│        _____        │
│        _____        │
│        _____        │
└─────────────────────────────────────────────────────────────────────┘
```

After careful study, write up your own personalized lesson plan.

Note well! You may find that the lesson plan in your text meets your needs and you feel quite comfortable following it more or less as it is. With a good textbook this should not be surprising. However, you need never feel bound to following the textbook rigidly. You know yourself, your students, and your situation better than anyone else.

Personalized Lesson Plans

The personalized lesson plan, which we will call PLP, can help you draw upon the sound curriculum process and structure of your textbooks while inviting you to develop your own creative resources.

Here's how it works. First, make up a personalized lesson plan form (see sample). The form can be duplicated so that you have one or more for every time you meet with your students. It has three major sections, plus space to describe the aim or goal, and space for after-class notes. What the three major sections are called depends upon the text being used. Throughout this chapter we will use a sample fourth grade lesson from *This Is Our Faith* series (Silver Burdett and Ginn Company, 1991).

The first and in many ways the most important item on the PLP form is the aim (goal or objective in other texts). Read the aim as printed in the text for the lesson in question, and with that in mind read through the whole lesson plan (including the very important Reflections for the Teacher (in some texts called Teacher Background). Then go back to the aim as stated in the book and sit with it a bit. What does it say to you? What is it expecting of the children as the end result of the lesson? How would you say it in your own words? Do you agree with it? How might you modify it because of your own priorities?

For example, in our sample fourth-grade text, the objectives or aim of Lesson 5, "The Great Commandment," reads this way: To help the students

• Explore the needs that people have

• Learn the Great Commandment

• Recognize that love for God can be expressed by showing love for our neighbor

• Think of ways to love our neighbor.

Reflect on the objectives in your text and rewrite them in your own words on the personalized lesson plan form. If you truly make the objectives your own in this way, they will more easily guide the development and the actual teaching/learning of the lesson.

Many catechists do better if they can rework the objectives into one clearly understood and personally-owned goal for a lesson.

The First Movement

Together let us explore how, having formulated your objectives or goal, you can now create your own personalized plan. You will draw upon the texbook's resources to stimulate your own creativity while resting on the textbook's structure and process as a security base.

For example, the first movement in Lesson 5 on the Great Commandment—like the first movement in each lesson of our sample text—deals with the youngsters' experience. The textbook presents a sequence of possible activities to help the children explore their experiences of people's needs by sharing a personal experience, reading a story, discussing it, listing needs people have, and exploring ways to help.

You need to judge which if any of these activities you will use. You may prefer to create your own activity to achieve the in-depth exploration of experience that the first step calls for. (Note that even in textbooks that present a number of activities, not as alternative options but to be done in sequence, catechists may often want to make selections, omissions, or replacements.)

In choosing activities, think very realistically about yourself, your learners, and your situation. What are your strengths? What do you do best? What can the youngsters do? What do they most enjoy doing? How many pupils are in the group? What resources are available?

Weighing such questions carefully, you might, for example, adapt the first or second of the above activities

suggested in the textbook to look at people's needs and people's responses to those needs. You may prefer to give the children a drawing assignment, but you will not provide enough papers and crayons. Once the children experience the tension of sharing or not sharing with those who lack drawing materials, you can plan to guide them toward talking about what happened.

Perhaps you will then use the story in the textbook to help your students get deeper in their own responses to people's needs. After discussing the story, you can then plan to do what the textbook suggests in listing various kinds of needs people have.

Whatever your choices, you are now ready to write these activities in your own words on your personalized lesson plan form under "Learning About Our Lives."

The Second Movement

The second step in most contemporary religious education plans relates the experience in the first movement to some aspect of our Catholic faith tradition. It may be a Bible story or quotation, a liturgical symbol or ritual, a doctrinal or moral teaching, the example of a saint or other admirable person. The key in building a lesson is to be sure that the second movement honestly relates to and builds on the first movement—always in pursuit of the stated objectives.

In Lesson 5, our sample text, movement two brings Jesus' call to love, his Great Commandment, directly to bear on the children's experiences of people's needs and their own selfish or unselfish responses. The textbook suggests a sequence of activities: explaining the meaning of "parables" and Jesus' use of them, reading a Gospel story, discussing it, role-playing the story, placing it in a contemporary setting, reading a brief interpretation of the story, memorizing new words, and discussing the doctrinal summary.

After carefully studying each activity in relation to the aim and the first movement, instead of reading the Good Samaritan story from the textbook and discussing it, you may decide simply to tell the Gospel story, using a favorite work of art to touch the students' hearts and illustrate the story. Then you plan to have them act out the story in a contemporary setting.

Afterwards you might have them read the brief interpretation of the story in the textbook, memorize the "Great Commandment," and simply read the new words and the doctrinal summary.

Then write down just those activities—in your own words—on your personalized lesson plan form under "Learning About Our Faith."

Third Movement

Move on to the third movement in the textbook. Again using our Chapter 5 as a sample, you see that it suggests several activities: reading the scriptural verse on the page, discussing it, looking at the pictures on the page and talking about how to be a Good Samaritan, reading the poem that is there, the child drawing him or herself acting like a neighbor to a person needing the child's love, listening to a song, praying, and reviewing the chapter.

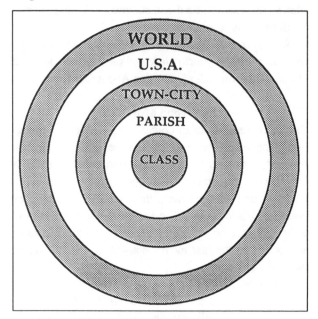

After thinking through these activities, you might focus on the poem, having the youngsters learn it by heart. You might feel that the drawing activity will help them internalize and concretize the poem as well as Jesus' call in relation to their own situations. Knowing a good musical version of the Good Samaritan story, you decide to build a simple prayer experience around it and the art work you used earlier. Using the lists of needs people have (from the first movement) you could end the prayer experience with a litany of prayer for the various groups of people whose needs the youngsters have listed.

You then write down your adaptation in your own words on your personalized lesson plan under "Learning How to Live Our Lives."

The Lesson's Context

An important further step is to take a serious look at the context in which you will be teaching your lessons. That is, consider the life of the community, the parish in which your catechesis takes place.

Look at three areas especially of your parish's life:

the liturgy, the social ministry, and the community life. If you look ahead, you will see what liturgical seasons, feasts, holy days, and sacramental celebrations are coming up.

Find out what major service projects are being planned by the social service ministers, and what major events of community life—e.g., celebrations, parties, social events—are being planned.

With these aspects of your parish's life in mind, look over the textbook lessons. You may want to change the sequence of lessons in the textbook so that particular lessons relate more immediately to parish events: liturgical, social service, community life. In this way you take advantage of the profound reality recognized by the church in our country, namely that "every pastoral activity has a catechetical dimension" (*National Catechetical Directory*, 30).

Then as you plan individual lessons, relate them more clearly to what is going on of importance in the parish community and the church at large. (For further insights on the importance of the community context in catechesis, see Chapter 2: "Context of Catechesis: Community.")

Finally, consider upcoming events important to the broader community: national holidays, local celebrations or customs, and try to integrate these with your lessons to the extent that it is possible. Included in these community events should be birthdays, anniversaries, and special events in the lives of those you catechize.

The back of the PLP (see sample on next page) can be used for this kind of integrated planning. In the light

(On the backside of the PLP)
I will do the following things during the lesson to relate it to other important community experiences:

1. Parish community-building events:
_____
_____
_____

2. Parish liturgical experiences:
Advent is a great time to balance the kids' preoccupation with getting gifts with awareness of other people's needs.

3. Parish social service actions:
Tie the lesson into the parish Advent "Toy Sunday." Encourage kids to bring in good toys they no longer use -- to give to those who have none.

4. National, cultural events:
_____
_____
_____

5. Local events in neighborhood, town or city:
_____
_____
_____

6. Personal events in the lives of the students:
_____
_____
_____

of parish community, liturgical, and service events, as well as events in the broader community and in the lives of your learners, you enrich your lesson plan to take account of these events or experiences. Some of these experiences you then place in the finished PLP, as in the accompanying example.

Complete the Form

The only thing remaining to be filled in on your personalized lesson plan form is the estimate of time (on the left side of the page) and a listing of materials and resources you will need (on the right side of the page).

With that you have a personal plan that draws upon the strengths of your textbook while adapting what is there to your own situation. You are getting the most out of your text and at the same time challenging yourself to

draw upon and develop your own creativity. The plan is now yours, not just the authors. With your PLP form you are not dependent on the teacher's manual while you are catechizing the children. Place the completed form on a desk or table where you can easily glance at it. You can now be much freer, and even more secure. The textbook now becomes an unseen bridge between you and the children, rather than a potential barrier between you.

After you have taught your lesson, take a few moments to evaluate how it went. Filling out the section "after-class notes" on your PLP form can be a helpful means of learning from your mistakes and discovering your strengths.

With such planning, you will find that you actually save time and conserve energy often wasted in panic at the last minute. You will also be doing a more personal and professional job, using the rich resources available to you. When you are ready for class, be sure to pray to the Holy Spirit and then confidently enjoy what you are doing.

Catechists Plan Together

One of the catechist's greatest resources in becoming more effective and collaborating in a more effective parish program is sharing with other catechists in the preparation and evaluation of catechetical efforts. The previously described stages of lesson planning can be more effective if done as a group. In this way, catechists become for one another a source of mutual growth. Working sessions in accord with the stages of planning—for the whole book at the beginning of the year, for each major unit each month or six weeks, and for each lesson every week or few days, can be very valuable, especially if catechists group themselves according to grade levels or different courses.

Begin a session with one of the songs or hymns that you will be using with the students, making use of recordings if available. All can sing, rotating in leading the singing, so that you all will become more confident in singing and leading others in song.

Sharing positive experiences and successes from previous units or lessons is important to create a growing sense of confidence. Sharing together less successful experiences or downright failures will encourage you catechists to suggest to one another how you might have handled the same situation with alternate approaches.

Next look at the material to be prepared, and share together any questions about the material or the approach. Also share creative ideas, activities, resources, and alternatives that may help in adapting the lessons, and discuss the major questions that occur in the text.

Included in this working together should be moments of genuine prayer similar to those to be introduced into the lesson with the students.

Some general questions you might share during this kind of meeting include:

- What are we trying to do? What is its value?
- What difference can this make in our lives?
- What is our personal experience and belief in relation to what we will be teaching? What questions do we have?
- What will be necessary to achieve the aim of the lesson?
- What resources do we have as a group to help one

another with this lesson or unit?
- What are the strong points in the lesson plan? What appears weak? How can we adapt it to our needs?

The three-stage planning model—long range, short range, immediate—not only saves time in the long run but frees you to maximize the resources within yourself, within your learners, and in the world around you. Integrated planning draws on the resources and life of the whole parish. Planning in groups maximizes the gifts of many and helps to foster a sense of community and shared ministry.

A final consideration might be: Where should an individual catechist do the preparation so necessary for good classes?

A Planning Place

If you are going to plan lessons that are effective, you might as well go first-class. Dream a little. Create an ideal place in which to work out the details of each plan.

Let's begin with the actual place. Creative lesson plans can develop more easily in a "growing place." We advise catechists to take a tour of their houses or apartments and look carefully at all the space to decide on one room or area of a room that could be made into a private place, an inner sanctum, for lesson planning.

You will want enough space for a work table and/or desk, a bookcase, a supply cabinet, and a large bulletin board. If possible, choose a room that you can use without having to put away work in progress. Liken your lesson planning room or space to an artist or writer's studio, and decorate it in a style that is particularly inviting and attractive to you. It should be a place in which you will enjoy working.

A lesson planning place can take on the personality of each plan that is being put together. For example, if an activity in a lesson calls for pictures of welcome, we transform our lesson-planning area into a place that says, "welcome." We place a welcome mat at the entrance and welcome sign over the door.

If we intend to use a recorded song in our lesson, we play it while we're working on the lesson. If we're using resource books and research materials on initiation rites, these books become prominent on our book shelves. Should a creative project, like making a large fish from wire, be part of the plan, we will hang our finished model somewhere in the room. Should the prayer experience include a renewal of baptismal vows, we tack the prayer to the bulletin board, or type it on a card, and place it in plain view on the desk. Every time we notice it, we pray it.

Every part of a lesson that is "feelable," "hearable," and "seeable" can become part of the lesson-planning area. This is what we mean by a "growing place."

A plan as it is laid out in your teacher's manual is like a seed. It needs to be cultivated. As you cultivate the seed, it should blossom into a lesson that is truly yours, one that is tailored to the children and in tune with the life of your parish.

Questions for Reflection and Discussion

1. How do you feel long-range planning might help you become a more effective catechist? What would such planning make possible for you?

2. How familiar are you with the major themes of the textbook you are now using? How well do you understand the author's approach and principles?

3. Why might short-range planning be helpful? What would be its chief benefits?

4. Why is it so important to become sensitive through planning to the wealth of things all around you and within you that might relate to your lessons?

5. Why would it be desirable to write up your own personalized lesson plan?

6. What do you need to consider most in selecting, discarding, or adapting activities from the textbook?

Ways to Respond

1. Actually plan. After reading this chapter, sit down with your textbooks—the book for students, the teacher's manual, and other components of your curriculum. Follow the steps outlined in this chapter. In all three stages keep alert to integrating your lesson with the realities of the church and world.

2. Start a personal resource center. The threefold planning model facilitates the development of your own personal resource center. Once you have become familiar with the major theme of your textbook, the major themes of each unit, and perhaps the themes of the individual lessons, set up a simple system for preserving resources that are relevant to your themes. You may want to use a box or drawer, a file system, or any system that works for you. What is important is that you begin your system and keep on using it to improve your teaching.

3. Make a calendar. Make a calendar that includes all of the days on which you will be catechizing. Highlight and write in the kinds of events mentioned in the chapter. Then go through your textbook and note which lessons you feel will best be taught and when. Working out such a calendar helps remove the tension that arises when you have a limited time to plan a lesson. It also frees you to begin looking for resources in advance.

16

USING MEDIA

> The collaboration of catechesis and the arts and media deserves close attention and encouragement. From the very beginning, the church has used the arts to communicate Christ's message and fix it in people's minds and hearts. Biblical stories, saints' lives, and religious themes of all sorts have been depicted in stained glass, mosaics, painting, and sculpture. Music, poetry, dance, drama, architecture, and other art forms have also served catechetical purposes. Contemporary media such as television, films, photography, filmstrips, slides, and tapes do so today.
>
> The communications revolution has had a profound impact on our world, with implications as great for religion as for any other area of life. Contemporary media offer marvelous new opportunities for catechesis, but they also present serious challenges and problems. They can unite people, foster the sharing of ideas, promote mutual help, justice, and peace, and carry the Gospel to those who otherwise might never hear about it.
>
> *National Catechetical Directory*, 251, 252

Frederick is one of our favorite creatures. He is a small gray field mouse with light gray ears. He lives with a chatty family of field mice in an old stone wall along a meadow. Frederick looks just like the other field mice, but somehow he is different. Instead of gathering food for the winter he sits in the window soaking up the sun.

Naturally the other little mice are angry. They wonder why Frederick doesn't work with them. Frederick tells them he is hard at work gathering sun rays for the cold dark winter. He says he is collecting bright colors for the long gray winter. When they think he is just daydreaming, Frederick assures them he is gathering words for the long winter evenings.

Winter comes and the field mice retreat to their warm home in the old stone wall. They happily munch on their store of supplies and chat about foolish foxes and silly cats. But before long they have eaten up the corn and berries, nuts and wheat. It is very cold.

Shivering they turn to Frederick. What about the supplies he said he had gathered. So Frederick stands up proudly. He asks them to close their eyes and imagine the rays of the sun and to feel its warmth. The four little field mice begin to feel less chilled. The dismal winter gray takes on bright colors as the little mice listen to Frederick's poem about the richness of their surroundings.

Frederick lives on in Leo Lionni's classic child's book *Frederick* (New York: Pantheon Books, 1967).

The Role of Media
A recent rereading of this charming story led us to reflect on the role of media in catechesis. For us, artistic media arise out of the kinds of creative contemplation Frederick practiced amidst the flurry of work and worry. They are not so much a matter of electronic technique and complicated machines as sensitive insight into life's mystery and the delightful expression of that insight through creativity. The use and creation of media is radically contemplative and creative, based on looking, hearing, feeling, and touching common reality with uncommon sensitivity.

Media are not merely "audio-visual aids" to enhance a more abstract, philosophical message, or to entertain a group of bored students, or to fill in for a catechist's lack of preparation. Media are themselves valuable windows into life's mystery—into the reality beyond and within life's shifting seasons.

Before going into a discussion of the rich catechetical

potential of media, we would like to share with you what we mean by media. When we used to hear the word, we spontaneously thought of rather complicated, fearsome machinery—projectors, recorders, cameras, television. Like many catechists we somehow feared machines, were puzzled by them, were never sure just how to run them. So for a long time we were turned off by media in our catechetical work.

Gradually from experience we learned that media is not just sophisticated electronic machines that generate and project materials. We learned that *media is everything that can touch a person deeply and delightfully through the senses.* We also became aware that the church during all its history has used media in catechesis and worship— that is media in the broad sense of our definition.

Catechesis in every age used all manner of media to touch minds and hearts through the senses. Early catechesis was a close partner of liturgy and used all its media to draw upon the symbolism and communication potential in the liturgy. Even printed catechisms—a very late development in the church—were normally illustrated with art. Catechists at home and in mission countries used music and song to convey the message of Christ in a delightful form. "Holy pictures" are something many of us remember from our own early catechism classes.

The more sophisticated modern media—photography, film, television, and video—are but further developments of the same basic media. But the principles of their use in catechesis or liturgy are the same.

Simplicity

For us simplicity is the clarity of relationship between the parts of a presentation or experiences around a single theme. Simplicity allows for depth and insight. Simplicity is not a matter of using simple media or having technically simple experiences. Simplicity can be achieved through the most sophisticated, complex use of multimedia. Simplicity is in the clear focus on a theme, a recurrent question, or a point of view. It can be achieved, for example, by using one photo and one word, or in a film using thousands of visual images, verbal statements, music, and audio effects. It can just as easily be lacking in the use of a single photo and a single word as in a lengthy film.

We need simplicity to center rather than dissipate concentration, because the purpose of catechesis is to lead to greater depth into life's mystery. The danger of careless use of media in catechesis is that the media may remain on the surface and scatter one's perceptions. If used simply, with a clear theme, focus, perspective, or question, media can deftly and delightfully penetrate below the surface and stimulate wonder, deep appreciation, profound insight, deeply felt attraction. If the theme or question is confused and clouded, media can actually accentuate the superficial.

The first question to ask in using media, therefore, is what does one want to say; what does one want to be experienced? Once that is clear, then every word, every picture, every sound needs to be tested against that straightforward objective. If this is done rigorously, then the result is the kind of simplicity we discover in Jesus' parables. They go right to the heart of the matter and encourage reflection, invite commitment, and provide insight.

A corollary of the simplicity principle is disciplined restraint. One picture may be better than a thousand words; it may also be better than two pictures, or a filmstrip, or film. The underuse rather than the overuse of media is often the key to success. Only considerable skill and long experience make possible a profoundly simple presentation using a multitude of various media. Better to have less than more, at least until the ability to achieve simplicity has been developed. Until one can sensitively achieve simple impact with one photograph and one word or phrase, there is little chance of producing more complex multi-media experiences.

Depth Appreciation

Simplicity in the use of media allows for the kind of depth appreciation that nurtures genuine religious experience and insight. Media may well be used simply for entertainment, but their use in catechesis is to involve the students in the faith-process described in earlier chapters. The media simply used can draw students into a deeper sensitivity to and appreciation of life's mysteries in the light of the Gospel. Media can invite more profound pondering and questioning of the meaning of the Gospel in the light of life's depth experience.

Involvement is the key. Media in catechesis are not meant to be mere passive instruments of passing on information—although this is one of their legitimate functions. But even in giving information, the catechetical media should be raising questions, digging below the surface to issues affecting the feelings and touching the heart, hinting at the mystery that underlies life's experiences. This is precisely how Jesus used media. His appreciation of field flowers and birds opened up an awareness of the Father's gracious care of them and more so of people (Matthew 6:26-34). He finds seeds, pearls, nets, weeds, and grain capable of drawing people to ponder the mystery of God's kingdom in their lives (Matthew 13:1-53).

And likewise Frederick. He draws the other field mice into experiencing more deeply the mystery of their lives through involvement in the experience of poetic words evoking the sun's rays and the world's beauty.

In addition to enabling in-depth appreciation, media make possible the creative expression and sharing of such appreciation. Media can stimulate growth in faith through active participation. Meditating on a photo or work of art, listening to music, responding to a film can also help further deepen that faith by creative media expression.

Photos may not only be pondered, but they can be created with simple cameras. Paintings can be created as well as enjoyed. So too can stories, books, songs, music. A most effective use of media in catechesis is in their creation by the students. The goal is to guide them to deepen their faith by creative expression and at the same time share that faith through the media they create. Even young children can draw, paint, photograph, write stories or books, make collages and displays. Older children can create newspapers, books, filmstrips, films, TV shows, dramas. Media allow for expressive communication of personal insights and feelings in such a way that the felt idea is deepened in the creator of the media.

Use With Care

The effective use of media requires careful planning, whether one is using published media or those one makes oneself. The use of media in catechesis is liable to increase rather than shorten preparation time for classes. That is not a disadvantage but an experienced fact suggesting the possibility of even better classes because of the careful preparation required. Some approaches to planning to use media follow.

1. Relation to program   It is vital that the proposed use of media be closely related to the textbooks and catechetical programs being used. Specifically the media used must fit into the aim and theme of the particular lesson or unit to be taught, as well as the overall approach and philosophy of the program. This may appear obvious, but is often overlooked. To assure such correlation demands that you preview any media before you select them. It is not safe to go by titles or by advertising copy or even by reviews. You personally must discern the media's appropriateness to the lesson and to the whole approach you and your program are taking.

2. Determination of theme   Particularly when preparing to use existing media or to create media, it is imperative that you carefully think out a single theme, question, or issue you want to explore. This, too, may seem self-evident, but is often not followed. To be sure you are focusing on a clear theme with clear developments, it may help you to write out in a sentence or two what you see the media as saying. This needs to be precise. It is not enough to say the theme is "freedom," but what about freedom is to be stressed and explored. Once the theme is settled, then every aspect of the development needs to be tested against the theme. Does it fit? Does it distract?

3. Clarity of aim   Related to the determination of theme is the need clearly to determine the aim or purpose for using media. Use of the selected media will differ significantly if the aim is to inform, or to entertain, or to motivate, or to stimulate reflection and discussion, or to raise questions, or to create a mood, or to support prayer. It is a helpful discipline to write down in one sentence just what you hope to achieve by the media use.

4. Previsualization   Once the theme and aim are clear, it can help you to previsualize the whole presentation step by step. A storyboard can be very helpful for this. On a paper, have one column for the script, another column for visual elements, another column for audio elements like music and sound effects, and another column for any physical or staging elements. Then go through step-by-step filling in the parallel columns to see the entire progression.

5. Timing   Once there is a clearer idea of the probable development of the media presentation, it should be timed. This may be a matter of simply estimating approximate times in rather simple media uses or a precise measurement in the case of more complex media presentations, such as joining slides with songs.

6. Criticism beforehand   The presentation should be viewed beforehand (perhaps by several catechists). This allows you to feel the effect, to alter parts, to change the rhythm or pace.

Summary

For us, these are the keys to effective use of media in catechesis: simplicity, involvement toward depth appreciation, and creative expression, all carefully planned. They rest on the very dynamic we find in the story of Frederick, an ability to look at the world with freshness and to express what one sees in some creative media. Frederick took time to notice colors, to feel the sun, to ponder his own reactions to the beauties of the meadow and to the on-coming cold and winter drabness. His contemplation opened up life's meaning for others.

So, too, Jesus opened his mind and heart through his eyes and ears and feeling to the wondrous world of Palestine. After pondering what he saw and felt, he shaped his profound glance at life into memorable parables, entertaining stories, provocative actions, and searching questions. His simplicity reveals the richness and depth of his perceptions. He involved his hearers and continues to do so. The rich heritage of Christian creativity reveals how his own use of media inspires the creative expression of faith through an outpouring of multimedia.

Jesus is an apt model for us in using media simply to encourage a living, maturing faith. Frederick may help us, too.

Questions for Reflection and Discussion

1. What are your reactions to the summarized story of Frederick? What does the story say to you about your own life?

2. What has been your experience with media in catechesis? What questions do you have?

3. How would you define media?

4. What are some practical ways to insure simplicity in the catechetical use of media?

5. How do you attempt to involve your students in an in-depth appreciation of life through the use of media? What success have you had?

6. How does Jesus exemplify a good catechetical use of media? How can you imitate him in this?

Ways to Respond

1. Read about Frederick. The story, *Frederick*, by Leo Lionni (Pantheon Books, 201 E. 50 St., New York, NY 10022) is available in most bookstores. A six-minute color film version, also by Leo Lionni, is available from Connecticut Films, Inc., 6 Cobble Hill Road, Westport, CT 06880.

Share reactions to the book and/or film with other catechists. Use questions like these for your discussion:

•What did you most like about the story? Why? What did you dislike?

•What do you think of Frederick's approach to life? What about it attracts you? What puzzles you?

•What very important value for all of us—as Christians and as catechists—does Frederick exemplify? How do we incorporate it into our lives? Into our catechesis?

•What do you think is the point of the story? How true is it? How important to your life?

If time permits, your group might want to draw thoughts together into a position paper, or group resolutions, or some other form of creative expression.

2. Imitate Frederick. After you have read this article, try to imitate Frederick's awareness of beauty. Take some time, quietly, in silence just to look around, to absorb the beauty around you as Frederick did. This is a kind of quiet contemplation. Share the beauty you discovered with others by creating a more beautiful environment, writing a poem, or taking pictures.

After you have experienced the beauty around you and creatively shared it, enjoy what you have created. Talk about your experiences with other catechists in the light of the ideas in this article.

3. Create media. After assimilating the principles stated in this article, create a media statement. This might be as sophisticated or unsophisticated as you wish, but it should stimulate the kind of in-depth appreciation the article describes. Any subject matter may be selected.

Once you have completed your work share it with another catechist. After time to enjoy and appreciate work, invite honest criticism—positive and negative—in the light of the principles enunciated in this article. A first step in this critique would be to have the person attempt to articulate what she feels your creation attempts to communicate.

4. Do verbal-visual exercises. To explore the unique potential of both verbal and non-verbal communication, it helps to try to translate a basic message from one medium to the other. What is suggested here for visual communication may apply as well to other forms of non-verbal communication such as music, gesture, movement, dance, spatial arrangement, architecture, and symbol.

Select a picture that you feel really says something about life. Now try to come up with a verbal statement that conveys what the photo says to you. If you want to begin with a verbal statement, find or take a photo that expresses the same insight. In place of photos, other forms of visual art can be substituted; for example, paintings, sculpture, or drawing.

When you have created a verbal-visual statement that is harmonious and complementary in expressing a single insight, explore the differences between the verbal and visual media of communication. Which do you find more meaningful and why? Which touches you most deeply?

17

USING PICTURES

The fine arts are among the noblest products of human genius. Ideally, their highest manifestation is sacred art. Things used in divine worship "should be truly worthy, becoming, and beautiful, signs and symbols of heavenly realities."

The Western Church has never adopted a particular style or school of art as peculiarly its own, finding virtually all to be suitable instruments for expressing Christian values and truth. The church has admitted fashions from every period according to the talents and circumstances of peoples and the needs of the various rites. Catechesis should include an introduction to the religious art of the past, such as music, painting, sculpture, mosaics, and frescoes.

In expressing their faith, the Eastern Churches have developed and found great significance in the traditional forms of icons (images). Iconography views redeemed creation as a manifestation of the creator. This art form seeks to express in painting what is divinely mysterious in reality. The composition, perspective, color, and lighting, and the decorative elements of icons all take on a religious sense.

Contemporary art is as suitable for the service of religious worship as the art of past ages, provided it expresses the reverence and honor which are due the sacred.

National Catechetical Directory, 146

"If Christ is as great as Christians claim he is, we should be able to see him or his influence in all things." We were a bit startled to read these words in an old issue of *Popular Photography* (June 1968). They were written by a well-known photographer and writer, Ralph Hattersley.

He went on to assert that "anyone trying to see better is on the way. The closer one is to good seeing, the closer he [sic] is to God."

Hattersley's point in the article is to suggest the religious potential of photography. As a marvelous technological aid to seeing more sensitively, photography seems to him a natural ally of the contemplative thrust of all the major religions.

We were struck by the similarity of this contemporary photographer's words to the language of the great Christian contemplative of Reformation times, St. Ignatius of Loyola. Ignatius urged his followers "to see Christ in all things." In that directive he sums up centuries of Christian spirituality.

Underlying the contemplative stance of Christianity is the faith-conviction articulated by Saint Paul: "Since the creation of the world, God's power and divinity have become visible, recognized through the things he has made" (Romans 1:20). In more poetic words Gerard Manley Hopkins echoes Paul: "The world is charged with the grandeur of God." Learning to see God in all things, to see Christ in all things, is therefore critical to growth in Christian faith.

It is not surprising then that catechists from the earliest days of the church have recognized the faith-potential of visual media. One of the great early catechists, Cyril of Jerusalem, wrote that "faith by seeing is stronger than faith by hearing." Cyril, in the 4th century, was speaking particularly of the visible actions, symbols, and rituals of the worshipping community.

Cyril's basic catechetical principle of "faith by seeing" applies as well to sacred art—mosaics, stained glass, paintings, statues—that later filled the great cathedrals and wayside shrines and had their beginnings in the ancient catacombs. Even the post-reformation catechisms were filled with drawings and sketches to help one see in image what one reads in words.

It is in keeping with this long catechetical tradition, rooted in the belief in creation and incarnation and closely related to the spirituality of contemplative seeing, that contemporary catechists continue to turn to the visual media of art and photography.

Photography

The use of pictures in catechesis has then as its primary purpose the fostering of the kind of seeing that opens one's mind and heart to the presence of the divine in human experience and in our religious tradition. Pictures are particularly valuable for fostering the discernment process that is at the heart of catechesis (see Chapter 3).

The use of photos in catechesis requires a growing sensitivity to strong photographs. Confucius said that "one picture is worth a thousand words." But most of us, deluged daily with a ceaseless flow of photos in the news media, need consciously to stop and really look at them in order to experience the truth of Confucius's famous saying. So the first step for a catechist wishing to use photos more effectively in religious education is to sharpen her or his sensitivity to the unique power of good photos.

Corita Kent has made a helpful distinction between *strong* and *weak* photos. Photos may be weak in their subject matter, for example, infants, puppies, kittens, sick persons. Or they may be of strong subject matter, like a lion, a mountain, an athlete. In addition to the strength or

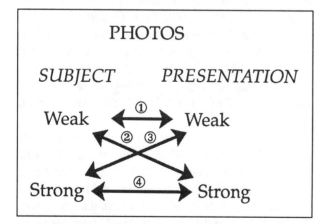

weakness of their subject matter, photos may be weak or strong as photos. A strong photo has impact, stopping-power. It has the ability to provoke wonder, to raise questions, to move us, to force us to think, to give insight. Weak photos lack these qualities, tending to be senti-

mental, superficial, dull, obviously posed or artificial.

Weak photos, whether of strong or of weak subjects, have little value in catechesis. Strong photos, of weak or strong subject matter, have religious potential because they draw one deeper into life's meaning and mystery. These are the kinds of photos to look for and use.

Religious Art

Growing sensitivity to religious art is equally important. Not all art is good for catechesis simply because it depicts Jesus, Mary, or Bible stories. The great theologian Paul Tillich gives a fourfold division of religious art which is not unlike Corita's four categories of photos.

Tillich distinguishes between an art work's *content* and its *style*, each of which may be *religious* or *non-religious*. That leads him to categorize art in these four types: 1) non-religious content (e.g., landscapes, portraits) done in a non-religious style (i.e., with little

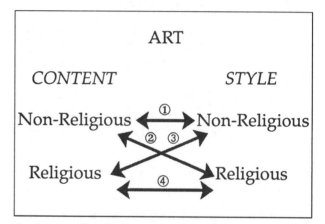

depth, superficial); 2) non-religious content (e.g., landscapes, portraits) done in a religious style (i.e., goes beneath surface, suggests mystery); 3) religious content (e.g., Jesus, Mary, Bible stories) done in a non-religious style (i.e., superficial, sentimental, without revealing depth dimension); and 4) religious content (e.g., Jesus, Mary, Bible stories) done with religious style (i.e., penetrates below surface, suggests mystery).

Tillich maintains that category 3—religious content without religious style—is actually detrimental to faith growth and is dangerously irreligious. Unfortunately, much so-called sacred art is of this kind. Go into most religious goods stores and you will find an abundance of this kind of sacred art. Tillich includes in this category even famous Madonnas by great artists like Raphael and Rubens. Beautiful in color and composition, they fail to convey the reality and mystery of Mary as Mother of God.

He sees category 4—religious content with religious

style—as truly sacred art. Such art would be very valuable for catechesis, but not abundant. As examples Tillich cites El Greco's "Crucifixion," the "Crucifixion" of Mathias Gruenewald, and the modern "Crucifixion" of Rouault.

Category 2—non-religious content with religious style—is also of great catechetical value. Its function is similar to Corita's "strong" photos. While the subject matter is not explicitly religious—portraying scenes from daily life—its style is profoundly religious. By religious style Tillich means a style by which "something is always breaking through out of the depths of the surface." He singles out as typical of this type of art Picasso's famous painting of war's destructiveness, "Guernica." He also cites the works of modern artists like Edvard Munch, Van Gogh, Chagall, and older artists like Michelangelo, Goya, Breughel, and Bosch. While "secular" in content, such art stirs religious questions that grapple with the deepest mysteries of life.

Tillich's level 1—non-religious content with non-religious style—while less useful catechetically, can be helpful at least for opening the eye and heart to the world of beauty.

Both Corita's analysis of photos and Tillich's analysis of art recognize the importance of distinguishing subject matter and style. Subject matter is easily recognized as weak or strong, non-religious or religious. But the ability to discern photographic and artistic style as strong and as religious is not as simple. We need to train our sensitivities to recognize photos and art that are strong and religious in their style.

"Reading" Pictures

How do you, as catechist, develop this needed sensitivity? Here are a few practical steps—many from Corita Kent—addressed directly to individual catechists. The better you learn to "read" visuals, the more effectively will you be able to use pictures in your catechesis.

1. Make a rotating exhibit. Find four photos and/or art works that you really like and feel are strong. Hang them up in a place where you can see them conveniently and often. Keep them up for a week. At the end of the week replace the one you find you like least with a picture you feel is stronger, more truly religious. Repeat this process each week, gradually developing your ability to select good visuals.

2. Try selective stacking. Take a magazine that has many photos. Start at the front and tear out every photo as you page through the magazine. As you tear out the photos, place them in two stacks. Do this quickly as you

tear them out. One stack is for photos you like and feel are strong. The other stack is for those you do not like and consider weak. Afterwards examine the two stacks of photos more carefully. Try to discover why those in one stack seem stronger than those in the other stack. Go through a similar process with religious art, tearing/ cutting out art works from magazines or inexpensive books of art.

3. Practice cropping. Make two cardboard forms, each in the shape of an "L." Place one on top of the other to form a moveable frame. Place the cropping frame on top of a photo or art work. Move the two "L's" so that you can see only selected parts of the picture. Continue looking for just that part of the visual that comes through most simply and powerfully. In this way you will be growing in your ability to select or create more effective visuals.

4. Meditate. Find a time and place where you can quietly—and regularly—spend a few minutes looking at a piece of art or a photo. Hang the picture where you can see it comfortably. Relax as much as possible. Breathe deeply and slowly, rhythmically. Let the tensions flow out of your body. Then look for a moment or two at the visual. Let it reach into you. Let it touch your feelings. Then close your eyes. Give in to the feelings that the picture has stirred in you. Imagine the picture if you can. After a moment or two, look at it again. Begin to notice details—the arrangement, color, lines, relationships. Close your eyes again while letting your feelings and mind and heart open to the picture's impact. Be aware of what the picture is saying to you, what questions or insights about life or Christian tradition it is surfacing. Look at it once more. Perhaps make notes of your observations and reactions. Do this as long as you find it profitable. Repeat the experience with the same picture or with other visuals another day. Get into the habit of meditating on different pictures. Gradually you will find yourself more sure in your selection of pictures to use in your religion classes.

5. Visit museums. Make time to occasionally visit an art museum or an art gallery. If you have no museums or galleries in your vicinity, visit them through art or photo books. Excellent reproductions of good art and good photography are available at libraries and at most book stores. (Many in bookstores are available at half price or less after their first year or two of publication.) A key to learning from such experiences is to learn to look carefully at a few photos or works of art at a time rather than scanning many works quickly. Let each picture speak to you globally before trying to analyze its details and form.

6. Classify photos and art. As you look at art works, try to classify them into one of Tillich's four categories. Do this after you approach the art openly, letting it work on you. Only then get analytical. Sensitivity to religious style comes only with looking at and responding to many works of art over some time. If you find art reproductions for use in your teaching, file them in terms of subject matter and also in terms of Tillich's four levels of religious art.

7. Take photographs. One of the most enjoyable ways of becoming more sensitive to the power of photos is to take photos yourself. Invest in a moderately priced 35 mm. camera with a built-in flash and zoom lens and begin taking pictures more consciously. Study your photos. Learning from your mistakes, try to take better photos each time.

In these and similar ways, you will find yourself growing in sensitivity to the kind of strong photos that have potential for use in catechesis. In the process you will discover that your use of photos in your teaching will be growing in effectiveness.

Four Areas for Use

Use of pictures falls into four broad areas that can facilitate the four basic catechetical strategies: 1) reflection, 2) dialogue, 3) prayer, and 4) action. Here are some ways to use visuals in each of these strategies.

1. Reflection A good picture is an invitation to reflect on life. A visual's gift is its immediacy and impact, its ability to capture one of life's fleeting moments, allowing that frozen moment to reveal something of life's mysteries. A picture's suggestive power—whether photo or religious art—lies in its symbolic character. One moment expressed in film or paint becomes a symbol of the inner reality or "inscape" of that moment and others like it. A strong picture has a kind of sacramental quality, making present and revealing the deeper reality of life that surfaces in its lines, composition, and color. Good visuals allow one to move from sight to insight. They raise questions as well as record facts or features. Photos are contemporary culture's most characteristic means of stimulating reflection. Good art has done this through the centuries. Here are some ways to use pictures to stimulate reflection in catechesis.

Focusing Hang a photo or art work in a prominent place, or project a slide, so all will see it as they enter the room. This can create an atmosphere, stimulate curiosity, suggest a theme, become the focal point of an entire lesson. Nothing need be said about the picture until the appropriate time within the lesson or unit. Such a photo or work of art may be displayed for several days or weeks without comment. Be sure to look at it yourself from time to time. Its very presence can silently reach out to the minds and hearts of the group until you or they are ready to deal with it more explicitly.

Captioning Show your group a carefully selected photo or piece of art. Ask them to look quietly at it for a moment or two. Ask them to write down in only a few words a caption that captures what the visual says to them.

Integrating Have your students study a photo careful-ly. Ask them to search out a biblical quote, part of a prayer, or a doctrinal statement that they feel the photo illustrates or exemplifies. That text may become the cap-tion for the photo. Or have them see how many biblical quotes speak to the photo.

Or reverse the process. Give the group one or more biblical, liturgical, or doctrinal texts and have them search for photos that suggest the meaning of that tradi-tional insight for today's life.

Or show a work of religious art. Ask what experienc-es in daily life the art suggests. Or have the group retell the religious story in contemporary terms. Or have them place side by side a photo and a work of sacred art.

Juxtaposing Provide one photo. Invite the students to find another photo that says the same thing or that says the opposite or that qualifies or builds on the first. In this way relationships may be discovered visually that might not be suggested verbally. A similar activity may be done with art works.

Storywriting Let your students look quietly at a care-fully selected photo. Ask them to write a story based on what they see in the photo. Or have them write an edito-rial, a poem, an ad, or an essay that will help them probe deeper the aspect of life revealed in the photo. With art that depicts biblical stories, have the students tell the sto-ry from the details of the artist's picture.

Questioning Show a strong photo or art work. Let the students look at it quietly. Then question them about it, moving from the picture to their own experience. For example: "What seems to be happening in the picture?" "Who are the people?" "What are they doing?" "How do they seem to feel?" "Have you ever been in a situation like that?" "What was it like?" "How did you feel?" "Why?" In this way let the picture draw them deeper into their own experience, which at first they may be hesitant or unable to think about.

Used in an open, reverent fashion, strong photos and pieces of art are evocative of deep reflection on life within the catechetical process.

2. Dialogue Pictures are particularly apt for encour-aging dialogue and building communication. Because a picture is more than simply a factual record, it can sug-gest different thoughts and feelings in each of those who view it. A group looking at the same visual will see a rich blending of meanings in the same picture. Photos and art thus become powerful catalysts for dialogue. It has been said that the primary use of all media in cat-echesis is to foster communication within a group.

Most of the techniques mentioned above for encour-aging reflection are equally effective for encouraging di-alogue. Done in a group the reflection stimulated by a photo or art work may actually be deeper and richer be-cause of the sharing. Here are some additional ways of using pictures for group sharing.

Making collages This is an overused but still valid way to use visuals in catechesis. Photos and/or art and words are arranged on poster board in order to make a strong statement. When done by a group this involves considerable sharing and communication. Variations suggested by Corita Kent are using a whole wall or the sides of cartons which may be stacked like blocks, or making books, like prayerbooks, with photos, words, and possibly sacred art.

Creating shows Have the group create together a presentation using slides, recorded commentary, and music. Such a presentation can sum up an entire unit, theme, or year. It may be quite simple or very sophisti-cated. (Note: video may be more exciting now than slides.)

Photographing Have the students go out and take photos. Give an assignment related to your topic or theme. For example: "Walk around your neighborhood. Photograph anyone or anything that suggests hope for the future." After the photos are processed, encourage the group to share and talk about them. They might then create with the photos some form of creative expres-sion—collage, photo-essay, sound-slide show, exhibit— for sharing with others.

3. Prayer Just as visuals lend themselves to encour-aging reflection and dialogue, so too are they valuable helps for prayer in catechesis. Prayer is a radical re-sponse to life. Art and photos present slices of life. Pic-tures help us identify with the deepest of human yearn-ings, the most pressing of human needs, the most marvelous of human giftedness, and the riches of our re-ligious tradition. Therefore they are valuable helps to prayer in catechesis. Following are suggestions for prayerful uses of photos and art.

Meditating Present a visual. Encourage each to look at it in a relaxed, unhurried manner, letting the picture "speak" to heart and mind. Invite each to take paper and pencil and write a meditation on what the picture sug-gests. Those who wish may share their meditations with the group. The shared meditations may lead to shared prayer arising spontaneously from the heart or based on a traditional prayer form.

Visualizing psalms Have the students select a psalm, psalm verse, or other prayer. Ask them to find one or more photos or works of art that illustrate the meaning of the psalm in today's world. Pray the psalm together while looking at the picture. In similar fashion they might match pictures to hymns or prayerful songs.

Sparking spontaneous prayer Have the students look carefully at a photo or piece of art. Allow time for the picture to touch them. Perhaps play a carefully selected recording of music. Then ask each to offer a brief prayer suggested by the visual.

Composing litanies Use a sequence of pictures or a random sampling of photos from magazines and newspapers. Allow time for the students to look meditatively at the visuals. Using a familiar litany pattern as a group refrain, e.g., "Lord hear us," invite individuals to pray whatever a given picture suggests. After each individual prayer, sparked by an individual visual, all pray the refrain.

4. Action Visual experiences can also lead to actions which flow from the shared reflection, dialogue, and prayer. Photos and art can provide powerfully motivating images as well as being part of actual actions suggested in lessons. Here are several ways we have used pictures in various actions as catechists.

Giving gifts Give your students good prints of strong photos or good art. The students may display them in their homes, helping them remember the insights originally gained from the visuals. Inexpensive but excellent reproductions may be had by mail from leading art museums and photo exhibitions. Encourage the students to also give similar photos or pieces of art to friends and relatives, for example, as part of a "get well" card for a sick friend or family member or as a gift on a special occasion like a birthday or First Communion.

Making ads or posters Individuals or groups of students might make striking posters or large ads—using strong visuals and striking words or a caption—for use in relation to the parish or school liturgy, or as part of a parish festival celebrating cultural diversity, or for calling people's attention to suffering, societal injustice, and violations of human rights.

Creating beautiful environments Visuals can add an element of beauty to almost any setting—a church, school, classroom, home, apartment, room. Adding beauty to any segment of space can be a boon to all who enter or use that space.

You can draw on your own creativity to find other and better ways of using pictures to encourage reflection, dialogue, prayer, and action in catechesis. Pictures—photos and other art—thus become more than "visual aids." They become a major language, a unique media for penetrating life's mysteries and meaning. They provide an expansion of our ability to see. Used sensitively in catechesis pictures can be a significant help in our learning "to see God in all things," "to see Christ in all things." Photos and art can help us grow in "faith by seeing." Photography is a modern help to healing spiritual blindness—as good art has been for centuries. All of us experience the profound need voiced by the blind man of the Gospel: "Lord, I want to see!" (Luke 14:41)

Questions for Reflection and Discussion

1. What visible things most strongly suggest to you God's invisible presence? Why?

2. What has been your experience with visuals in religious education?

3. What visuals have had the most impact on your thinking and feeling? Why?

4. Why are visuals uniquely suited to stimulate reflection?

5. Why is it easier to talk about people in a photo or picture than about one's own experience?

6. What experiences of prayer have you had using visuals?

Ways to Respond

1. Study the textbook. Go through your textbook carefully examining the photos and art works that are used in it. Pencil by each work the words "weak" or "strong," "non-religious" or "religious" in the sense used in this chapter. Consider how the textbook suggests that the pictures are to be used. How do these uses mesh with the principles and examples found in the chapter?

2. Start a picture file. Make folders or envelopes for each lesson in your text or of the more important themes you will be considering with your students. Then be alert as you read newspapers and magazines for pictures that reflect those themes. Cut out such visuals and file them for use at the appropriate time. You will be building a personal picture file that may well have more meaning to you and your students than the visuals in your textbooks.

3. Invite a photographer, artist, picture editor, or media consultant. Depending on the resources at hand, invite someone who specializes in visual media to a meeting with you and your co-catechists. Ask what your guest looks for in a good picture, what can be done to make good pictures, how to exhibit or use good visuals, etc. Some technical information about photography and painting will also be helpful to you in discovering really good pictures—e.g., the impact of composition, lens choice, focus, grain, and color.

18

Using TV, Video, and Film

> Because television occupies so much of the time of so many people in the United States, catechesis should seek to foster critical understanding of this medium in particular. Viewers need to know, for example, how programs are planned and produced; techniques used by advertisers and others to influence and persuade; whether and to what degree TV gives a true picture of life or distorts reality; and the role of profit motives in determining policy in commercial television.
>
> Because people grow in maturity and because there are frequent changes in the media, continuing education is necessary to keep abreast of the changes.
>
> *National Catechetical Directory, 261*

Several years ago we spent two weeks in Honduras in Central America with close Honduran friends. We had the opportunity to go to places many tourists would not normally visit.

One evening we were in a remote town. The poverty was appalling. Our "hotel" was most primitive. It was a hot evening so we strolled around the town square with our god-children, whose mother is Honduran.

They wanted some candy. We noticed a small store that was still open. We walked in and looked around. There was just one bare light illuminating several old glass cases with a few bags of candies inside. A few naked children gazed at what was behind the glass.

Off to the left was a door to another room. It was totally dark, except for a small black and white TV in one corner. As we stepped through the door, we realized the room was packed with people, young and old. They were watching an American sitcom rerun.

New Media, New Age, New Language

Being in that dark room for a few moments, in a foreign country overwhelmed with poverty, looking with poor peasants at a show made in our wealthy nation reflecting our consumer values, brought home the importance and power of the electronic media in today's world. Television is not only all pervasive, but helps shape a kind of global culture, instantaneously bridging vast gulfs, providing a new world language. Marshall McLuhan two

decades ago summed it up in his famous phrase: *The medium is the message.*

The nature and power of this new technological language strongly impacts the church and its ministries. It is no accident that in a culture of the *spoken word* catechesis developed as oral proclamation. Later as cultures shifted to the written and then the printed word, catechists needed to learn new methodologies based on manuscripts and books.

Now, in a culture shaped by mass communications media, catechists are challenged to "echo God's Word" through the electronic media—film, television, video, and computers. New methods are needed to supplement those based on oral communication and the printed word.

Avery Dulles, S.J., suggests that the church and its ministries in this age of electronic communications need to be more *dialogic, democratic,* and *secular,* balancing previous approaches that were more overtly religious, authoritarian, biblical, and philosophical.

Pierre Babin—French media expert and expert catechist—seems to share that conviction. He believes the electronic media work strongly through *visual sensory images* created to influence *feelings,* unlike earlier media that stressed words and concepts aimed at convincing the reason. As such the new media can foster a healthy *emotional response* to reality. Audio-visual media *evoke* more than they define, and encourage *creativi-*

ry. The genius of film, TV, and video in catechesis is that the electronic media invite *involvement* and *participation* (even though passivity seems the more typical response). Since images evoke different feelings and ideas in each viewer, electonic communications media have a marvelous *democratizing* power. They have the innate ability to foster a richly varied *community* (even though most often TV viewers seem lost in their private worlds). And they can develop *critical awareness* when used properly.

With these strengths of the new media Babin notes some negative effects. The electronic media *lack clarity* and *precision*, and *lack structure and synthesis*. For a balanced catechesis these negatives can be offset by carefully developed textbooks and knowledgeable catechists. He stresses that electronic media can never replace *personal contact*, must always be a *medium for communication* between human beings, and need the balance of *systematic, reflective thinking*.

With these insightful observations in mind we need to look at creative, practical ways of using the electronic media in catechesis—ways that maximize the inherent strengths of the media while countering their weaknesses. Although *film, television*, and *video* each have some unique characteristics, what they have in common seems much greater. We will explore some practical principles and techniques that apply to all three. We will not explicitly treat *computer programs* or *computer games*. Nor

will we touch on the constantly developing electronic equipment and hardware.

Our experience is that *filmstrips,* which were one of the major catechetical media in recent decades, have much less appeal to today's youth, so accustomed to film and TV. Some of the following principles and techniques can also be applied to filmstrips where they are still used.

Fundamental Principles

The fundamental principle guiding use of electronic media in catechesis is that their use must be such as to foster growth in faith. A film or video clip must fit honestly into the essential process of faith growth—associating some dimension of human experience with some related aspect of Catholic tradition—at a level below the superficial.

The primary value of the electronic media in catechesis is their sensory and experiential power to suggest and evoke involvement in the deeper mysteries of life and our Catholic faith tradition. They invite a personal response within a community.

Secondarily the electronic media are catechetically useful for conveying information—historical, biblical, liturgical, theological, scientific.

Most catechetically useful films, TV, or video presentations fall into one of the two basic dimensions of the catechetical process—either explore some *mystery of hu-*

man experience or some *mystery of Catholic tradition*. They are usually secular or explicitly religious in content.

Using Paul Tillich's categories of art—religious or non-religious in content and style (see chapter 17)—we want to find media that are *religious in style,* whether their content be explicitly religious or not. That is, whatever the content of a media work useful for catechesis, its style, form, presentation needs to be strong and religious, suggesting the deeper mysteries of life and Catholic tradition.

Unfortunately many "religious" films, TV, and video presentations tend to be illustrated lectures or conversations, "talking heads" with visual illustrations.

We normally use a film, TV, or video expressing an overtly secular content (but presented in a strong religious style) during the first step or movement of a lesson, Learning About Our Lives. Sometimes, if short enough, it can be repeated in the third step, Learning How to Live Our Faith, either to deepen its insight into one of life's mysteries or as part of a prayer experience.

Explicitly religious films or video/TV presentations—about the Bible, prayer, liturgical rites, Catholic doctrinal or moral teachings—normally fit best in the second step of a lesson, Learning About Our Faith.

Many media creations are designed actually to engage the viewer in making precisely that faith connection between daily experience and our tradition as Catholics. These may be used as the basis of a whole lesson, or as a review, or as part of a prayer service.

Some Practical Approaches

Here are some steps we have found helpful for using electronic media effectively in catechesis or religious education.

1. Preview. Absolutely essential is that you preview whatever you are hoping to use. Do not depend on written descriptions or evaluations of a given film, TV show, or video. Actually take time to view it and reflect on it in relation to your class.

Notice:

• *its overall impact on you.* Did it touch you, move you, give you new insight? What did it say to you?

• *its relevance to your students.* Is it appropriate to and understandable by your students? Do you feel it would really speak to them?

• *its relevance to your lessons.* Does it truly fit the theme and purpose of your lesson?

• *its length.* How much time would it take in your class if you showed the whole piece? Are particular seg-

ments more meaningful and suggestive than others? How long are they?

2. Plan carefully. Once you have previewed the media and decide to use it, take real care in planning how to use it most effectively. Consider:

• *when to use it.* In which part of the lesson would it best work—exploring life experience, sharing Catholic tradition, or integrating and responding to both?

• *how to use it.* Which of the essential catechetical learning strategies does it seem best suited for—to foster reflection, stimulate dialogue, facilitate prayer, or motivate to action?

• *what else is needed.* Depending on your intended use, you will need things (a) *before* showing the media, to lead into it—like questions about the human experience or Bible story central to that media, hints as to what to focus on during the viewing, questions to keep in mind during the viewing, (b) *during* the presentation of the media—like paper and pencils to take notes, a prayerful environment if its being used primarily for prayer, and (c) *after* viewing the media—like paper and pencils or crayons for doing something in response to it, worksheets with questions to guide reflection on it, activities to help the students relate it to their lives or to their Catholic faith.

3. Prepare. Prepare long enough to be sure the media selection you want to use will be available when you need it.

Carefully prepare and test any equipment so you, an assistant, or one of the students, can run it comfortably.

Prepare the film or video cassette for viewing—set to where you want to begin, marked clearly where you want to stop.

Prepare the environment so all can comfortably view the presentation and respond to it according to your plan.

4. Present. The impact of a good film, TV show, or video presentation comes chiefly from the work itself. However, you can enhance its power within your catechetical session by your careful planning.

Perhaps most important in relation to the actual showing or presenting of the media selection is how you introduce it. For example:

• *cold start* Some works are most effective as the initial experience of the session, with no comment, no preparatory experience. Simply begin your session with the media piece. Everything that follows will then hinge on the impact of that opening work.

• *warm start* More often, perhaps, a film or video/TV presentation's impact in a lesson is enhanced by a preparatory experience. If you have carefully planned where to show it in a particular lesson, there will be a natural preparation flowing from the lesson plan itself. You may want to build in some specific preparation for a particular work. For example:

Depending on the nature and purpose of the media itself, we find at times a *moment of quiet reflection* beforehand can be helpful to focus attention.

At other times we ask *questions* of the students and engage them in initial discussion. The questions center on the theme or topic of the media presentation which in turn will provide answers to those questions at at least lead the youngsters into deeper exploration.

Sometimes we prepare a *worksheet* on the topic of the film or video/TV selection, with something from a recent newspaper or magazine, together with questions that lead into the media presentation.

• *start/stop/start* A very effective way of presenting some media works is to begin them, then stop them at an appropriate point to allow the students to respond to it, and then continue it, perhaps stopping and starting another time. You will have questions or a worksheet prepared to guide their reflection, dialogue, or prayer during the breaks in the presentation. The pausing can greatly increase student involvement with the media work and help them relate it to their lives.

5. Ponder. Sometimes a film, TV, or video work may be used at the *very end* of a class. If it is well done and fits the preceding dynamic of the class, closing with a strong media work can send the youngsters out pondering, reflecting, making their own what they experienced through it and the whole lesson.

More often, perhaps, the media is used within the lesson's development. Then its catechetical power can be enhanced by guiding the youngster to reflect on it in relation to their own lives and faith tradition. You may find prepared questions helpful for stimulating thought or discussion.

We like to prepare worksheets that draw upon the words and images of the media. For example, we often ask our students to *Draw the image of the film/video/TV show which touched you most (do you most remember, did you like best)?* This has proved very revealing since the selected image is normally very powerfully, emotionally as well as cognitively.

The worksheet then continues with questions related to other dimensions of the media piece. These questions encourage deeper reflection and help the youngsters relate the issue, experience, or value explored in the media presentation with something in their Catholic tradition; or vice versa, if the media was biblical, liturgical, doctrinal, or moral in its content.

6. Pray. Because the electronic media can have a strong impact on the whole person, they often lead quite easily into prayer. Some media presentations are so beautiful and insightful, just viewing them is a prayerful meditation. Others lend themselves to a prayer experience, either by exploring a dimension of reality in depth or by powerfully presenting a biblical story, liturgical ritual, Catholic doctrine, or great Christian's life.

7. Promise to act, to do something motivated by the media work. Ultimately catechesis is aimed at fostering in people a maturing faith that shows itself in action—in love, compassion, justice, honesty, commitment. One of the special powers of the electronic media is their ability to invite response, involvement, participation. We need to keep in mind this call to action, to lifestyle, in our use of media in religious education.

New Skills

The new media challenge is to develop new skills as catechists. They tend to reshape our overall approach and methodology to one that is less directive and more suggestive, more balanced between images/senses/emotions and words/concepts/ideas, more respectful of each student's ideas and therefore less authoritarian, more oriented to exploring in depth than to surface learning of facts, more balanced between subjective and objective, contemplative and active, imaginative and rational.

Questions for Reflection and Discussion

1. What has been your experience with television, video, and film in religious education, as a student and as a catechist?

2. What do you see as the greatest strengths and the greatest weaknesses of the electronic media in catechesis?

3. How do you think the electronic media have affected your life, your family, your children, your faith? American culture? the Catholic church?

4. What are your biggest hesitations or anxieties about trying to use media more in your catechesis?

5. What would most help you feel more comfortable in using the electronic media more in your catechesis?

Ways to Respond

1. Become more sensitive to media. You probably watch a certain amount of television, film, and videos. Try occasionally to view them, more consciously aware of how they affect you, how they achieve their effect. Give attention to the images that move you, the way music is used deliberately to heighten emotional responses, what techniques they use to keep your attention, the pacing. The more conscious you are of the way the media communicate, the more sensitively you can use them in your lessons.

2. Study TV ads more critically. Become aware of how much commercial interests affect the media. Notice what ads are shown with what shows and ask yourself why? who is the audience? Be attentive to the proportion of emotional appeal relative to objective information. Observe the actors and actresses, what kind of persons are used to see what kind of products? Ask yourself what life-style, what values, what world-view a particular ad assumes.

3. Compare TV and reality. Reflect on how many ways the world presented in television shows differs from the real world as you experience it. Chart what values different programs consistently present. Become more aware of the sometimes subtle, often quite direct, commercial messages in various shows. Examine how sex and violence are portrayed.

19

USING STORIES

Experience is of great importance in catechesis. Experiential learning, which can be considered a form of inductive methodology, gives rise to concerns and questions, hopes and anxieties, reflections and judgments, which increase one's desire to penetrate more deeply into life's meaning. Experience can also increase the intelligibility of the Christian message, by providing illustrations and examples which shed light on the truths of revelation. At the same time, experience itself should be interpreted in the light of revelation.

The experiential approach is not easy, but it can be of considerable value to catechesis. Catechists should encourage people to reflect on their significant experiences and respond to God's presence there. Sometimes they will provide appropriate experiences. They should seek to reach the whole person, using both cognitive (intellectual) and affective (emotional) techniques.

National Catechetical Directory, 176

Over the years we have experienced a growing belief in the power of storytelling. We find we learn as much or more about life from children's literature as from any other source. We have come to share the conviction of G.K. Chesterton, the great Catholic writer of the early twentieth century. In a marvelous chapter, "The Ethics of Elfland," in his very serious book entitled *Orthodoxy* (Garden City, NY: Doubleday Image Books, 1959), Chesterton writes, "My first and last philosophy, that which I believe in with unbroken certainty, I learnt in the nursery.... The things I believed most then, the things I believe most now, are the things called fairy tales." From fairy tales Chesterton claims to have learned the deepest realities of the "eccentric privilege" which is life. Fairy tales led him to wonder at life's mysteries and gradually to sense life's ultimate mystery. "I had always felt life first as a story, and if there is a story there is a storyteller."

Chesterton's appreciation of fairytales is echoed in the comprehensive work of the great contemporary child psychologist Bruno Bettleheim, *The Uses of Enchantment: The Meaning and Importance of Fairy Tales*. Other experts, representing a variety of disciplines, like theologian John Shea, sociologist Andrew Greeley, liturgist James Dunning, pastor William Bausch, and writer Madeleine L'Engle, have popularized the importance of story in human and spiritual development.

What Stories Teach

What is true of fairy tales is true as well of other good stories. They help us in a delightful way to discover that life is full of good and evil, and hint that no matter how great and many the evils, ultimately life is good. Good stories and tales can clothe all who have the heart of a child with a religious perception of life's mysteries. For example, the "fool" of the fairy tale is not necessarily the one who is witless, but rather the one who spontaneously does what is caring, selfless, and thoughtful. The "ugly duckling" turns out to be the most beautiful of all the swans. The life of the "selfish giant" is one of perpetual winter until he is able to open his heart and his garden to others. *Hansel and Gretel* evokes the reality of evil and the triumph of innocence and goodness.

From fairy tales, good stories, and literature, the childlike of all ages can discover that there are special rewards for being loving, upright, responsible, faithful, and industrious. One can learn that sacrifice is an important part of enjoying the good things of life. Story is a natural way of uncovering and entering into life's mysteries. Stories are a delightful source of human and religious wisdom.

Through stories we can look at slices of life up close and experience life by walking vicariously with another. We find our own story becoming clearer as we enjoy good stories about others. People in stories take all kinds of risks and live with consequences. People in stories make both good and bad choices, but they make them. People in stories have their feelings hurt and hurt others back or they find a better way.

People in stories survive the ambiguity of adolescence, fear, shattered hopes, death, loneliness. People in stories grow in wisdom through their experiences, and their struggles carry the reader along. People in stories learn that there is more to life than meets the eye.

Stories, if they are good, allow one to gaze more deeply into ordinary experience. Through the eyes of a skilled storyteller one is led to identify with the characters, enter into their responses, and share the consequences of their choices. Stories make available segments of life in such a way as to stir imaginations and hearts to sense the deeper story in all our stories.

Jesus Told Stories

Anyone doubting the power of story to break open life's mysteries need only to open the Gospels. Jesus speaks of the most profound realities of God's kingdom in deceptively simple stories of farmers sowing seeds, housewives baking bread, shepherds caring for sheep, children obeying and disobeying, rich and poor men praying, fishermen fishing. After some 20 centuries we have yet to exhaust the riches of Jesus' parables.

Christian catechesis has traditionally followed Jesus' example of teaching through story. The New Testament is made up of stories of Jesus' life, death, and resurrection, of the stories he told, and of stories of his early followers. Down through the centuries catechists have told and retold these stories, and added others recalling the lives and teachings of great Christians of later times.

Today theologians and catechists are more conscious of the importance, too, of our own personal stories, and less obvious religious stories about life's deeper experiences. Story is recognized as a primary way of approaching the mystery present in life's sorrows and joys, successes and disappointments, satisfactions and frustrations, loves and hates.

Catechists today tend to describe their task as helping people relate their own stories with the traditional stories of the faith community. For the traditional stories are best

grasped in the light of our own experienced stories, which in turn are illuminated by the traditional stories. In a real sense the traditional stories are our stories. We all need to face the insecurity of life with trust in God as Abraham did. We all struggle for freedom in our lives as Moses did in his. Each of us lives out Zacchaeus's search for recognition, the blind man's yearning to be able to see, the rich farmer's lust for bigger barns. Sometimes we may be the Good Samaritan, yet at other times may pass by the hurting as quickly as did the priest and Levite.

Catechesis is the process of helping us to interpret our stories in the light of the great Judaeo-Christian stories. Good stories of all kinds are immensely helpful to this process because good stories are about the mysteries of life we all experience.

Perhaps a few examples of this process would be helpful. We would like to sketch briefly three lesson plans, one for very young children, one for older children, and one for adolescents or adults. With minor adaptations, however, all three could be used with adult groups.

Stories With Young Children

First, a class for young children. Our aim might be to help the children grow in appreciation of God as someone who cherishes them just the way they are and loves to be with them always. Using the typical lesson structure (as discussed in Chapter 3 and 15), we begin with the children's life experience. We read Margaret Wise Brown's beautiful classic, *The Runaway Bunny* (New York: Harper & Row, 1942). This charmingly illustrated story is about a baby bunny who repeatedly runs away only to find that his mother searches him out and welcomes him back to their den and feeds him as before. After listening to the story, the children are invited to talk about the bunny's experience and feelings. The children will begin talking about their own experiences and feelings as they talk about the bunny and his mother. The story of the runaway bunny touches down on their own stories. The children might want to draw their favorite part of the story, or they might want to act it out.

Next we move to the church's tradition. Building on the children's stories and the story of the runaway bunny, we share with them one of the most beautiful poems in the Bible, Psalm 139, verses 1-13, a story poem about God's loving presence to us wherever we may go. This could be read directly from a simple version of the Bible or from an adaptation of the biblical text. For example, *Where Are You, God?: Psalm 139 for Children* by Elspeth Campbell Murphy (St. Louis: David C. Cook, 1980).

We would then draw from the children their feelings about the image of God found in the psalm. We might learn a short phrase or two from the psalm by heart.

The final movement, the integration of the children's experience with the Christian tradition and their response to God's Word in both, might be to make buttons that say something about God and the children. This simple activity integrates in a personal way the story of God from the psalm with their own stories. The buttons can be made of circles cut from construction paper.

When we used this lesson once with six year olds, one little boy looked for a moment at the blank paper circle, then took a fat red crayon from the box nearby and quickly made his button. "He drew a "smile" face and printed below it: "God loves me." Finally, we might end prayerfully with the catechist rereading aloud the verses of Psalm 139 (used earlier in the lesson) as the children actively enter into it with simple gestures and movements.

For Older Children

This second sample lesson plan is for older children, perhaps in the middle grades. The aim of the lesson is to help them know Jesus better as someone who welcomes and forgives those who are guilty—or are presumed guilty by others. A secondary aim is to reinforce the values inherent in the commandment "You shall not steal."

Beginning with the youngster's life experience we read a poem together, for example, Cindy Herbert's "The Theft" from her book *I See a Child* (New York: Doubleday, 1974).

Everyone knows I took your money.

I don't show it and they don't show it.
But everyone knows I did it.
THIEF.
All I wanted was a little money to buy a ring.
I didn't know it would make me a thief.

We would talk about the poem, letting the youngsters share the feelings, ideas, and experiences suggested by it. They could write stories of a time when they took something or were accused of taking something. The following two stories were written by sixth-graders with whom we did this lesson.

Mom realized that the coffee candies were gone and she knew that I positively love coffee and so, right away she accused me. I told her and I told her that it wasn't me but she still thought it was. When my brothers came home I asked them what coffee candies tasted like and right away one of them spoke up.

Mom noticed that her radio was missing, when she asked my sister she said, "Ann probably did it." When she asked my brother he said, "Ann did it." When she asked my other brother he replied "Probably Ann." Then my mom came to my door and accused me of taking her radio. As it came out, my father brought it to work!

Using these stories as a basis for sharing, we talk about how it feels to steal or to be accused of stealing.

Once we are well into their experiences we move to the second stage of the lesson, Catholic tradition. A perfect story from the Gospels is the one about Zacchaeus (Luke 19:1-10). Whether Zacchaeus was in fact guilty of graft in his tax collecting or not may be open to question, but everyone presumed he was a thief. There is a beautiful telling of this story in the biblical series by Kort de Kees (Augsburg Press). However, the story might also be read directly from a good translation of the Bible.

The youngsters then talk about the story of Zacchaeus, what it says to them, how they feel about Zacchaeus, the other people, and Jesus. They might do some research into the background of the story to better understand Zacchaeus's role and why people were so hostile to him. They might dramatize the story to get deeper into Zacchaeus's feelings and Jesus' attitude.

To help the youngsters enter into the integration-response stage, we might suggest that they "become" Zacchaeus. They are each to write a letter in Zacchaeus's name to someone who is a thief or is accused of being one. The letter would tell what Zacchaeus experienced in meeting Jesus. In this way children can relate the Gospel story with their own stories. The class ends with the sharing of at least some of their letters and a prayer.

Older Students and Adults

A final example of the use of story in catechesis is with adolescents or adults. This lesson would be appropriate for confirmation preparation or for the feast of Pentecost. The aim would be to help the students grow in appreciation of how the Holy Spirit is present and active in their lives.

To get into the life experience of the students, ask them to tell or write a story of the most important, or most difficult, choice they have ever had to make. When completed, the stories are shared and discussed. When we have done this lesson with Confirmation candidates, their choices ranged from relatively small ones like what kind of bicycle to buy, to major choices like which of their separated or divorced parents to live with.

To enrich and broaden their own experiences of personal choices, we read together the fascinating story by Max Odorff and Louis M. Savary, *The Wind and the Dwarfs* (Winona, MN: St. Mary's College Press, 1970). We then talk about the story and ponder why the dwarfs finally chose the wind to be their friend.

Within the context of personal choice, enriched by the story of the dwarfs' choice, we get into our tradition by telling the Pentecost story from Acts 2:1-13. Discussion of the biblical story follows, along with any background needed to better understand it. What did the disciples experience? How is their experience of the wind like the dwarfs' experience? Why is the Spirit described as wind and fire? What choices did the disciples make? Why did they choose the way they did?

Now participants are ready for the integration and response. They might be invited to write a letter to their Bishop requesting confirmation and describing why they chose to be confirmed. Or if they are not preparing for confirmation, they might make some choices about the Spirit's guidance in their own lives. Perhaps some choice of an action or project might be made to help those in need, thereby responding to and revealing the presence of Christ's Spirit. The lesson could end with prayer to the Holy Spirit to be with them in their choice or project—or with the prayerful singing (with gestures) of a Holy Spirit hymn.

These sketches of three lesson plans need fuller development, but they suggest how story can be woven into catechesis using the students' personal stories, biblical stories, and the stories or poems told by poets and storytellers about life's mysteries. The sketches show how we as catechists can help our students associate their own stories with the stories of our Judaeo-Christian tradition and respond to God's word speaking through both.

Practical Suggestions

Ten practical hints on storytelling follow. Feel free to adapt them in the light of your own experiences.

1. Finding good stories is perhaps the first step. Once you have decided that "story" will be an important part of your future catechetical efforts, you will become more sensitive to good stories that come into your lives from a variety of sources. Your own daily experiences are filled with possible stories useful in catechesis. Other stories will come from the daily newspaper, from magazines you read, and from radio and television. Stories are everywhere, but you need to be alert to recognize them and to jot them down or clip them for future use.

Libraries or local book stores can become a constant source of valuable stories. Getting acquainted with the librarian and browsing around the library or bookstore will help you find stories that appeal to you. The children's section of any good bookstore or library is a goldmine. Other valuable sources of good stories are friends, neighbors, and school teachers. The world is full of stories that can enrich your own life and the lives of those you catechize, but you need to learn to recognize and collect them.

2. You should use only stories that you enjoy and find delightfully enlightening. You shouldn't use a story just because it is recommended unless you actually like it. Unless stories touch your heart and imagination, your sharing of them will probably not touch your students.

3. Before reading or telling a story you will want to become thoroughly familiar with it, reading it over and over until it is a part of you. You will begin to see the setting and the characters, and feel with each of them. If you are going to tell the story, you may find it helpful to sketch out in outline form the main steps of the plot. Be aware of how the story builds to a climax and familiarize yourself with any unusual names or expressions.

4. The use of stories in catechetical lessons should be true to each lesson's particular aim and faithful to the story's own message. Take care not to bend or force a story to fit a catechetical purpose. Unless a story fits the theme and objective naturally and honestly, don't use it in the lesson.

5. Telling or reading stories with interest and conviction is essential. If you really like and react to the story, moving and feeling with the characters, imagining the action, you will be able to tell or read it in a lively manner. The key is living or experiencing the story as it is communicated, keeping eye contact with your listeners and varying your tone of voice, speed of talking, facial and bodily expressions. Some people find it helpful to practice reading or telling a story beforehand, either alone, perhaps in front of a mirror, or with family or friends. Storytelling is an art; it is perfected by practice.

6. Using visual aids where appropriate further stimulates interest. The illustrations in children's books are often exquisitely beautiful. These could be shown to listeners as the story is read or told. Sometimes sacred art depicting a Gospel story can help in the telling of it. Many catechists like to use flannel-board figures to add a visual dimension to their storytelling. Some like to write key words or names on the chalkboard, or even draw the story with stick-figures. Sometimes it is best simply to tell the story and let the listener's visualize it in their imaginations. Recording the story beforehand and playing the recording in class is another way of adding interest.

7. After the story, let the listeners be silent with it for a moment or two. Encourage them to share the ideas and feelings stirred in them by the story. Ask questions and allow free interpretation. Let the listeners ask questions. Do not tell them what the story means or expand on the moral of the story. If the story is a good story, it will convey its own meaning and moral.

8. Encourage your listeners to react to the story, at least at times, with some kind of creative activity that will help them move deeper into it. For example, some stories lend themselves to acting out. The listeners can draw the story or their reactions to it. They might rewrite it by changing its ending or modifying the action or characters. They might interview one of the story characters and write the reflections or reactions of this character. Such activities are meant to help them enter more fully into the story and probe its meaning.

9. With older children, adolescents, and adults it may be that some of them can tell the stories as well or better than you can, and they should be encouraged to do so.

10. You might want to encourage students to write stories from their own experience and imagination. The very writing of an experience as a story can enable the students to enter more fully into their experience and become more able to grasp the meaning and shape of their lives.

Years of experience have confirmed for us the vital role of "story" in catechesis. It is indeed close to the heart of this important process.

Questions for Reflection and Discussion

1. What have you learned from fairy tales and other good stories?

2. How do stories help you better know yourself and your world?

3. What is the unique power of stories? Why are they often so meaningful and memorable?

4. Why do you think Jesus used stories so much in his teaching?

5. What Bible story speaks most strongly to you? Which seems most "your" story? Why?

Ways to Respond

1. Begin a story file. Set aside a box, drawer, or series of file folders for your story collection. Whenever you discover a story that speaks to you, for example in a newspaper or magazine, clip it out and put it in your file. When you hear a good story on TV or radio, or experience one in your life, jot it down and file it. The file can be simple or complicated, neat or messy, depending upon your style. If you collect stories, you will find yourself using them, to the improvement of your catechetical classes.

2. Read stories. Begin the habit of reading stories each week. Begin with whatever kind of story appeals to you—novels, short stories, children's literature. Gradually expand your reading into kinds of stories you are not as familiar with. A librarian or knowledgeable bookstore person can be an invaluable help, as can teachers, friends, and neighbors.

3. Try writing stories of your own. You may enjoy trying to write stories of your own based on experiences you've had or created out of your imagination. Don't worry at first about grammar or style. Just try to tell an interesting story. You might begin by trying to rewrite or adapt existing stories, even Gospel stories. Or you might prefer to begin from scratch to build your own story from your own resources.

CHILDREN'S LITERATURE

The following list is offered as a starter menu of children's literature, stories that may be used with most ages, including adolescents and adults, as well as with younger children. *All of them are of a length so that they could be used within the time span of a lesson.* The list is arranged according to some of the themes common to catechetical programs.

Community/Friendship

Ackerman, Karen. *The Tin Heart.* Atheneum/Macmillan, 1990.

Bell, Martin. *The Way of the Wolf.* "Barrington Bunny," pp. 1-8, Ballantine, 1970.

Boddy, Marlys. *The Glassmakers of Gurven.* Abingdon Press, 1988.

Brown, Marcia. *Stone Soup.* Scribner, 1947.

Freedman, Florence. *Brothers.* Harper & Row, 1985.

Goffstein, M.B. *Our Snowman.* Harper & Row, 1986.

Kantrowitz, Mildred. *Maxie.* Parents' Magazine Press, 1970.

Lionni, Leo. *Little Blue and Little Yellow.* Ivan Obolensky, Inc., 1979.

_____. *Frederick's Fables.* "A Color of His Own," pp. 105-112; "Swimmy," pp. 71-80. Pantheon, 1985. (Each also published as separate books.)

Rose, Deborah Lee. *The People Who Hugged the Trees.* Roberts Rinehart, Inc., 1990.

Roy, Ronald. *A Thousand Pails of Water.* Alfred A. Knopf, 1978.

Ryland, Cynthia. *The Relatives Came.* Bradbury, 1985.

Steig, William. *Amos and Boris.* Farrar, Straus & Giroux, 1971.

Spier, Peter. *People.* Doubleday, 1980.

Compassion and Justice, Sharing, Serving Others and Sacrificing For Them

Bang, Molly. *The Paper Crane.* Greenwillow Books, 985.

Carlson, Natalie Savage. *Surprise in the Mountains.* Harper & Row, 1983.

DePaola, Tomie. *The Legend of the Bluebonnet.* G.P. Putnam's Sons, 1983.

Goffstein, M.B. *Natural History.* Farrar, Straus & Giroux, 1979.

Keats, Ezra Jack. *Louie.* Scholastic Book Services, 1975.

Lindgren, Astrid. *My Nightingale Is Singing.* Viking, 1985.

Lionni, Leo. *Frederick's Fables.* "Tico and the Golden Wings," pp. 51-50. Pantheon, 1985. (Also published as separate book.)

McLerran, Alice. *The Mountain that Loved a Bird.* Picture Book Studio, 1985.

Olson, Addie North. *The Lighthouse Keeper's Daughter.* Little, Brown & Co., 1987.

Price, Leontyne. *Aida.* Harcourt Brave Jovanovich, 1990.

Ringgold, Faith. *Tar Beach.* Crown Publishers, 1991.

Silverstein, Shel. *The Giving Tree.* Harper & Row, 1964.

Steptoe, John. *Mufaro's Beautiful Daughters.* Lothrop, Lee & Shepard, 1984.

_____. *The Story of Jumping Mouse.* Lothrop, Lee & Shepard, 1984.

Tolstoy, Leo. *Shoemaker Martin.* North-South Books, 1986.

Love, Cherishing

Bornstein, Ruth Lercher. *A Beautiful Seashell.* Harper & Row, 1990.

Bunting, Eve. *The Wednesday Surprise.* Houghton Mifflin Co., 1989.

Flourney, Valerie. *The Patchwork Quilt.* E.P. Dutton, 1985.

Hest, Amy. *The Ring and the Window Seat.* Scholastic, Inc., 1990.

Martin, Bill & John Archambault. *Knots on a Counting Rope.* Henry Holt, 1987.

Munsch, Robert. *Love You Forever.* Firefly Books, 1988.

Pearson, Susan. *Happy Birthday, Grampie.* Dial Books, 1990.

Rylant, Cynthia. *Birthday Presents.* Orchard Books, 1987.

_____. *Every Living Thing.* Aladdin, 1985.

Shecter, Ben. *Grandma Remembers.* Harper & Row, 1989.

Wittman, Sally. *A Special Trade.* Harper & Row, 1978.

Presence

Ackerman, Karen. *Song and Dance Man.* Alfred A. Knopf, 1988.

Brown, Margaret Wise. *The Runaway Bunny*. Harper & Row, 1942.

Joose, Barbara M. *Better with Two*. Harper & Row, 1988.

Littlefield Hoopes, Lyn. *Half-a-Button*. Harper & Row, 1989.

Winthrop, Elizabeth, *Are You Sad, Mama?* Harper & Row, 1979.

Zolotow, Charlotte. *If You Listen*. Harper & Row, 1980.

Prayer

Baylor, Byrd. *The Way to Start a Day*. Charles Scribner's Sons, 1978.

Bitney, James & Suzanne Schaffhausen. *Sunday's Children*. Resource Publications, 1986.

Cohen, Barbara. *Yussel's Prayer: A Yom Kippur Story*. Lothrop, Lee & Shepard, 1981.

DeGastzold, Carmen Bernos & Rumer Godden. *Prayers from the Ark* (1955), *The Creatures Choir* (1965). The Viking Press.

Hague, Michael. *A Child's Book of Prayers*. Holt, Rinehart and Winston, 1985.

De Paola, Tomie. *The Clown of God*. Harcourt Brace Jovanovich, 1978.

Larrick, Nancy. *Tambourines! Tambourines to Glory! Prayers and Poems*. Westminster Press, 1982.

Murphy, Elspeth Campbell. *David and I Talk to God—Psalms for Children Series*, and *God's Words in My Heart Series*. David C. Cook.

Royds, Caroline. *Prayers for Children*. Doubleday, 1988.

Stevenson, Rosemarie. *A Day to Pray—A Collection of Poems, Prayers and Praise*. Melbourne Australia: The Joint Board of Christian Education, 1988.

Overcoming/Hopefulness

Aurelio, John. *The Garden of Life*. Crossroad Publishing, 1989.

Bunting, Eve. *Fly Away Home*. Houghton Mifflin, 1991.

Kraus, Robert. *Leo the Late Bloomer*. E.P. Dutton, 1971.

Lionni, Leo. *Tillie and the Wall*. Alfred A. Knopf, 1989.

Walvoord Girard, Linda. *At Daddy's on Saturdays*. Albert Whitman & Co., 1987.

Death

Clifton, Lucille. *Everett Anderson's Goodbye*. Holt, Rinehart and Winston, 1983.

Coerr, Eleanor. *Sadako and the Thousand Paper Cranes*. Dell, 1977.

Donnelly, Elfie. *So Long, Grandpa*. Crown Publishers, 1980.

Douglas, Eileen. *Rachel and the Upside Down Heart*. Price Stern Sloan, Inc., 1990.

Kantrowitz, Mildred. *When Violet Died*. Parents' Magazine Press, 1973.

Miles, Miska. *Annie and the Old One*. Little, Brown, 1971.

O'Hanlon Nunn, Rebecca. *Tom's Remembrance*. The Westphalia Press, 1987.

Park, Barbara. *Don't Make Me Smile*. Alfred a. Knopf, 1990.

Thurman, Chuck. *A Time for Remembering*. Simon & Schuster, 1989.

Viorst, Judith. *The Tenth Good Thing about Barney*. Atheneum, 1971.

Zolotow, Charlotte. *My Grandson Lew*. Harper & Row, 1976.

Identity/Character

Blue, Rose. *Wishful Lying*. Human Sciences Press, 1980.

Demi. *The Empty Pot*. Henry Holt & Co., 1990.

De Paola, Tomie. *Oliver Button Is A Sissy*. Harcourt Brace Jovanovich, 1979.

Goble, Paul. *The Gift of the Sacred Dog*. Bradbury Press, 1980.

Howe, James. *I Wish I Were a Butterfly*. Gulliver Books, 1987.

Munsch, Robert. *The Paper Bag Princess*. Firefly Books, Ltd., 1980.

Schenk de Regniers, Beatrice. *The Way I Feel Sometimes*. Clarion Books, 1988.

20

USING ROLE-PLAYING, DRAMA, DANCE

> Sound methodology...includes providing continued opportunities for concrete experiences of lived faith, in which the message of salvation is applied to specific situations. Such things as field trips, meaningful social action, weekend retreats and programs, group dynamics of a sound and tested nature, simulation games, audio-visuals, and similar techniques can be very helpful. Constructive interaction and personal involvement are extremely important, and are present in gospel-based value clarification, group discussions, programs for the development of communication skills, and group prayer.
>
> *National Catechetical Directory, 181/10*

One seventh-grade class of ours was particularly challenging. We met each week on Tuesday evenings with twenty-five tired youngsters. After all day in classrooms they were not overjoyed to be in another classroom with rows of chairs one behind the other.

We tried a variety of approaches to engage the group in learning about their faith. But everything seemed to fail.

Then one evening near Pentecost, workers were repairing the classroom floor. We had to move out to another room. Fortunately it had more open space.

We took advantage of the opportunity to invite the youngsters to act out the Pentecost story in whatever way they wished. We first quietly read the story in the Acts of the Apostles. Then they began their free-flowing dramatic interpretation of Pentecost.

The first moments were chaotic. Gradually something touching took shape. They gathered close together and began slowly to shuffle in a circle, waving their hands in a soothing, undulating motion, softly repeating over and over the sacred sound, "Om...Om...Om...Om."

It was a prayerful moment of unity and harmony, based on the Bible, but freely interpreted. Through their own creative acting-out they allowed the Pentecost experience to touch their lives. They referred back to this class from time to time as the year pressed on.

Learning Through Bodily Movement

That special evening convinced us anew of an oft neglected reality—our bodies are a marvelous learning tool. We learn in a unique way when our whole bodies are involved in purposeful movement. Some call it "kinesthetic" or "haptic" learning. For many individuals it is their preferred learning-style.

Traditional catechesis recognized and respected the power of bodily learning. Early "mystagogical" catechesis hinged on the experiences of the liturgical rituals. Saint Jerome wrote in the fourth century: "The joy of the Spirit finds expression in bodily gesture." Medieval catechesis used "miracle plays" and "morality plays," processions and dance, to great advantage. Contemporary catechesis builds on these traditional ways of bodily learning with contemporary techniques.

Gesture

Perhaps the easiest place to begin exploring kinesthetic learning in catechesis is with simple gestures. Sitting properly in one's chair can foster an alertness and openness to learning and to meditation. Kneeling or standing can facilitate an attitude of prayer. Bowing and genuflecting may deepen a sense of reverence and respect.

Simple gestures such as holding the Bible reverently, kissing it, raising it high, all have the power to actuate the attitude of reverence that is expressed bodily.

We frequently hold hands in a circle as we pray the Our Father. At other times we create gestures to accompany each part of traditional prayers.

Role-Playing

Role-playing is a way of freely expressing inner feelings and personal interactions through bodily movement. Role-playing has no script, no predictable gestures or movements. It is meant to honestly and freely flow out of inner experiences. Role-playing allows for a great variety of expressions with varying degrees of difficulty and complexity. It may include words as well as gestures, but normally the "actor's" own words. It may also be wordless, like charades or mime.

Simplest, perhaps, are role-plays like this: "Imagine you are a flower seed, and show with your body alone how it feels to grow into a flower." "Imagine you have done something wrong and asked God's mercy; act out how you feel as you experience God's forgiveness." "With your finger draw in the air Jesus' face." "Express with your body what God is like for you, or what faith in God looks like."

Groups can do bodily sculptures, like what it means to be church. "Think of what church is and how it feels to be Church. Without words, use your bodies to create a sculpture that shows what Church really is."

We have often used similar expressive movements in our catechesis with children, youth, and adults. Such simple experiences enable people old and young to sense the relationship between inner ideas, feelings, and attitudes with bodily expression, and they are thus more free to learn or pray in fresh ways.

More complex forms of role-playing involve acting out more of a story or interpersonal encounter, often of a conflictual nature. It is an excellent way of helping youngsters express and deal with situations in which they have deep or confused feelings, particularly moral choices.

For example, in one of our fourth grade classes several years ago, we role-played "temptation." We knew the youngsters loved a certain kind of potato chips popular at the time. We placed a bag of potato chips on the desk and asked them to play out their reactions to seeing the bag of potato chips.

One of the boys jumped up, ran to the front, grabbed the bag and began to rip it open. We asked him to stop and put it back.

A girl began to get out of her desk, hesitated, slowly walked toward the chips, stopped, looked around sheepishly, quickly picked up the bag, hid it under her arm, and slipped back to her desk, with her eyes down.

Others acted out variations of the same theme—always taking the potato chips.

Then we stopped to talk about what their role-playing suggested about temptation. They gradually formulated a definition: "Temptation is when you see something irresistible and take it." "Irresistible" was their word. They filled in with examples—sneaking money from a mother's purse, shoplifting a popular rock cassette. Each temptation was irresistible.

At one point a boy who had been silent and had not entered into the role-playing spoke up. He insisted none of those things were irresistible. He assured us he knew how to handle temptations. We asked him to show us.

He moved out from his desk, walked up toward the potato chips, and stopped. Then he pushed upward toward his head with both hands, whispered something inaudibly, spun quickly around, and walked directly back to his seat.

He then put in words what he had just showed with movement and gesture. "When you see something that is 'irresistible,' you push all your energy up into your head, say 'NO!' and walk away. Pretty soon you forget it."

For us it was an unforgettable moment. We all learned surprisingly much from that simple, spontaneous role-play.

Role-playing can be particularly useful in exploring interpersonal situations, like problems with parents or teachers, encounters with someone selling drugs, interviewing a current star or political personality, meeting Jesus or Mary or a saint, or deciding between two choices.

To engage the students in role-play:

• Be sure it fits meaningfully into your lesson.

• Be sure all understand clearly the feeling, situation, moral choice, conflict, or challenge that is to be role-played.

• Be sure all feel free to express through bodily movement and gesture what they actually think and feel. Role-playing needs to flow honestly from inner experience to bodily expression. There is no scripting, since its main value is to enable children to express through movement what they genuinely experience.

• Allow a moment for silent reflection before the actual role-playing.

• Take time afterwards to allow your students to share their reactions and new insights gained from the role-play.

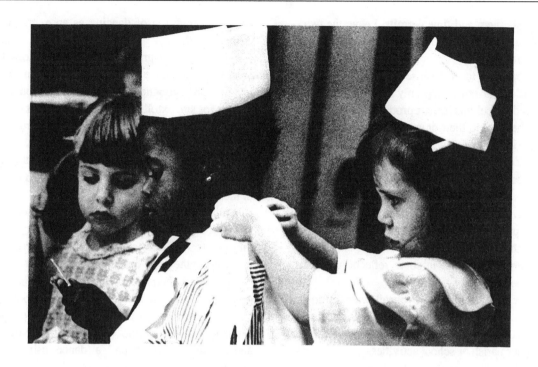

Somewhat similar to role-playing are simulation games. These are educational games that simulate real situations, inviting the players to enter into real-life situations and to make choices. For example, we created a simple simulation game using M & M candies to teach basic insights into the injustices of world food distribution and to help eighth graders experience some of the consequences for everyone if, for example, almost all receive just 1 M & M, while several receive 2, 3, 4, or 5, and one receives 42! It was most effective with the youngsters because they learned accurate information about the unequal sharing of food worldwide, and they felt the pains of injustice.

Drama

Dramatizing is similar to role-playing in that it involves acting out inner experiences through bodily movement, word, and gesture. But dramatization normally interprets an already completed story or play, for example, a piece of children's literature, a song with a story, or a Gospel story.

Like role-playing, dramatizing needs to express real feelings. Instead of the uniquely personal feelings evoked in role-playing, the actor in a drama tries to give expression to the feelings and ideas of a character in the story with whom the actor identifies.

Dramatizing may quite literally express the plot, even the actual words, of the writer. For example, students might memorize and then act out the parable of the Good Samaritan, using the exact words of the playwright or storyteller. Or they might have considerable freedom within the broad lines of the plot—as we allowed our seventh graders in dramatizing the Pentecost story from the Acts of the Apostles.

Or, somewhat in between, they might act out the Good Samaritan story, but write in their own dialogue.

Sometimes it can be exciting to read students a story—from the newspaper, children's book, Bible, or other source—but stop before the end. Ask the youngsters to dramatize the story, adding their own ending.

It can be interesting, too, to invite the youngsters to dramatize their own modernized version of a Gospel parable or biblical event.

We have found that some dramatizations developed in religion class occasionally also fit well into the Liturgy of the Word at the Sunday Eucharist.

Processions may be considered a form of drama. They usually center on an historical event, reenact some sacred story, or celebrate a great person.

To use drama effectively in catechesis:

• Be sure what you dramatize fits meaningfully into the development of your lesson.

• Read and talk about the story to be dramatized. The better the youngsters know the story, the better they will be able to dramatize it in a convincing way.

• Work with the youngsters in selecting the cast, including "backstage" workers. Help them to develop a simple "set" and simple "props"—only to the extent that the story needs them and time permits. Leave the working out of the drama's actions and words as much as possible to the students.

• Give them time to practice several times. Intervene with suggestions or other help only as absolutely needed. They need to feel this is their production.

• Invite them to do their dramatization. If short, they might repeat it, perhaps changing roles or involving other students. You might give the "audience" a question or two to answer from what they observe in the dramatization.

If you or one of the students photograph or make a video of the presentation, you will have a creative visual to use at another time.

• Afterwards engage all in some reflection and discussion on their drama.

• Consider together whether you all want to do the dramatization again in other circumstances, e.g., during the Liturgy of the Word some Sundays, in other classes, as part of other parish or school activities.

Dance

Dance is a vital form of learning, communicating, and praying through bodily movement. It has a long history of use in catechesis and liturgy. King David danced joyfully before the Ark of the Lord (2 Samuel 6:14-15). The Psalms came alive as the community danced them, accompanied by timbrel and harp: "Let them praise his name in the festive dance" (Psalm 149:3). Early Christian teachers called Jesus the "Lord of the dance"—echoed beautifully still in the popular Shaker hymn with that name.

Dance is a dramatic language of inner feeling. The great modern dancer Martha Graham saw her dance and choreography as "charting the graph of the heart."

For young children, simple dances are relatively easy and enjoyable because the children are so uninhibited and unself-conscious. In upper grades dancing may be more difficult in religion classes, but it nonetheless remains important and possible. It is worth experimenting occasionally with dance in your classes. It can add a dimension of freedom, joy, physical activity, and fun.

To use dance effectively in catechesis:

• Be sure it fits your lesson meaningfully.

• Be sure your students grasp something of the value and tradition of dancing as an expression of our Catholic faith.

• Be sure they grasp the faith dimensions to be expressed in the dance you are inviting them to do—e.g., joy in God's goodness, celebration of God's presence, sorrow for sin, extolling the freedom Christ brings us.

• Spend time becoming familiar and comfortable with the song or music to which they will dance.

• Encourage children to focus on honestly expressing their genuine feelings as they are suggested or expressed in the music or song.

• Give them much freedom to create their dance. Involve yourself only to the extent necessary. Ultimately they are to feel free to work out whatever gestures and movements they feel best expresses their inner feelings.

We find it helpful at first to provide some simple guidelines, like these which we learned from Sister Micaela Randolph, O.S.B. She taught us her "ABCs of Movement" as a simple way of helping young people and adults "choreograph" a dance using four basic movements:

• moving up—raising arms or whole body, stretching, looking up...

• moving down—bending knees, bending over, bowing, lowering arms, head...

• moving forward or backward—walking, crawling, sliding...

• turning around—left to right, right to left, full turns, partial turns...

We can play with these four basic movements, putting them together into one flowing line of movement expressive of whatever we wish—with or without a song or instrumental music. With these four movements almost any group can create a meaningful dance. Sometimes it may turn out so well you will all want to incorporate it into the Sunday Eucharist as a liturgical dance.

Creative Movement

Creative movement in all of the above ways centering around role-playing, drama, and dance has a proud tradition in Christian religious education or catechesis. It remains a most effective way of hearing and responding to God's Word. As our seventh graders experienced in dramatizing Pentecost, and as Saint Jerome put it long ago: "The joy of the Spirit finds expression in bodily gesture."

Questions for Reflection and Discussion

1. What has been your experience with creative movement in your religion classes—as a student and as a catechist?

2. Name something you have learned primarily or solely through bodily movement or gesture?

3. Why do you feel creative movement of various kinds is so important in religious education?

4. What hesitations or fears do you have about trying to use more gesture and movement in your teaching?

5. What is there about American culture that might inhibit many of us from expressing ourselves more freely with our bodies?

Ways to Respond

1. Try it. Perhaps the best way to experience the power of "kinesthetic" or "haptic" learning is to try it out. If you find it difficult to do at first with others, experiment in the privacy of your room. Begin simply with one of the simple bodily role-plays described in the text. Or try to dance how it feels to be free, happy, sad. Let yourself experience your feelings and express them as best you can through your body.

2. Reflect by yourself or with other catechists on your experience of a professionally done dramatic presentation or dance that you really responded to and liked. Try to discern what it was in the production that moved you. Why would a lecture or discussion or study not have the same impact on you? What was the power of the acting and/or dancing on you that words alone do not have?

3. Choreograph a song. Take a song you like very much. Play it several times, letting your body resonate and move with the music. Then work out simple movements freely, or use the four basic movements described in the text. Play with it until you have a simple pattern of movements that capture the feelings of the song.

21

USING MUSIC AND SONG

Singing hymns and religious songs is also a form of prayer. Parishes should provide opportunities for people to learn hymns. The rich musical heritage of the church, including Gregorian chant, should be preserved and made part of the parish musical repertoire.

Today most people, especially the young, are accustomed and even expect to experience much of their learning through sophisticated media presentations. The church needs to make creative use of these tools in communicating with them.

Instrumental media are of many kinds, both print and nonprint, and include activities such as arts, crafts, dramatics, mime, dance, role playing, simulation or instructional games, music, storytelling, visuals such as posters and charts, videotapes, films, filmstrips, slides, cassette tapes, and overhead transparencies. All instructional materials used in catechesis should be artistically sensitive and technically competent. They should also be theologically accurate and should reflect the insights derived from good catechetical research.

National Catechetical Directory, 143, 265

Shirley walked into her third-grade religion class weighted down with a heavy accordion. She had used it during a previous lesson to help teach the children the melody to a song. The attempt had gone fairly well, she thought, but as she was unpacking the accordion this time, Steven—in the very front row—turned around to a friend and in a stage whisper exclaimed, "She's not going to play that thing again, is she?"

Shirley went on as if she had not heard. As she was strapping the accordion over her shoulder, Steven raised his voice so that all could clearly hear. "I know someone who can *really* play the accordion!" Laughter and general chaos followed.

That brought a quick end to Shirley's attempts to pick out notes on her long unused accordion. She was frustrated and angry. But she remained convinced of the importance of music for religious education. So thereafter she looked around for records to replace her accordion.

This true experience illustrates in very practical terms several important facts about the relationship between religious education and music.

Catechists in every age instinctively sense the value of music for religious education. The earliest catechesis, recorded in the New Testament, is sprinkled with psalms and original Christian hymns. Later catechesis centered around the liturgy, much of which was music and song. Missionary catechists like St. Francis Xavier created or adapted simple melodies for equally simple lyrics that summed up the essentials of the Christian faith.

In this same tradition catechists today work hard at making music an integral part of their catechetical efforts. By and large they do so, like Shirley, with limited musical skills and inadequate knowledge of musical resources. They also lack principles or guidelines. The Vatican's *General Catechetical Directory* (1971) and our own *National Catechetical Directory* (1977) make only passing mention of music. Catechetical journals rarely devote much attention to music in religious education.

Very Important Resource

Yet there is a growing awareness that music is one of the most important media in religious education. Music makes up in our time almost the atmosphere in which the young live, move, and have their being. Contemporary music is in a real sense the privileged language of young people around the world, bridging languages and cultures. Music, then, has perhaps an even more vital

place in catechesis and religious education today than in previous ages. Catechists need to become familiar with the language of music today as much as missionaries need to learn the language of those they serve.

Music has a unique power to touch a person's whole being—body, feelings, mind, heart. It brings a fullness, a depth, a richness that words alone, or photographs and art by themselves, lack. Music has a rare ability to move people, especially when it is used sensitively with words and visual images.

In religious education—as in liturgy—music is not just a secondary complement to word, gesture, and image. Music blends with all three to become a real part of the experience and the message. Music and song bring out the full meaning of the message by expressing its inner feeling and attitude. Music, then, is a dimension of the word spoken by God in catechesis as in liturgy. It is a natural and normal means of expressing personal and communal faith in response to God's gracious initiatives.

The goal of catechesis is, in the words of Vatican Council II, "to make faith become living, conscious and active through the light of instruction" *(Bishops,* 14). The living, maturing faith at which catechesis aims is a personal bonding with God whom one knows and loves in the intimacy of one's heart and in the community of believers. The instinctive language of personal affection and dedication, of group commitment, is song—poetry embraced by music.

Along with words, silence, visual images, gesture and dance, music is a vital aspect of catechesis as a dimension of God's word to people and of their faith-response to God. The various roles of music in the religious education process may help clarify its value for that process.

Mood Music

One of the more common uses of music, with or without lyrics, is to create environment controlled by sound, an atmosphere dominated by what is heard, a mood. Carefully selected music can create a sense of peace for better hearing of God's Word from the Bible, or for more sensitively hearing God's word rising up within one's interior, or for more surely noticing it in the world in which one lives. Music can add poignancy and depth to reflection on the sorrows of life, or lightness and exhuberance to meditation on life's joys.

Selected to resonate the single theme or mood of a lesson, music appeals with subtle directness to the whole personality. This is true even if no words or images are used to accompany the music. When music is used with visual images or with words, it significantly deepens and enriches their impact. It tends to spark movement, gesture, and dance.

So catechists use music, for example, to create a thematic mood at the very start of class, to deepen that mood during periods of reflection, meditation, or creative work, to interpret slides of human experiences or of sacred art, to permeate moments of quiet prayer or of listening to God's Word, to invite and inform dance or expressive gesture.

Message Music

Catechists also use music through songs that sum up the message of a lesson. Contemporary catechetical programs frequently include original songs written precisely to express the central meaning of a given lesson or unit. Catechists have apparently done this from the very beginning of Christianity.

The melody tends to make memorization of the words painless and readily recalled. It is not unusual to hear children and their catechists—sometimes even their parents—singing spontaneously the more catchy of these songs at work or play.

But more than that, putting the words to music captures something essential to the message itself. The medium truly is the message. Song is particularly appropriate for Christian catechesis because the message of Christ is truly "good news."

Another type of message music is found in the catechetical use of popular songs, particularly those currently heard on local radio stations. Many of the better songs—including rock, rap, and country—touch real-life issues, ask honest questions, and invite reflection on human life. Even though the majority of these songs enjoy a very brief lifespan, they have the advantage of immediacy, impact, and relevance. The better of them may be relatively popular for long stretches of time. The best become classics and are regularly heard. Since they are drawn from the everyday world and are not limited to religion, these songs can often side-step feelings of apathy or hostility, particularly on the part of adolescents.

The use of such secular songs also has a proud history in religious education. St Robert Bellarmine, one of the most influential of the Post-Tridentine catechists, regularly adapted contemporary love songs for religious purposes. Actually, in the catechetical use of message music, the distinction between "sacred" and "secular" music becomes almost meaningless. Any song that touches down on significant values, gropes toward insight into life's mysteries, or raises questions about life's deeper meaning is essentially religious. Sometimes "secular" songs are in fact more profoundly religious than "sacred" songs because they are more attuned to life, more honest, or are simply better songs.

Story Songs

Similar to message music is music that helps relate a story. Some of the most popular songs used in catechesis are those that tell biblical stories. An entire Gospel story can be learned, enjoyed, and responded to by learning a song that skillfully and delightfully unfolds the story's details. Protestant religious educators have perhaps in the past made more use of this kind of music than have Roman Catholic catechists. Negro spirituals and traditional Gospel music are excellent examples, expanded by more contemporary Christian rock and rap. Recently Roman Catholic song writers are also creating more and better story songs of Gospel events.

Such songs not only aid recall of the story, but capture something of the inner attitude and affective pull of the story. The musical dimension helps people identify more fully with the characters in the story—to feel with them. Story songs often draw students quite naturally to movement and gesture, to acting out the story. This is particularly helpful with younger children.

Prayer Music

Perhaps the most obvious use of music in catechesis is the use of hymns, songs written precisely as expressions of prayer. The more modern of these prayer-songs sound more like folk songs, jazz, rock, rap, or country music than like Bach, Handel, or Gregorian chant. But they have essentially the same purpose; additionally they help people become better pray-ers.

Prayer-songs or hymns have always had a part in Christian catechesis, evident already in the New Testament. Hymn singing, long the pride of Protestant worship and religious education, is experiencing a dramatic renewal in many Catholic parishes, schools, and homes.

Contemporary religious education programs include hymns, psalms, or other prayer-songs in almost every session. Sometimes used to begin or end a class, hymns are more typically used today at any point in the learning experience where prayer is an appropriate response.

Use Music With Care

Despite the values of music and song in catechesis many catechists hesitate to build them into their lesson plans because they feel inadequate. "I can't read music," "I can't sing." These are the most common reasons for neglecting music and song.

Undoubtedly it helps to be able to read music and to sing, but it isn't necessary to be able to do so. What is necessary, first of all, is to believe in songs as an absolutely necessary ingredient in religion classes. Secondly, it is necessary to have a record player, cassette or CD player and records, cassettes or CD's on hand as supportive equipment. Thirdly, it is necessary to have a reasonable amount of "know how" regarding the use of music and song in a class.

The successful use of music in catechesis not only requires careful preparation but an ongoing effort to raise one's own awareness of and appreciation for the value of music and song.

We recommend that you set aside some quiet time in a comfortable place, allowing no interruptions if possible. When playing the music allow yourself to flow into it, move with it, become aware of how your feelings change with the music, how it affects your mental images, letting it flow into and through you. Afterwards you might try to reflect more consciously on your reactions to the music and to consider possible uses for it in your classes.

Songs, popular and traditional, provide a wealth of material, particularly for use with teenagers. The key to successful use is again to become sensitive to the songs—lyrics and music. Radio gives instant and constant access to the ever-changing world of popular music. Some songs are gems for catechetical use, but many are not, and some are even junk. But the time spent listening and selecting can be very worthwhile. It may take some effort to be open to modern songs that may not fit comfortably into every listener's musical tastes. A resource like Fr. Don Kimball's *Top Music Countdown* (Taylor Press) provides invaluable help toward evaluating, selecting, and using contemporary music in your catecheics.

Song can be used in a variety of ways and can be used over and over again the same way. Suggestions for use are made in lesson plans, but you need not follow every suggestion. You should use songs in ways that you feel will be easiest and most enjoyable for both you and the children, doing it that way over and over again. The more you use song, the more you'll vary your use of it. However, the strength of song does not depend upon clever uses. Actually using a song in the same way over and over again tends to add to its power.

A significant tip regarding the use of song in a lesson plan is to decide very definitely in the planning stage how it will be used and then to follow some simple guidelines. For example, if you decide that you will have the children listen to a song because it tells a story, or creates a mood, or summarizes the lesson, here are some guidelines.

• Play the song softly, so the children will have to listen carefully.
• Give the children one or more things to listen for precisely.
• Have enough time built into the plan to listen to a piece completely, even two and three times.
• Be sure that everyone listens intently to the piece.
• Take time to share what everyone or at least some of the group heard.

Or, should you decide that you will have the children sing a song as part of the class's experience and it is a song that is new to them, follow these guidelines.

• Print or write the words of the song on a chalkboard, chart, or overhead transparency, or give each child a copy of the words. Read or say the words together until they are memorized. If the song is short or the children are too young to read music, simply have them listen to and repeat the words line-by-line until they know them.
• Then repeat the words of the song adding rhythm. Have the children do this until they get a feel for the song's rhythmical pattern. They usually do this quite easily.
• Play the song through as they listen to it to capture the melody.
• Finally, sing and enjoy it!

Or, if you plan to have the children draw a picture of the story or an impression of the song, here are some guidelines for doing this.

• Give each child a large sheet of paper, crayons, marking pens, or paints.
• Tell them very clearly what is expected of them.
• Have a moment of silence.
• Play the music or song once or twice, depending on what seems to be happening in the group.
• Wait until all or nearly everyone has finished his or her picture.
• Share by putting the drawings in a display area so that all can see.
• Play the song again in the context of the fuller understanding expressed by the drawings.

Or, you may want the children to gesture, pantomime, or dance with a song. These can be done spontaneously, free form without a design. Or you can work out movements ahead of time that express the feeling and message of the music or song and teach these to the children, inviting them to add to and vary the movements. In this type of response to song and music, it is important that the movements express outwardly what is being inwardly spoken, felt, experienced.

One final tip: Just as song can be used in the same way over and over again, so can the same song be sung again and again. This is particularly true if you and the children like a particular song and it addresses a theme in a general way.

What Else Is Needed?

A good record, stereo, cassette, or CD player for your use (every time you meet with a class) must be considered standard equipment for a program in which music is a priority. This does not mean one per catechist, unless the whole school of religion is in session at the same time. The audio equipment needs to be a good one, which means it's dependable so that it projects sound well.

If records or cassettes accompany the textbook series your parish is using, you should have a personal copy. This is necessary because you should be able to listen to the songs again and again, to reflect on their relationship to lessons so that you can include music in each of your teaching-learning experiences.

A library of music for catechetical use should be gradually built up in parishes so catechists can familiarize themselves with the selections on these works, and see their relationship to the theological and human themes that are developed in the religious education program the parish uses.

What about the possibility of inviting the parish music minister to work with you, the other catechists, and your classes on a rotating basis? This is not to turn the catechetical experience into a music class, but to give music its proper place in a program. It will assist and encourage you to use music as a resource for sharing, celebrating, and praying.

And finally don't forget to build a musical bridge between the songs sung during Sunday Masses and the music you use in your religion classes. Very often the liturgical music will relate directly to the topics you are covering, and the children will enjoy seeing this relationship.

Questions for Reflection and Discussion

1. What has been your experience using music with your classes?

2. Why does music seem to be neglected in so many religion classes?

3. What are some current popular songs that you might use in your lessons?

4. What hymns touch you most deeply? To which do your students seem to respond?

5. How do you feel in general about music? Do you enjoy it? Do you listen to it much? Why or why not?

6. What resources are available to you from your parish or school? How much use do you make of them?

Ways to Respond

1. Draw on your textbook. The better religion textbook series all incorporate music and song into their programs. Go through your teacher's manual and examine how music and song are used in the lessons. Read the author's explanations and practical tips. Some weeks before you teach a particular lesson, get and listen to the recommended music and songs.

2. Find out what students like. Ask your students what music they like, what songs are popular among them. Invite them to bring in songs or music they feel touches them and fits in with the themes you are studying together. This is especially helpful since you may not be able to keep up with the current top hits.

3. Get help. Find someone in your parish, school, or neighborhood who is gifted at playing a guitar or other instrument, or who sings well. Invite him or her to assist you from time to time in introducing music and song more fully into your catechetical lessons. Draw on helpful resources like *Top Music Countdown* by Rev. Don Kimball.

4. Go through your parish hymnal. Determine which songs sung in the parish fit the themes you will be teaching. Plan how you might introduce some of these hymns into your lesson plans during the next few weeks. This not only draws upon music your students may be familiar with, but integrates catechesis and liturgy.

22

Drawing, Writing, Questioning

> Experiencing is of great importance in catechesis. Experiential learning, which can be considered a form of inductive methodology, gives rise to concerns and questions, hopes and anxieties, reflections and judgments, which increase one's desire to penetrate more deeply into life's meaning. Experience can also increase the intelligibility of the Christian message by providing illustrations and examples which shed light on the truths of revelation.
>
> The experiential approach is not easy, but it can be of considerable value to catechesis. Catechists should encourage people to reflect on their significant experiences and respond to God's presence there.
>
> *National Catechetical Directory,* 176

We were frustrated. We had never met as challenging and unruly a group of third graders as the 22 unsettled youngsters we were attempting to teach. After six or seven classes with them we were tempted to give up. Their two previous teachers that year had done just that.

It was clear that we were not reaching these children. Somehow we were not touching their experiences and interests. So we decided to give them a chance to let us into their world. We gave them drawing paper and crayons with these simple instructions: "Each of you draw for us a picture of your world and what is most important to you in it."

The children went to work with considerably more interest than they had thus far invested in anything we had suggested. They filled their pictures with computer games, Nintendo, dinosaurs, footballs, friends, guns, bicycles, pets, airplanes, rocket ships, and themselves.

As they shared their drawings with us and with each other, something striking surfaced. Not a single drawing showed an adult relating with a child. The world of these third graders, as revealed in their drawings, seemed devoid of caring adults. Their busy, affluent, successful parents, relatives, and neighbors apparently had little impact on their lives.

This discovery helped explain much of their distracted, attention-seeking behavior. What their drawings revealed helped give us a point of contact with their experience. We tailored the remaining classes with them to touch down on this missing dimension of their lives. Our catechesis improved because we were more in touch with what they were living and feeling in their sadly empty world.

Importance of Drawing

This experience suggests what is perhaps the most important value of drawing (and painting) in catechesis. Drawing allows children, youth, and adults to surface experiences, express insights and feelings, questions and concerns, that they may not be as able to articulate in words. Drawings provide colorful windows into the mysterious world of below-the-surface experience. Drawings have a kind of "sacramental" reality, revealing and allowing contact with the deeper mysteries of people's daily lives.

The students' drawings become vital means for themselves and their catechists to hear God's Word expressed in their experiences. Drawings, too, can put us into contact with the "natural signs" of God's presence and self-

revelation in the lives of our students. The two accompanying drawings reveal the pain of loneliness in the lives of two of the fourth-graders, a pain they were unable to articulate verbally.

Drawing or painting also allows young and old alike to express their faith, their understanding, their feelings and questions about the Christian tradition. For example, drawing a Gospel story engages children in identifying with and responding to the people in the story. In so doing they may come to feel and express a need of healing or of trust in Jesus. The act of drawing allows them to make the story personal in terms of their own feelings and experiences.

We have found that teenagers and adults, as well as children, find drawing a creative, valuable catechetical experience. They are often surprised at what they reveal about themselves in their drawings. One of our most successful catechetical approaches to adults is to have them draw, for example, what "faith" or "sin" means to them.

Drawing or painting in catechesis is not just an entertaining way of filling class time or keeping the students occupied. The expression of one's self, one's feelings and insights, understandings and questions, experiences and concerns through color, shape, and line is an important means of allowing ourselves and our students to discover and respond to God's Word in our lives and in our Catholic tradition.

The completed drawings become excellent media for group sharing. Talking about and gently questioning what each has drawn provides a valuable resource for dialogue and mutual enrichment. The drawings become a bridge linking student to student, students to catechists, and linking what happens in class to what happens at home.

Practical Uses

Here are some practical hints for a more effective catechetical use of drawing or painting.

1. Focus on the experiences, ideas, and feelings that the drawings reveal rather than on the artistic quality of the work. Artistic excellence is not the main criteria in the catechetical use of drawing or painting. Our concern is that the students express themselves honestly through their drawings. Artistic technique is secondary to spontaneous, honest self-expression. What you should look for in the drawings is the student's communication of the mystery of their experiences.

2. Encourage free drawing of situations, stories, experiences, feelings. Coloring of predrawn figures is of limited catechetical value, as is mechanical copying or imitating of art works. Occasionally coloring a biblical story or a liturgical symbol may be a helpful means of allowing the students to become more familiar with details of the story or symbol. But generally in catechesis, spontaneous free drawing allows for more honest, deeper engagement.

Simply give the students blank drawing paper—large enough for drawing big pictures—and crayons or paint. Give them clear but open instructions like: "Draw how it feels to be lonely." "Draw someone in need of help." "Draw Jesus' story of the Good Samaritan." Or "Draw yourself praying," or "Draw yourself helping someone."

3. Normally give only the most basic mechanical or technical help. Do not suggest what a student might draw or how the student might draw what he or she wishes to express. Encourage free, honest, creative expression.

4. Music can be a helpful mood-setter for drawing. Select instrumental music—at least on occasion—that expresses the feelings of the lesson: peace, joy, sadness, excitement, love.

5. Encourage your students to show their drawings and talk about them. Sometimes a child or adult, in describing his or her drawing, may for the first time be able to articulate an idea, feeling, or question. The sharing of the drawings becomes a simple means of enabling group sharing and reflection.

6. Whenever possible, display your students' work in the place where you are teaching. Such displays can become places for prayer and can even stimulate prayer. They also remain for a time a point of reference that the students can go back to for still deeper insight or questioning.

At times you will want to display drawings in a place that other classes or other parishioners can visit. Displays may be set up in the vestibule of the church during Sunday liturgies or in school corridors for a week or two.

7. Students may want to save their drawings by including them in a journal or workbook that they build as the year unfolds. Such a book of their own becomes a rich resource for review, for observing growth, and for bridging their catechetical learning with their families.

Writing and Faith Learning

Drawing and painting can be simple yet highly valuable catechetical tools. Similarly, writing also facilitates faith-learning. We have found writing to be one of the surest ways for students to express significant feelings and ideas about particular topics or experiences.

When they are asked to write a sentence, a paragraph, a story, a poem, or an answer to a question, students are forced to reflect. Each time the challenge is met productively, growth may occur. Repeatedly we have witnessed amazement in children, youth, and adults at what they drew out of themselves by writing. Writing is a catalyst that can awaken sleeping giants that rest within ourselves and our students.

The things students write will bring into the learning process what is already known, experienced, and felt. The writing also allows for questions and concerns to emerge. These important data become part of the content of catechesis. They also provide a bridge to new learning, new perceptions, new answers and questions.

Writing helps bring each learner into the learning experience. Their hearts and imaginations as well as their brains are involved with the class content. The spin-off is greater involvement, interest, and learning.

The accompanying example of sixth-grade writing suggests how writing can add to the catechetical process.

Another value of writing in catechesis is that the writings reveal the growth that occurs week after week during the year. What students write gives surprising evidence of how much they know and are learning.

What is written by each student has another benefit. Such writings provide the individual and the group as a whole with a reference point and memory of what was learned earlier. Children, youth, and adults tend to read over again and to remember what they have written. The writings allow you to recall and refer later to significant insights gained by individual students. Parents are often pleasantly surprised at what their children have written about life and faith.

Helpful Hints

A few helpful hints on writing in catechesis follow.

1. As with drawing, honest and spontaneous expression should be encouraged. Avoid suggesting what you expect your students to write or what would be the right or acceptable answer or expression. Instead, simply pose a question or give a direction that allows for free expression. For example, give the students paper and pencils and ask them to answer "Who do you feel Jesus is?" or "How do you pray?" Or ask them to write a story about a time they were unfairly accused, etc., allowing and encouraging honest feelings and benefits.

2. Just as drawing in catechesis is not primarily an artistic exercise, so writing in a religion class is not primarily a grammatical or literary exercise. At times a profound insight may be expressed in poor handwriting or with bad spelling and grammar. At other times the written expression will be striking in its accurate and beautiful expression, as when a teenager wrote just one sentence about the wedding feast at Cana: "The water saw its master and blushed."

In catechesis, spelling, grammar, and literary style are secondary. Focus less on the quality of writing than on the experiences, feelings, and insights put into words.

3. Communicate to the students a sense of expectancy. Some students feel inhibited when challenged to write a page or even a few lines in their own words. A key to freeing them to write is an attitude that expects that they can do it, which the students sense. This attitude in effect can assure them that they really can do something they fear they cannot do, namely express themselves in written words.

4. Avoid telling students what they are to write or how to write it, except for a few technical helps. Don't hesitate to help with spelling or simple grammar questions. If students have been asked to write poems or cinquains or haiku, they may need some technical information about these forms. In short, help those who ask grammatical or technical questions, but do not become overly concerned about spelling and grammar in religion class.

5. A great help for students to express themselves in words are worksheets, prepared beforehand. These worksheets can be quite simple or increasingly sophisticated. The simplest might be a blank page with space for the student's name and with a single clear direction: "Write here a prayer of thanks to God." The addition of four lines forming a block within which to write adds a note of expectancy. So too might lines within the block on which to write. Ask students to fill all the lines with their writing.

More sophisticated worksheets might include a short excerpt from a news story in the local paper or popular magazine. The instructions might be as follows: "Read this story. Write why you feel the people in the story did what they did." If the news item is longer, you might have it on the front of the worksheet and place several questions on the back. In place of a news report, a Gospel story or doctrinal teaching could be placed on the worksheet with challenging questions about it to be answered in writing.

6. Invite students to share their writings with you and with each other. They may need some guidelines for discussing what they have written. Some will be most comfortable just reading what they have previously written.

7. Help the students gather their writings and drawings into a kind of journal, workbook, or personal religion textbook. Entries could include what they have written in class, but could also contain additional personal reflections, meditations, and prayers. As they build their own books or journals during the year, they will be providing evidence of what they are learning and how they are growing.

Writing remains one of the most readily available methods of helping students explore and share their experiences, insights, feelings, and faith. Take seriously what they write and use their writings in the teaching-learning process, praising their insights and questions. You and your students may well be surprised at the wealth of experience and wisdom they have to share.

Asking Questions

Drawing and writing are most effective when they are a response to good questions. In a sense the key to the success of any creative activity in catechesis rests on the quality of questioning with which it grapples.

Theologian Karl Rahner called questions "signs of transcendence" because good questions open one's experience to life's ultimate mystery. Questions help probe beneath superficial understandings of Christian faith. The chief catechetical value of questioning is to open the mind and heart to the mysterious presence within yet always beyond experience. A good question is in many ways one of the most vital elements of good catechesis. Such questions stimulate reflection, dialogue, prayer, and action—the four critical learning strategies of catechesis. Only when we go below the superficial grasp of our experience and of our faith tradition is there a realistic possibility of linking the two in a living faith process.

For many years in recent religious education practice we were so preoccupied with passing on right answers that honest questioning was not encouraged. The questions of the Baltimore Catechism are restatements of the expected answers rather than questions meant to provoke deeper exploration.

Today many catechists have rediscovered the importance of questioning to foster mature faith. A good catechist poses questions that invite students to think more deeply, to probe below the superficial. Students are encouraged to question, not to create doubts or loss of faith, but to encourage faith that responds to the deep mysteries of our lives. The religious dimension of daily living and church tradition is revealed through challenging questions.

In catechesis there are several kinds of important questions. We will look at these briefly.

1. Factual questions Questions of fact are important in catechesis because our Christian faith is a historical faith. It matters greatly to be able to answer questions about what Jesus said and did, what the church teaches, how the Christian community prays. So you need to ask factual questions such as Who is Jesus? Why was Jesus executed? What are the two great commandments? How many sacraments are there?

Answers to questions like these provide us with the essential data for deeper probing of our experience and faith heritage. We all need to keep going back to these factual questions about the basics of our Christian faith. Important as they are, however, they are but the first step in the art of catechetical questioning.

2. Meaning questions The answers to factual questions more often than not raise new questions. Having named the seven sacraments children may be curious to know just what is meant by "sacrament." The intriguing facts of our faith tradition continually give rise to deeper questioning about the meaning of those facts. Why was that? How can that be? and What does it mean? are natural questions that lead behind the facts to their meaning.

Meaning questions are the next stage of catechetical questioning. Such questions need to be directed to life experience as well as to the riches of Catholic tradition. What does it mean to be truly free? What does Paul mean when he writes that wherever the Holy Spirit is, there is freedom? (2 Corinthians 3:17). The task of catechesis is to invite students to probe their faith tradition and their daily experiences through such meaning questions. "Why? What does that mean?" are perhaps the simplest, most direct expressions of meaning questions.

But meaning questions can be presented in many other ways, too, for example, by simply not accepting superficial responses, by redirecting students' questions back to them, by posing situations or cases that give rise to questioning, by using strong photos or works of art, by writing, drawing, or more sophisticated multi-media creations. In whatever form, the meaning question is meant to challenge students to reflect more deeply, to open their minds and hearts to more than superficial knowledge.

Every effort to formulate good meaning questions will pay off in more effective, faith-nurturing catechesis.

3. Value questions Even more challenging and closer to faith commitment are questions that lead the students to look at their personal stance toward the mean-

ings they have discovered. Value questions are simply more personalized meaning questions. "What is the meaning of the Eucharist?" is a meaning question. As such it can be reflected on quite dispassionately. But as a value question one's personal attitudes and convictions are engaged: "What does the Eucharist mean in your life?" One can discuss at length without personal commitment Jesus' question, "Who do people say I am?" But his more insistent question can only be answered by a personal response: "But who do you say that I am?" (Matthew 16:15).

To answer that question involves not just what one may understand or believe, but what one values, what one considers important. Since religious faith is basically more a matter of commitment than of disinterested understanding, value questions approach the core of faith growth.

Because they are so personal, value questions need to be asked with respect and care. No student should be forced to answer such questions. Students should know that they have the right not to answer questions about their personal values. Yet in an atmosphere of mutual trust, value questions can help students look more closely at what really matters to them and their personal faith commitments.

4. Limit or faith questions Catechetical questioning ultimately comes to those profound questions that stretch the human mind and heart to its limits. Faith questions bring one face to face with life's mystery. They probe human experience and God's revelation to the point where ultimate meaning and value escape adequate definition. These are the questions that open out to the mysterious presence that envelopes us and at times seems to abandon us. To these ultimate questions of life, death, good and evil, sin, suffering, and love there are no satisfying rational answers. Each answer is in fact the catalyst of further questions. "Why do good people suffer?" is "answered" not by reason or logic as much as by silent self-surrender, trust, prayer, and courageous struggle against the evil. Limit or faith questions are best answered, as Job discovered, in awe, wonder, and praise. Stories and rituals, such as Jesus' parables, leave us with further questions even as they provide us with answers.

Truly religious answers are most often found in prayer, in self-surrender to the loving presence that may so warmly embrace us or seem so coldly absent, and in actively trying to live Christ's way. The response to ultimate faith questions is found in that "cloud of unknowing" that reassures yet unsettles us. Symbol, story, gesture, ritual, silence, and lifestyle reveal partial answers to these profoundly religious questions.

It is a great injustice to leave our students with the false impression that clear, distinct answers are available for life's deepest questions. To lead our students to touch life's mystery in an environment of faith is what catechesis is all about. We must never block access to mystery by providing apparently conclusive answers to life's deepest questions.

To "define" the Trinity risks never knowing the God whose oneness is so rich as to explode in a community of love. To "define" Jesus Christ as "true God and true man" raises more insistently the awesome questions of his personality.

Factual, meaning, value, and *faith* questions have an important place in catechesis, and here are some practical hints about using them.

How to Use Questions

1. Try never to ask questions that may be answered by a simple yes or no. These tend to stifle reflection and conversation. Rather, introduce questions with words that encourage further reflection and dialogue, words like *why, how, what if?* Such questions invite personal, individual reflection and allow for a variety of responses.

2. Normally it is more effective to pose a question to the whole group before indicating who should answer it. Instead of calling on "John" to answer the question, ask it first and then pause so that all can think about it. Then perhaps call on John.

3. Take time in preparing lessons to focus on the underlying question or questions that lead to the heart of it. Structure lessons so that one question prepares the way for another and arises from the answer to the first question. In this way you insure a kind of dynamism in the movement of the lesson, a dynamism that nurtures faith and models the process of ever deeper questioning.

In Summary

Draw, write, question—three methods of accomplishing the same catechetical goal, namely, to help students uncover the deeper mysteries of their lives and their faith. All three are readily available, cost little or nothing, and have rich potential for faith growth. All three allow and enable students to reach into their experiences and knowledge in ways that surface deeper feelings and insights. All three methods foster reflection, stimulate dialogue, and can lead to prayer and action.

Questions for Reflection and Discussion

1. What has been your experience in drawing or painting with your classes?

2. What have you learned about your students, about yourself, through drawing and painting?

3. What has been your experience with writing in catechesis?

4. What are some effective ways you have found of encouraging those you teach to write?

5. Why are good questions important for successful lessons?

6. What "meaning question" about your faith would you most like to find an answer to?

7. What religious "value question" do you find most challenging?

8. What "limit questions" interest you most?

Ways to Respond

1. Practice drawing. Get out some paper and crayons and give yourself some quiet time. Draw the same kind of situation, experience, or biblical story you will be asking the students to draw. It is important that you as a catechist know from experience the power of the process of drawing. It may be a bit uncomfortable and embarrassing if you are not accustomed to doing free drawings about life or about your faith. Yet the experience can be very enlightening and helpful.

2. Experience writing. Look ahead to the kind of writing you will be asking your students to do. Do those assignments yourself. Again the experience of writing out of your own daily life feelings and situations can be very valuable. You may be surprised at how easy or how difficult you find this kind of personal writing. You may be surprised as well at what you discover about yourself in the written word.

3. Read any biblical story. Take, for example, Jesus' parable of the Good Samaritan (Luke 10:25-37). Read the parable. Then formulate one or more of each of the four kinds of questions mentioned in this chapter: factual, meaning, value, and limit or faith questions. Write your questions down and then try to answer them yourself.

23

PRAYING

Inasmuch as it seeks to lead individuals and communities to deeper faith, all catechesis is orientated to prayer and worship. The deepening of faith strengthens the covenant relationship with God and calls Christians to respond in worship and ritual. By the nature of their ministry, catechists are often called to lead the community to prayer.

Catechesis promotes active, conscious participation in the liturgy, helps the faithful to meditate on God's Word, and provides opportunities for praying.

Catechesis for prayer begins very early in childhood by hearing others pray; even small children can learn to call upon the Father, Jesus, and the Holy Spirit. In time, the child will become familiar with the various prayers and prayer forms mentioned earlier and make them part of his or her life. Catechesis encourages daily prayer, family prayer, and prayer at special times, e.g., before and after meals.

Building upon the sense of wonder, catechesis leads people to a sense of the sacred and to recognition of God's presence in their lives. This is the source of both spontaneous and formal prayer.

To lead others to pray, the catechist must be a prayerful person.

National Catechetical Directory, 145

It was Yom Kippur, a day of prayer and atonement. Yussel, an orphan boy who cared for the wealthy Reb Meir's cows, longed to go to the synagogue to pray. But Reb Meir thought it best for Yussel to take the cows to pasture. Besides, Yussel had no education and could not read. How could he pray with everyone at the synagogue?

So Yussel led the cows to pasture. In the synagogue the congregation prayed with their beloved Rabbi hour after hour.

Reb Meir prayed aloud the prayers, but his mind was on his business. Reb Meir's oldest son said the prayers, too, but his heart was on ways to have a good time. By sunset Reb Meir, his sons, and the whole congregation were ready to go home. Yom Kippur was over.

But the Rabbi did not close the service. He prayed and chanted on and on as darkness filled the synagogue.

Out in the pasture Yussel watched the sun set. He did not know any prayers. But he could play his reed pipe. So he played a tune of his own. His heart and mind were on God. He played for God whose beauty and peace he felt in the evening stillness.

Just then in the synagogue the Rabbi chanted the Ne'lah prayers, bringing the day-long service to an end.

Reb Meir and his sons were relieved—but puzzled.

"Why did you delay the ending so long," Reb Meir boldly asked the Rabbi.

"In a vision I saw that the gates of heaven were closed to our prayers. Our prayers were not pleasing to God."

"But, why then did you finally end the Yom Kuppur service?" Reb Meir asked.

"In another vision I heard a simple melody played on a reed pipe. The gates of heaven opened. Our prayers went in to God with that melody. The simple melody was a true prayer; it came from the heart."

Reb Meir and his sons left the synagogue. On their way home they met Yussel with the cows. Reb Meir saw the reed pipe in Yussel's hand.

"*L'shana tova*, Yussel," said Reb Meir, wishing the orphan boy a good year. "Come into my house and share our meal."

This ancient rabbinic tale is retold beautifully by Barbara Cohen and sensitively illustrated by Michael J. Deraney in *Yussel's Prayer: A Yom Kippur Story* (New York: Lothrop, Lee & Shepard Books, 1981). It is a moving story of the meaning of prayer, an appropriate starting place for considering prayer in catechesis.

Prayer as a Goal

Father Gerard Sloyan, as we have already mentioned, taught us that the very goal of catechesis may be stated thus: "to help people learn to pray." Catechesis is not primarily the teaching of basic truths, biblical facts and stories, or church teachings—although these are important aspects of catechesis. Rather catechesis aims most basically at helping people enter into a relationship with God, our Father, with Jesus Christ, and with the Holy Spirit. Prayer is the natural lifeline of such a relationship.

Yussel exemplifies this heart-to-heart communication. Without knowing the words of the formal prayers, the orphan unites himself with God through a simple melody rising from his heart and expressed through his reed pipe. Jesus encourages us to pray like that, not necessarily with many words but from the heart, expressing love, thanks, praise, sorrow, and petition. Jesus' own prayer—a prayer echoed by the Spirit in our own hearts (Galatians 4:6)—is one of intimate relationship: "Abba," "Dad," "Daddy."

This is not to underplay the value of formal, traditional prayers. These cherished expressions of openness to God are an integral part of catechesis. We are impoverished if we do not know the prayer Jesus himself taught his followers, the Our Father or Lord's Prayer. We lack a tremendous prayer resource if we are not familiar with the psalms. Not to know the Hail Mary, Glory Be, Sign of the Cross, Apostles' Creed, Prayer of St. Francis, and other prayers of faith, hope, love, and sorrow, is to lack points of contact with the rich spiritual tradition of the Christian community.

Cherished Prayers

While saying traditional prayers is not automatically the same as learning to pray, Jews and Christians alike have long cherished the psalms and other formal prayers as vital means of learning to pray. Jesus gave his disciples the words of the Our Father precisely to teach them to pray as he himself prayed. The psalms have traditionally been a school of Christian prayer inside and outside of monasteries. Every Catholic has a right to learn the basic traditional prayers. They are to be learned, not as relics of the past, but as helps to learning how to pray and as valuable expressions of our prayer.

The traditional prayers become true prayer when they genuinely express the response of the praying person to God's presence and Word in his or her life. The catechist's task then is to help people become aware of God's gracious presence and life-giving Word in their daily experience in such a way that they are led to respond to God.

The psalms and other traditional prayers give us hints about how and where we can find God, and how to respond to God's ever-present Word. We might look at some of these hints in order more creatively to guide our students in prayer.

1. Feeling loved   Judaeo-Christian prayer rests on the experience of being loved. God takes the initiative, searching us out, delighting to be with us, alluring us. God loves us so that we may love in return. The teaching of prayer needs to be rooted in helping students sense how loved and lovable they are.

Since God's love is normally experienced through human love, a first step in helping people learn to pray is helping them to feel loved. The experience of being loved provides the key to sensing the loving presence of God with us in life's up and downs. Feeling loved is the natural source of prayers of faith, hope, and love. It is hard to overestimate how important is the experience of being loved in helping people discover and respond to God who is best known as love: (1 John 4:8). So, if you want to lead others to prayer, love them.

We learned this working with delinquent adolescents in a state rehabilitation center. The youngsters shrugged off homilies about God's love and exhortations to love God in return simply because they had never experienced being loved in any sustained, reliable manner. Our first work with them as catechists was to let them feel that we really cared for them. The same approach is needed in more normal catechetical settings as well.

2. Appreciating beauty and goodness   A second direction suggested by traditional Judaeo-Christian prayer is that God's gracious presence is with us always and everywhere, that God's insistent Word may be heard in any experience or event. Every bush may be another "burning bush," every meal, every meeting with a stranger or friend, every journey may be another "Emmaus event." But we tend not to notice.

Catechesis in prayer is therefore an effort to become and to help others become more aware of their experiences. We need to learn to notice, to appreciate the world within us and the world all around us. For it is in these worlds of experience that God is with us and speaking to us.

There are many ways of encouraging awareness and appreciation. All of them in a way are forms of meditation or contemplation, to use traditional terminology. They are all ways of nurturing more sensitive awareness to the mystery clothed in life's mysteries.

Help Find Beauty

We can help our students, for example, become aware of the beauty around them by giving them time and opportunity to stop and look at a sunset or sunrise, flowers, a tree, snow, mountains or streams, skyscrapers, lovely lawns, a city's lights at night, and most of all, people. We can help them smell, taste, touch and feel, listen and observe. Natural beauty leads to wonder at the world, to praiseof the source of life's beauty and mystery.

Becoming aware of beauty, of the wonderfully good things in life—a baby's smile, a loved one's touch, a word of love, a handshake of trust and friendship, a helping hand, good music and art, tasty food and drink, warm sun in winter and cool shade in summer's heat, someone's creativity, dedication, self-giving—help to praise and thank God. They lead us to wonder at the love who makes people lovable and loving, the creator who creates them to be creative, the beauty whose loveliness delights their senses and spirits, the giver whose gifts are in everything people know and experience.

You can facilitate this kind of awareness through a variety of means. Photography and art, for example, have the ability to capture a slice of life that we can contemplate. Both can help us become aware of the world in which we live. Looking at photos or works of art can be a form of meditation. Taking photos or creating art can become a prayer.

Literature is another rich means of becoming more aware of the mysteries of life that reveal the mystery at the heart of all creation. Good stories and poems can be a source of meditation. Writing can be a way of praying. The morning paper can become a prayer book.

Silence is a needed skill in the art of learning to notice and to meditate. Children and young people today are often "addicted to noise," according to expert catechist Richard Reichert. Stillness needs to be learned. Helping people become comfortable with silence is a valuable help to teaching them to pray. Initiate the students slowly into short periods of silence and gradually expand the quiet time.

As your students become more sensitive to God's Word in their lives and struggle to respond faithfully, they become ready to appreciate traditional prayers that echo the same word and express similar responses.

The psalms are a treasure of prayers of thanks and praise. The Glory Be, the Holy, Holy, Holy, the Te Deum are traditional, liturgical expressions of praise, wonder, and thanks. Saint Francis' Canticle of the Sun is a beloved hymn of praise. Grace at meals can bring thanksgiving into our dining rooms. All these help us express our response to God in words that bond us with millions of others who praise and thank God, present in the beautiful and fascinating world of experience.

Help Face Evil

3. Reacting to ugliness and evil   Life, of course, is not just a succession of beautiful, gracious, affirming moments. Our experience of life is filled with shadows. Ugliness mars the beauty of human beings, nature, and human creations. At times hate overwhelms love. Our senses and spirits may be wracked with pain. Catastrophes and tragedies at times outnumber blessings. Evil threatens to swallow up the good. Bad things happen to good people. Death extinguishes life.

Christian prayer needs to be nourished by life's ugliness and pain as well as by its lovely wholeness. As a catechist you need to help students not only face but question and struggle against evil of all kinds. Help them learn to pray for help to struggle against life's shadows and diminishments. The prayer of petition can rise out of the most painful questions and challenges of life. "Why?" "Why me?" can be profoundly prayerful questions. You do no service to your students—even young children—by trying to shield them from pain, ugliness, and evil.

The psalms are lamentations and petitions as well as prayers of praise and thanks. We do hurt. The world groans with injustice and hate. Disease does kill millions. Starvation is more common than satisfaction.

Our education in prayer needs to be an education to petition, to pray for help with hope in God whose love is matched by power, even when all looks hopeless. The Prayers of the Faithful or General Intercessions at Mass are a liturgical example of the community of believers, aware of evil and human needs, calling out to God for help. Petition is an expression, not just of our need, but of our trust in God's care and our hope in God's power. Jesus himself models this kind of prayer in Gethsemane and on the cross. Overwhelmed by suffering and feeling abandoned by his friends and even his Father, Jesus calls out with faith and hope.

The other side of this kind of hope-filled prayer of petition is that we take a stand in our lives against evil, particularly forms of pain and injustice that can be overcome. Our prayer needs to be prophetic as well as contemplative, active as well as mystical. We need prayerfully to cry out to God for help in the face of suffering and injustice, while at the same time we do all we can to overcome these deadly evils.

Our students have a right not only to learn prayers of

petition and hope, but to become acquainted with men and women of prayer, saints of past and present who knew how to praise and thank God for the goodness of life, but knew also how to call out in hope as they struggled against life's evils.

Be Honest Together

4. Being honest   As we come to notice how beautiful and good life is, and learn to question and struggle with the evils in daily experience, it is important that our education in prayer include an honest awareness that we share in the evil as well as in the good. Education to prayer has traditionally included prayers of sorrow and contrition. The mystery of evil is not just something "out there," but is found in each of our hearts.

The psalms are filled with expressions of honest sorrow and repentance. The eucharistic liturgy gives us additional expressions of contrition: Lord, have mercy; I confess; Lord, I am not worthy. The rite of reconciliation provides still more prayers of sorrow. The Jesus Prayer—"Lord Jesus Christ, son of God, have mercy on me"—is but one of the many traditional prayers that express honest awareness that we are sinners who have need for God's mercy.

5. Being united   Helping people learn to pray involves helping them become more united with others. Judaeo-Christian prayer is always a community reality, no matter how personal the prayer. The psalms give ample evidence of how individual prayer is united with the praying community. Jesus teaches us to call upon "Our" Father.

Education in prayer involves helping our students learn to pray together, and to be aware of their Spirit-filled union with others even when they pray alone. Lita-

nies have traditionally been prayers that naturally draw people together in prayer. More spontaneous forms of prayer highlight the blending of intensely personal prayer with the prayers of the community. The prayer of each member of the body of Christ is taken up into the prayer of the whole body.

Being able to pray together requires that people experience a sense of being together. Community prayer builds on and expresses the union between people that already exists. It can then deepen and enrich that very unity. Catechists can do much to help students become united in mutual care and trust.

From the treasure of traditional prayers, we have sketched five practical approaches to helping students learn to pray: 1) feeling loved, 2) appreciating beauty and goodness, 3) reacting to ugliness and evil, 4) being honest, and 5) being united. These approaches give rise to the four traditional forms of prayer: *praise or adoration, thanksgiving, sorrow,* and *petition.* These approaches can be worked out in a rich variety of creative prayer forms. Some of these ways of praying have already been suggested. Here are additional creative techniques for facilitating prayer in catechesis.

Creative Techniques

1. Writing   Have the students write their own prayers that rise out of the experiences explored in the lesson. These prayers may be free flowing or they may be patterned on the psalms, on liturgical prayers, or in imitation of some traditional prayer.

2. Litanies   This is one of the easiest forms of group prayer. Ask each individual to express a petition, for example. All pray a common response after each petition.

The individual petitions may be based on what the students have done up to that point in the session; for example, each drawing might suggest a petition, or every item clipped from newspaper, or each story written or told during the class. The General Intercessions of the eucharistic liturgy provide a model that can be adapted creatively. Litanies may be of praise and thanks or love or sorrow as well as petition.

3. Singing   Song has traditionally been an important form of prayer. Hymns are a valuable expression of prayer, whether listened to on records or actively entered into by singing aloud. Having the students write a prayer-song using an already known melody and drawing upon what has been learned in class is a fine way of helping students pray creatively.

4. Gesture and dance   The body is certainly a neglected medium for prayer. Many people are uncomfortable at first in expressing prayer through bodily movement. Raising one's hands upward, bowing low, kneeling, sitting, lying prostrate, genuflecting, bowing one's head, and joining hands are all traditional bodily prayer expressions. These can be expanded by more free flowing, expressive gestures and movements that reveal inner attitudes of prayer. More sophisticated movements may form dance, a traditional way of praying. Joined with music, such gestures, movements, and dance take on added power as prayer. Processions, too, involve the body actively in prayer.

5. Drawing   Ask your students to be still and let prayer well up in their hearts. Give them paper and crayons or paints and ask them to express their prayer in color, line, shape, or in a story-picture. They may add words if they wish.

6. Environment   Creating a prayerful environment can be helpful, particularly for quiet meditation and spontaneous prayer in groups. Darken the room and light a single candle as a focus of attention. Or show a single slide of a strong photo or work of art in a darkened room. Add quiet music if convenient. Or let the bright sun into the room, allowing all to feel its warmth. With pillows or small rugs create a more comfortable setting for prayer or use the hard floor or hard chairs to create a more austere prayer environment. When carefully positioned, flowers, plants, photos, and art, can certainly help people who want to pray.

7. Posters/banners/collages   Creative visual expression can embrace moments of meditation or contemplation. With or without words, visual creations like posters, banners, and collages can become moving expressions of prayer.

8. Modeling   Prayer can be expressed through ones hands and fingers working modeling clay or aluminum foil. Not only is the process of modeling a potentially prayerful experience, but the finished work may remain as a reminder and facilitator of prayer.

9. Newspapers   Give the students newspapers. Invite them to look through the papers as a form of meditation on life. They may focus, for example, on news items that suggest reasons for wonder, thanks, praise. Or they might look for items that inspire prayers of petition and expressions of hope and trust in the midst of evil. Use the clipped news items for further individual prayer or for creating a litany of prayers.

10. Photos/art   Photos and other good visual art are excellent helps to meditation. Display the visual so that it can be seen comfortably. Invite the students to become still, relaxing as they focus on the visual. Encourage them to let the picture speak to them and to be conscious of their own reactions to it. As they interact with the picture they may pray silently or aloud the prayers that well up within them. Their prayers might take the form of captions to use with the picture. Or they might express something one of the people in the picture might be moved to pray.

11. Symbols   Traditional and contemporary symbols can be important means of growing in prayer. The crucifix, cross, altar, candles, wedding rings, as well as contemporary cultural or advertising symbols can provide such stimulus for reflective meditation.

12. "Banking"   Memorizing short prayers, for example from the psalms, can become a valuable means of filling the memory with prayer expressions. Storing them up, memorizing them, can itself be a prayer. Students can learn to pray these brief prayers frequently during the day.

13. Breathing   Learning to pray in rhythm with one's breathing or with the heart beat has a long history in Christian prayer. Help the students to sit in a comfortable position. Encourage them to relax and gradually become conscious of their breathing. Let them spend a few moments just breathing more deeply, rhythmically, and consciously. Then suggest a word or phrase that they can silently pray with each breath. A traditional prayer of this kind is the "Jesus Prayer," in which one prays with each breath either the name "Jesus" or the prayer, "Lord Jesus Christ, Son of God, have mercy on me," or some variation of it.

14. Journaling   A more extended form of prayer and education to prayer is the journal. Each day students enter in their journals actual prayers or some experiences that spark prayer. The journals may include any kind of prayer or form of praying. Over a span of time such journals can become reliable sources of prayer and valuable records of progress in prayer.

There are, of course, many more ways of helping children learn to pray, and some are yet to be discovered. But keep in mind that the traditional prayers of the church provide clues to learning how to pray, clues grounded in centuries of experience of men and women responding to God's presence in the mysteries of their lives.

Our role as catechists is to share with others the rich heritage of prayer that we have inherited as valuable helps to our own prayerful response to God in our lives. Our goal should be to help our students combine the praying of traditional prayers (like those said by Reb Meir and his sons) with the ability to pray simply and from the heart (as Yussel did).

Questions for Reflection and Discussion

1. What is your favorite way of praying?

2. What do you mean by prayer? How would you describe or define prayer?

3. What is the primary value of having traditional Catholic prayers? Why teach them?

4. Where in your life do you most readily sense God's presence and hear God's Word?

5. Do you often notice the beauty around you? How can you become more aware of it and use it in your prayer?

6. Why is facing the evils of life so important for Christian prayer?

7. Why is Christian prayer basically a community reality—even when you pray alone?

Ways to Respond

1. **Look for textbook prayers.** Jot down the kinds of prayer that your textbook uses. Select several of them. Each day pray in one of the suggested ways. In preparation for guiding your students in a given form of prayer, pray that form yourself. In this way you will be expanding your own experience of prayer as you help teach others.

2. **Practice praying.** After reading this chapter, note each experience of prayer with which you are unfamiliar or uncomfortable. Set aside a few minutes each day and experiment with these prayer forms. Note for yourself in a journal or notebook the results of your experiences.

3. **Pray the psalms.** The psalms have been for Jew and Christian alike—and for Jesus in particular—a helpful resource for praying. Find a translation you like and pray a psalm each day, repeating it several times during the day. Perhaps read a book about the psalms to fire your enthusiasm and to give you additional background.

24

EDUCATING FOR COMPASSION, JUSTICE, PEACE

Throughout its history the church has catechized concerning the corporal works of mercy. The practice of these corporal works of mercy by Catholics has made the church more Christlike, more credible before the world...

The Second General Assembly of the Synod of Bishops in 1971 further expanded the understanding of the church's ministry in society. In *Justice in the World*, the bishops said: "Action on behalf of justice and participation in the transformation of the world fully appears to us as a constitutive dimension of the preaching of the Gospel, or, in other words, of the church's mission for the redemption of the human race and its liberation from every oppressive situation in Jesus Christ."

National Catechetical Directory, 160

It happened some 30 years ago, but the memory remains fresh. One day the speech team coach drove Jim and five other midwestern high school juniors across the city to a debate competition. He deliberately drove through a part of town his students had never seen, the inner city slums.

Jim was so moved by what he saw that the next day he drove slowly through the urban ghetto alone. He noticed a small girl standing shoeless in a grassless yard before a decrepit old house. He thought of all the shoes in his own younger sister's closet.

Jim looked for a shoe store, but could not find one. He bought a doll for the shoeless girl and drove back, but she was gone.

Jim shared his experience with the other debaters who were also in the Sodality. They talked about what Jim shared, prayed over it, and decided to go back to the slums together.

As they walked around, they met a crippled man who showed them his house. It was in terrible shape. The teenagers took his address and left.

They later met with their Sodality moderator, talked about what they had seen, and reflected together on the "Works of Mercy." They decided to spend most of each Saturday for six months fixing up the crippled man's

house. And they did.

This cherished story reminds us that education for compassion and justice is not new in the church. The story also sums up some of the guiding principles of education for compassion, justice, and peace.

Compassion

Before the Second Vatican Council in the 1960s, we Catholics typically grew up in families with a deep concern for the poor and needy. In catechism class we learned the "Works of Mercy." We practiced them by saving our pennies or nickels to "buy pagan babies" who were starving in far away places. In high school we collected food and prepared food baskets for the poor on Thanksgiving Day. We learned to admire great Christians who gave up life's good things in order to devote themselves to the poor—Francis of Assisi, Martin of Tours, Frances of Rome, and more recently Dorothy Day, Tom Dooley, and Mother Teresa.

Most of all we learned to love Jesus who dedicated his life to the outcasts of Palestine. He was found most often with the poor, the sick, the deranged, the lepers, the prostitutes. We memorized and acted out his great parable of compassion, the Good Samaritan.

Justice and Peace

Yet, like Jim, his friends, their speech teacher, and Sodality moderator, most Catholics were not educated to look beyond the immediate hurts of needy individuals. We did not try to discover the underlying systemic or institutional causes of their pain. We admired the Good Samaritan's compassion for the man beaten and robbed and left to die on the road to Jericho, but we never thought of probing the socio-economic-political-cultural conditions that led to the poor victim being assaulted in the first place.

If, as was actually the case historically, the unfortunate traveler in Jesus' story was but one of hundreds of people attacked each year on the winding road from Jerusalem to Jericho, we might ask some serious questions that have social, economic, political, legal, and cultural implications.

"Why are so many being assaulted and robbed?" "Who are the victims?" "Who are the bandits?" "Who is benefiting?" "Why are the bandits so uncontrolled?" "Who has power to do something about the situation?"

This kind of "social analysis" was normally not part of catechesis before Vatican II. It leads to a sense of social justice that Peter Henriot, S.J., defines as "to love people so much that you work to change structures that violate their dignity."

While we continue to share with our students compelling models of compassion, we can also encourage them to admire and imitate great Christians who struggled (and continue to struggle) against the institutionalized forces of injustice. These are women and men like Dr.

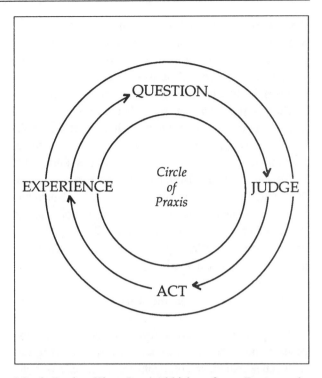

Martin Luther King, Jr., Archbishop Oscar Romero, the six Jesuits and four church women martyred in El Salvador, and the thousands of oppressed Christians in *comunidades eclesiales de base* in Latin America.

Two Dimensions Needed

What is needed is a catechesis that includes both dimensions: compassion and justice.

Education for *compassion* stresses love, care, and concern for suffering individuals. It tends to treat evident symptoms—hunger, thirst, illness, loneliness, depression. It looks at the hurting individual from the perspective of a compassionate person able to reach out and ease the pain. Its model is Jesus, the compassionate Savior.

Education for *justice* stresses human dignity and rights. It explores the causes of people's hurts and looks for remedies in the institutions of society. It approaches the situation from the side of the victims. Its model is Jesus, the "Suffering" or "Oppressed" Servant.

We need to teach our students to see the face of the poor, to feel their pain, and to walk with them. We also need to help them keep asking "Why?" "Why in a world so rich in resources do so many continue to suffer great want?" "Why?"

A Challenging Process

A very practical approach to compassion, justice, and peace education has developed during the past half century. Before and after World War I Joseph Cardinal Cardijn in France worked out for his Young Christian Workers and Young Christian Students the enormously influential three-step process: *see, judge, act.* It became widely used in North, Central, and South America—for example, in the Christian Family Movement.

Twenty years later, in Brazil, Paulo Freire developed and popularized a similar process which he called "praxis." Praxis simply means the constant connecting of reflection and action. In the United States during the 1970s and 1980s, Joe Holland and Peter Henriot, S.J., of the Center of Concern in Washington, D.C., adapted and popularized these three previous contributions as the "circle of praxis" or "pastoral circle." We find this ongoing process of reflecting and acting very practical for use with children and youth.

The pastoral circle has four steps:

1. *Experience.* Education for compassion, justice, and peace is not merely academic or theoretical. It begins with actual experience of, contact with, people who are hurting. Jim and his fellow debaters were quite comfortable with the world until they drove through the city slums and came into contact with poor persons for the first time in their lives. They observed the dreadful shacks, felt the cold inside the crippled man's "home," sensed the pain in the shoeless girl's eyes, compared what they saw with their own homes, clothes, and overall lifestyle.

That awareness through personal contact with suffering persons can ignite in people's hearts a tug of compassion. Further experience may foster a profound feeling of identification with the poor. Gradually one comes to *look at the world through the eyes of the poor.*

2. *Question.* The second step is one that Jim and his friends and teachers did not take. It was not an explicit part of the "see-judge-act" process common at that time. The questioning, more formally called "social analysis," arises from the awesome extent of human suffering and the complexity of its causes. Our lives are enmeshed in social, political, legal, economic, cultural forces and structures. These profoundly affect how much we and others earn, who can find jobs, where people may live, what kind of education, work, and positions people may achieve. We need to reflect critically, to systematically probe the causes for so much poverty, homelessness, hunger, inequality, violation of human rights.

Social analysis is simply doing just that, asking questions and searching out answers, looking for connections, anticipating consequences: "Why?" "Why are so

many hurting?" "Who are suffering?" "Who is benefiting?" "Who has the power to bring about changes?" "What would happen if...?"

In the second step we learn to *look at the world with more critical eyes.*

3. *Judge.* Once our hearts are moved with compassion for suffering persons and our mind analyzes the causes of their pain, we turn to Christ Jesus and his Way. We turn to the Bible, as did Jim and his friends, and to the church's social teachings, to judge the world we are now more aware of in the light of the Gospel. This is more formally called "theological reflection."

For youngsters this may be reading together, talking and praying about, biblical stories like the Good Samaritan, the Final Judgment, Jesus' "Great Commandment," one or more of his healing miracles. It might include the life of a famous saint or an unknown Christian they know who compassionately works for justice and peace. It might also draw on prayers from the liturgy and excerpts from the social teachings of a recent Pope or our Bishops.

In these ways we may come to *look at the world through the eyes of Christ, the Suffering Servant.*

4. *Act.* Once we see the world more critically through the eyes of the poor and of Jesus Christ, we need to *do* something. Our "experience," "social analysis," and "theological reflection" need to move to action. We need to take at least a step to help ease people's pain and to create a more just, peaceful, caring world—starting within the narrow radius of our home, school, parish, neighborhood. One step we all can do right in class is to pray for hurting individuals and for a more compassionate, just, and peaceable world.

What we do will depend very much on our situation and resources, the needs we have discovered, the causes and systems we have analyzed, and the impulses of Christ's Spirit. But do something we must. We may not be able to solve world hunger, but we may be able to help feed a hungry family, and in the process learn that even we can do something more to ease world hunger.

In short, we need to *do something to change the world we have come to experience, question, and judge.* And the new experiences that occur through that action start the "circle of praxis" all over again on a deeper level, as more a spiral than a circle.

Practical Tips

To use the "circle of praxis" within your present religious education program, you may find these tips helpful.
1. *Act justly in a peaceable classroom.* First and most important is that you act compassionately and justly in

your teaching and that you empower your students to do the same. Basic attitudes like respect, equal rights and opportunities, fairness, consistency, strong but gentle discipline, genuine caring—these teach louder than any words.

2. *Permeate all learning.* Education for justice is not simply another course, much less an "elective." All Christian education must be an education for compassion, justice, and peace. This means drawing out the justice implications of anything we teach. Jim's speech coach effectively did this by selecting a route to the debate tournament that would allow his students to see a whole new world.

3. *Enrich lesson plans.* You may have noticed that the "circle of praxis" meshes nicely with the process underlying the lesson plans of today's mainline textbooks.

Experience and question easily become part of the first step of the lesson plan: *Learning About Our Lives.* You may want to expand what is in most textbooks with actual experiences of contact with the poor or sick, or simulation games, and with the results of social analysis research (often available in the daily news media).

Judge becomes a dimension of the second step: *Learning About Our Faith.* You may want to update your textbook with more recent social justice teachings of the Pope or Bishops, or with contemporary examples of Christians working for justice and peace.

Act readily fits the third step: *Learning How to Live Our Faith.* Expand what is in the lesson plan to include real opportunities for action in your own area.

So do not think you need to learn a whole new way of planning lessons for compassion, justice, and peace. Use your textbook's lesson plans, but draw upon your insight into the dynamic of the compassion-justice-peace "circle of praxis" to enrich and deepen them.

4. *Exercise the four essential learning strategies.* You may have noticed also how the "circle of praxis" engages the very same learning strategies essential to the catechetical process most commonly used in today's texts: explore, share, pray, act. Education for compassion, justice, and peace simply focuses these four learning strategies on issues of human pain and systemic injustice. So, be

THE TWO FEET OF CHRISTIAN SERVICE

SOCIAL CHANGE (Works of justice)
- Working for full employment bill
- Land reform
- Getting bakeries & restaurants to reduce wasted food
- Challenging practices of corporations contributing to hunger
- Starting a food co-op or credit union
- Organizing workers & the poor
- Educating the public

DIRECT SERVICE (Works of mercy)
- Food pantries
- Food baskets
- Clothing centers
- Hospitality houses
- Visiting:
  —elderly
  —shut-ins
  —prisoners
- "Meals on Wheels"
- Transporting elderly to grocery store
- Tutoring children

James & Kathy McGinnis *Parenting For Peace & Justice* (Orbis Books, p. 109)

sure you are involving your students actively rather than simply giving them information or abstract principles.

5. *Educate the heart.* One of the most traditional aspects of teaching compassion, justice, and peace is the role of the heart as well as the mind. Emphasis on critical reflection and social analysis is welcome, but it should not lead us to lose sight of the importance of the heart. Action for justice is motivated and sustained not just by critical thinking. Jim and his friends were moved to action when the sight of a shoeless little girl and crippled man in a cold shack touched their hearts and carried them through six months of Saturday sacrifice and work. Compassion, love, a thirst for justice, are the motivators toward action for justice and peace. The courage to begin and the patience to endure rest in the heart.

6. *Stir the imagination.* It is imagination that opens the heart to be touched. It is imagination that bridges theory and practice. It is imagination that fires motivations and sparks hope that with God's help we can create a more just world. We live more by dreams, symbols, images than by clear, distinct ideas and logical analysis. Revolutions have been launched by a song, a poem, an image, a symbol.

Education for justice and peace needs to be rich with food for the imagination: story, poetry, song, symbols, images, photos, art.

Something Old But New

Much of contemporary education for compassion, justice, and peace is already an integral part of religious education theory and practice. What needs greater attention is personal contact with the poor, greater awareness of the structural and systemic dimensions of justice and injustice, greater exposure to Catholic social teaching, and creative, imaginative actions for justice and peace.

What Jim and his friends did under the guidance of their speech teacher and Sodality moderator exemplifies much of the basics of teaching justly. We hope that students today will act as compassionately as those youngsters did thirty years ago. But we also hope that while "repairing one house for one crippled man," they will also ask why, in an affluent society, people like the crippled man have no decent homes in the first place. Then we hope they will try to find creative ways to work for better low-income housing for millions of people like him in today's world.

Questions for Reflection and Discussion

1. What has most moved you to reach out to the suffering and to work for social justice and peace?

2. Why do you feel so many people are hungry, poor, unemployed, homeless in today's world and even in our own country?

3. What experiences have you had (or do you still have) that diminish your human dignity and violate your rights?

4. How central to the Bible do you feel is concern for social justice? What are some striking examples?

5. What have you personally tried to do for others individually or through efforts to change unjust social, legal, or cultural institutions?

Ways to Respond

1. Experience. Plan carefully with your students a visit to a nursing home, shelter for the homeless, soup kitchen or similar place where they may come into contact with people in need. Be sure to work sensitively with the staff of the institution. Prepare the youngsters for the experience. Let them know what to expect and suggest ways to act. Creatively plan together some concrete action they might take to show their care for the needy. Accompany them in the actual experience. Afterwards guide them in reflecting together on their experience. Include your own reactions and feelings.

2. Question. Join your students in a research project that might enlighten them and you about social, political, or economic causes of some aspect of poverty. Focus the research preferably on any type of human hurt with which they have had or may have some personal experience in your geographical area.

3. Read Chapter VII, "Catechesis for Social Ministry," of the *National Catechetical Directory*, or a book like that of Joe Holland and Peter Henriot, S.J., *Social Analysis: Linking Faith and Justice* (Orbis, 1980), or *Our Best Kept Secret: The Rich Heritage of Catholic Social Teaching*, by Michael J. Schultheis, Edward P. DeBerri, and Peter J. Henriot (Center of Concern, 1987), or *The Faith That Does Justice: Examining the Christian Sources for Social Change*, edited by John C. Haughey (Paulist Press, 1977), to enrich your own awareness of Catholic social teaching.

25

Evaluation

It was a shock! Three letters arrived on the DRE's desk the same day in early May. Each said almost the same thing: "The parish religious education program is dreadful." "My children are not learning anything about their faith. They are not being taught the basics." "Unless things change next year, I will remove my children from the program."

After recovering from the initial shock, our DRE friend decided to plan a systematic evaluation at the end of May. She devised a simple questionnaire which she sent to every family and to all the catechists, aides, and students. During June she studied the results.

To her satisfaction the overwhelming response was quite positive. Several deficiencies in the program surfaced, together with a number of fine suggestions for improvement.

That example suggests several things about catechetical evaluation: its importance, the need for broad involvement, and generally known and accepted goals and objectives (on which to base the evaluation). Periodic evaluation is a key to growth. It is important that each individual look into his or her performance, and that all who are involved in the catechetical work of the parish evaluate the entire program.

We have found it helpful to begin our personal evaluation with two strategies.

1. Personal reflection   Take some quiet time after the end of the teaching year. Think back over the year. Note your spontaneous feelings. Great? Awful? Exciting? Discouraging? Joyful? Sad?

Then reflect more deeply to get behind the feelings. Ask yourself questions like:

• What seemed to work consistently well?
• What did we seem to enjoy most?
• What definitely did not work?
• What seemed most to help? to hinder?
• How well do you feel you achieved your personal objectives?
• How eager are you to teach again next year?

2. Student evaluation   Take time the last class of the year to invite your students to evaluate the year. Suggest simple questions like the following:

• What did you like best about this year?
• What did you like least about this year?
• What would you suggest to make next year's classes better?

• Overall, how do you feel about religion class?

It is equally important that the whole catechetical team look at its successes and failures as a group. Such an evaluation reaches out to the whole parish. Catechetical work is only one part of the pastoral ministry of the parish and is intimately related to the overall parish ministry.

The following questions are suggested as a kind of checklist for group evaluation. Since each parish or school has its own particular philosophy of religious education, its unique assets and liabilities, its peculiar opportunities and obstacles, individual catechists may find it necessary to adapt the checklist.

Checklist

1. Goals and Objectives

• How clear are we on our goals and objectives? At what are we consciously aiming? As a parish? As a catechetical team? As individual catechists?

• To what extent have we been achieving our goals and objectives?

• What criteria do we use to judge our success or failure?

• What data do we have upon which to base our evaluation?

2. Context

•To what extent is the catechetical work carefully and consciously integrated into the overall parish ministry—community building, worship, and service?

• As catechists, what kinds of relationships are we creating among ourselves with the pastor? Parish priests? Sisters or Brothers? Parents? Parochial school? Other parish organizations? What can be done to remove obstacles to better collaboration?

• How well does the parish liturgy blend with the kind of catechesis we are giving?

• To what extent are parents interested and involved? What can we do to improve parent involvement?

• What influence on our catechetical work do we notice from other environmental sources? e.g., media, neighborhood, peer, and social pressures?

3. Catechists

• Are we knitting together as a creative working team? Indications? Hindrances? Area of improvement? Plans?

• Are we sharing more easily our own faith, ideas, feelings, successes, failures? How? Why? Why not? Remedies?

• Do we plan our sessions carefully? Individually? Together, in age-level or content groups? What can be done to improve personal and group planning?

• Do we pray together? Enough? Why not? Suggestions?

• What is our general level of satisfaction with our catechetical ministry? Individually? As a group? What are key positive factors? Which negative factors stand out?

• What three things would most improve our ministry in the next half year?

• Are we doing adequate professional reading related

to what we are teaching? Why not? What can we do about it?

• Does the way we relate with our students reflect the ideals of Christian respect, care, concern, understanding, and compassion that we attempt to teach?

• What kind of in-service training has been provided? How might it be improved?

4. Learners

• Is attendance generally acceptable? Any special problems?

• How about the students' attitudes? Eager? Interested? Questioning? Bored? Apathetic? Hostile?

• To what extent do they seem to be meeting the goals we have mutually agreed upon? Intellectual? Affective? Behavioral?

• Are there any special situations that need more sensitive handling? e.g., exceptional persons, behavior problems, unusual home conditions.

• Any specific recommendations for improving learner attitudes and/or achievement?

5. Content

• How well have the students learned what you set out to teach?

• How well have you balanced your content to include the "natural signs" (life experience), "biblical signs" (Scripture), "liturgical signs" (liturgy and other prayer), and "ecclesial signs" (creeds, doctrines, witness of Mary, saints and other Christians)?

• To what extent has all you taught centered on Jesus Christ?

• How well did your teaching and the student's learning blend "affective" and "nonverbal" content with "cognitive" and "verbal"?

• How well did the year's content meet the needs, readiness, and abilities of your students?

6. Resources

•Are we happy with the program or texts we are using? What do we particularly like? Dislike? Suggestions?

•Do we have adequate supplementary materials (e.g., media)? What is lacking? What can be done to improve?

•Are the necessary materials readily available and accessible? Any systems improvements needed?

•What ways can be found to acquire or make more and better educational resources?

•What religious education journals are available on a regular basis? What others might be helpful?

Evaluation Approaches

The above check-list may be used in any of the following ways or in various creative combinations of the four suggestions.

1. Individual questionnaires The checklist (after being adapted to unique parish situations) may be duplicated and distributed to each of the catechists individually. The items on it may be used by each person simply as an aid to self-evaluation. They may also be used as an instrument of team evaluation. In that case, the completed questionnaires will need to be returned to the director of religious education. They may then be used by the administrator(s) as helpful data for reviewing policies and programs, or they may be used in the following types of meetings.

2. Formal meeting All of the catechists and related administrators—director of religious education, pastor or delegated parish priest, and parish council members—meet formally to evaluate the first half-year. The checklist may be used as the agenda for such a meeting. Or the compilation of data from completed questionnaires may be used to provide an agenda for discussion and planning. Or use a simplified form with three questions: 1) What did you like best about this year? 2) What did you like least? 3) What positive suggestions do you have for making next year better?

3. Informal meeting Some parishes prefer a more informal, flexible approach to an evaluation meeting. A pot-luck supper may initiate the evening, either in one of the catechist's homes or in the rectory, convent, or other appropriate parish facility. After the supper, the catechists may be invited to share informally their impressions of how things have gone during the first months of the year. The checklist may be a loose guide to the kinds of areas to be considered. Perhaps the catechists could fill out the questionnaire as a preparation for this informal meeting. Simple, informal prayers and a song might conclude the evening.

4. Personal interview A valuable means of evaluation, morale building, and team-building is the personal interview. The director of religious education meets individually with each catechist to look over the past half year and plan for the coming months. The checklist might be filled out prior to the interview, used as a loose guide for the interview, or presented in the interview to be filled out later.

Such interviews, if done with understanding, respect, and trust, give the catechists a chance to share their own ideas and feelings about the program in general and their own contribution in particular. They may be more honest in private than they would be in a larger public meeting. The interview also provides the administrator a chance to gauge more closely the abilities of each catechist. This not only allows for the early detection of problems, but more important, provides an opportunity to discover and identify potential leaders.

Report Card Alternatives

The question of report cards for religious education has always been a thorny question. Some aspects of the catechetical ministry can readily be graded: knowledge of facts, memorization of definitions, capacity for research and reasoning, and overt behavior. Other dimensions escape ready measurement. No catechist can accurately judge the degree of growth in personal faith, hope, or charity within an individual, or safely translate that into a quantitative measure or grade. Neither catechist, parent, nor student should consider a grade in religion as a valid indicator of growth in genuine religious faith, hope, or love. On the other hand, a report card can give some indication of acquired knowledge and overt behaviors like attendance, discipline, listening, and cooperation.

The report card, or an alternative, provides a highly regarded moment of contact between parent—or other relative—student, and catechist. The catechist should try to maximize the positive impact of that moment for improving understanding and collaboration between home, school, and church. Some suggestions along these lines follow.

1. Parents' personal critique   Catechists may send home a simple instrument by which parents submit their own evaluation of a) the student's progress and attitudes, b) the catechist, and c) the entire parish catechetical program. Not only will this provide helpful insights, but it may increase parental involvement and responsibility toward the catechetical work of the parish.

2. Parent-catechist meeting   In addition to or in place of a report card, a formal or informal meeting with parents can provide an opportunity for more honest and complete sharing. In addition, such meetings make it possible to share with parents creative displays of the students' work, of the texts and other materials used, and offer a chance to get to know those directing the program.

3. Personal letter   In addition to or in place of a report card, a brief personal letter to each parent or relative can be helpful for both catechists and students. Receiving a personal letter usually conveys more insight than a formal report card, and tends to create or deepen the bond between parents and catechist.

4. Personal phone call   Perhaps even more useful than a personal letter is a phone call. The telephone allows catechists to talk with parents or relatives on a more personal basis. It is also a more direct means of sensing the attitudes of parents, their social situation, their feelings toward the parish and its catechesis.

On-going parental involvement is the key in many instances to the success of catechetical programs in parishes and schools. Several of the above report-card alternatives are designed to increase understanding and involvement of parents in the religious education ministry of the parish. In addition, the following suggestions may prove useful.

1. Prayer evening   An attractive evening of worship might draw some parents to greater involvement. The worship might be a Eucharistic liturgy or it might be any form of group prayer. Whether held in a private home, parish church, or meeting hall, it is important that the prayer evening be carefully planned. It should be simple, joyful, and adapted so that parents would feel comfortable.

2. Active involvement   Many parents simply are unaware of how they might be helpful. Do not hesitate to ask parents to get actively involved as catechist aides, librarians, phone contacts, drivers, record keepers, or media coordinators. Others would be delighted on occasion to share gifts or talents they have with students.

3. Cassette evenings   Parents can learn and share much through the use of video or audio cassettes. Preferably in small groups in private homes, parents can watch, listen to, and talk about recorded presentations that explore their role in religious education.

4. Parents' notes   Many catechetical programs provide materials or notes for parents. Sometimes these are separate books or spirit masters, at other times they are contained in the student's book. In any case they are often neglected valuable tools for involving parents more intelligently in the religious education of their children—as well as in their own ongoing religious education.

These and other techniques may be used for periodic evaluation of catechetical programs. Honest evaluation is important to ensure quality catechesis and continued growth on the part of all involved. Evaluating can be a very positive, creative experience when done sensitively.

Questions for Reflection and Discussion

1. How do you presently evaluate your catechetical efforts?

2. What is your feeling about report cards for catechesis?

3. Why are parents such an important part of the evaluation process?

4. How do your students get involved in evaluation? Do you offer them opportunities to discuss their honest feelings and reactions?

5. Do you evaluate your teaching after every class? How can you make this a habit?

Ways to Respond

1. Do a check-up. Take some time to think back over your past catechetical sessions. Before looking at detailed questions listed in this article, jot down your overall feelings about what has been happening. Think too of what you see your main objectives to be—in your own words. Compare these with what the textbook authors indicate as the major objectives of their program. Draw any conclusions that occur to you.

2. Revise your plan. An evaluation is primarily an opportunity for growth and improvement. Notice first the positive aspects that surface during your self-evaluation. Then take account of evident weaknesses. Building on your successes and strengths, revise your plans for your teaching in such a way as to minimize weaker areas or strengthen them.

3. Get outside evaluation. Invite a co-catechist, someone you trust and are comfortable with, to observe one or more of your sessions. Or invite the DRE or religion coordinator to observe you at work. Or invite observations from your students. Or use an evaluating instrument prepared by someone else as an aid to helping your own evaluation.

26

THE CATECHISM
AND THE CREATIVE CATECHIST

> This catechism aims at presenting an organic synthesis of the essential and fundamental contents of Catholic doctrine, as regards both faith and morals, in the light of the Second Vatican Council and the whole of the Church's Tradition. Its principal sources are the Sacred Scriptures, the Fathers of the Church, the liturgy, and the Church's Magisterium. It is intended to serve "as a point of reference for the catechisms or compendia that are composed in the various countries."
>
> *Catechism of the Catholic Church, 11*

As we Americans celebrated Thanksgiving in 1992, the bookstores of Paris posted eye-catching signs in their windows: *Le catechisme est arrivé!* (The *Catechism* has arrived!). The posters recall the yearly ads for the arrival of new wine: *Le beaujolais nouveau est arrivé!*

France's response to the *Catechisme de l'eglise catholique (Catechism of the Catholic Church)* was almost as enthusiastic as its response to the year's beaujolais nouveau vintage. The book stores quickly sold out of the new *Catechism.*

The response worldwide has been similar. Sales are in the millions in Europe, North and South America, and other parts of the world. The *Catechism* apparently has touched a widely felt thirst.

We received a copy of the French edition barely a week after its publication in France and have been reading, pondering, writing about and using it ever since. The English edition, *Catechism of the Catholic Church*, translated in the United States from the French original and revised by the Vatican, was published in 1994.

The Catechism: What It Is

Many purchasers may have been surprised to see the size, weight, and density of the *Catechism.* Although it is called a catechism, it is quite unlike the *Baltimore Catechism*, with its questions and answers, which was widely used in the United States from the 1880s well into the 1960s. The only cat-

echism like the *Catechism of the Catholic Church* in the church's history is the Roman Catechism, also known as the *Catechism of the Council of Trent*, or the *Catechism of St. Pius V*, published over four hundred years ago in 1566 for the whole Catholic church.

The *Catechism* arose in response to a desire expressed at the Synod of Bishops in 1985 for a single, comprehensive catechism for the whole church. Pope John Paul II took the Bishops' desire to heart, seeing such a catechism as "fully responding to a real need of the universal church and of the particular churches" (5).

Work on the *Catechism* took almost six years, nine drafts, and worldwide consultation before the Pope finally approved it in October 1992. He called it the "symphony of faith," reflecting the unity and harmony of the Catholic Church (p. 4).

The Pope himself describes the kind of catechism it is:

A catechism should faithfully and systematically present the teaching of Sacred Scripture, the living Tradition in the Church and the authentic Magisterium, as well as the spiritual heritage of the Fathers, Doctors, and saints of the Church, to allow for a better knowledge of the Christian mystery and for enlivening the faith of the People of God. It should take into account the doctrinal statements which down the centuries the Holy Spirit has intimated to his church. It should also help to illumine with the light of faith the new situations and problems which had not yet emerged in the past (p. 4).

This one volume is meant to contain, in a systematic and organized manner, all the teachings of the Catholic church. Essentially it is a compendium of Catholic doctrine, a reference book, providing a sound, reliable resource for creating catechetical materials.

Unlike the *Baltimore Catechism*, which was used mostly to catechize children and youth, this *Catechism* has a different purpose and audience. The Pope calls it "a sure norm for teaching the faith" and "a sure and authentic reference text for teaching Catholic doctrine and particularly for preparing local catechisms" (p. 5). It is meant to be used as "a reference text...for a catechesis renewed at the living sources of the faith!" (p. 3).

As such, the *Catechism* "emphasizes the exposition of doctrine" and "seeks to help deepen understanding of faith" (23).

Similar Organization

The *Catechism* organizes its immense amount of information in a manner not all that different from the way the *Baltimore Catechism* was put together: Creed, Sacraments, Commandments, Our Father. Both were influenced by the four-part division of the 16th-century Roman Catechism. Actually the traditional four-part arrangement of catechisms has even more ancient roots in the catechumenate process developed in the early church.

The *Catechism's* four parts, or "four pillars," are identified in its Prologue as:
The baptismal profession of faith (the Creed),
The sacraments of faith (the Sacraments),
The life of faith (the Commandments), and
The prayer of the believer (Lord's Prayer) (13).

While anyone can read it, the *Catechism* is chiefly meant "for those responsible for catechesis: first of all the bishops, as teachers of the faith and pastors of the Church.... Through the bishops it is addressed to redactors (authors/editors) of catechisms, to priests, and to catechists" (12).

The Catechism: What It Is Not

While noting what the Catechism is, it can also be helpful to keep in mind what it is not. It is not meant to be a textbook for actual catechesis, certainly not of children or youth.

Neither, according to Pope John Paul II, is the *Catechism* a tool "to replace (existing) local cat-

echisms" (a term that in our country includes catechetical textbooks and teaching materials) but to "encourage and assist in the writing of new local catechisms" (p. 6).

The *Catechism* insists that it needs to be adapted to the needs and gifts of individuals and cultural groups. This adaptation and inculturation is to be done through approved local catechetical materials and ultimately by individual catechists (see 24).

The *Catechism*, in effect, does not deal with who teaches whom, when, where, or how. It does not even claim to contain the whole of the "what," or content of catechesis. For such practical matters the *Catechism* refers catechists to the church's approved documents regarding catechesis. These include the documents of the Second Vatican Council, which, citing Pope Paul VI, the *Catechism* calls "the great catechism of modern times" and the *General Catechetical Directory*, published in 1971 (presently being revised), the third and fourth general assemblies of the Synod of Bishops, on evangelization (1974) and catechesis (1977), the apostolic exhortations *Evangelization in the Modern World* of Paul VI (1975) and *Catechesis in Our Time* of John Paul II (1979).

Documents in This Country

In addition to these documents meant for the entire church, there are similar official documents governing catechesis in our own country, especially *Sharing the Light of Faith: National Catechetical Directory for Catholics of the United States* (1979), and *Guidelines for Doctrinally Sound Catechetical Materials* (1990).

The *Catechism* also urges us to look to great catechists and important catechetical movements throughout the history of the church for models of sound, creative catechesis (8-9).

It is these very sources that guided us in writing (1983) and revising (1991) *Creative Catechist*, and continue to guide us in 1995. The principles and practical hints found in *Creative Catechist* remain valid and are in harmony with the *Catechism*.

The Catechism and Creative Catechist

It may be helpful to look at *Creative Catechist* in relation to the *Catechism*, keeping in mind that the two books serve quite different purposes. *Creative Catechist* is an example of the kind of catechetical materials for which the *Catechism* is meant to be a point of reference.

We will look at *Creative Catechist* chapter by chapter, and note sections of the *Catechism* that relate more or less directly to each chapter, in order to help you enrich your reading of both books as you strive to become a better catechist.

1. The Goal of Catechesis: Faith Growth

Creative Catechist describes the goal of catechesis as "growth in faith," aiming at a "faith that is living and maturing, affecting people's everyday responses, and grounded in the church's tradition." The text describes a dynamic catechetical "process of faith growth."

The *Catechism* also is oriented ultimately "toward the maturing of faith, its putting down roots in personal life and its shining forth in personal conduct" (23). The Prologue defines catechesis as "an education in the faith of children, young people, and adults" (3). The *Catechism* explores the dynamic of faith growth in more depth and detail in Part One, Section One, "I Believe"—"We Believe" (26-184).

2. The Context of Catechesis: Community

Creative Catechist stresses the community context of catechesis and makes the point that the believing community is ultimately the most effective catechist of its adults, youth, and children. The community catechizes not just through its formal catechetical ministry but by its "lifestyle, liturgy, service, hospitality, as well as by formal and informal sharing of God's Word" (10).

Similarly, the *Catechism's* Prologue points out that "early on, the name catechesis was given to the totality of the Church's efforts to make disciples" (4), affirming that "Catechesis is intimately bound up with the whole of the Church's life" (7).

The community context of faith growth is undergirded later in Part One, Section 1, Article 2, "We Believe," (166-169), summed up in St. Cyprian's words: "Believing is an ecclesial act....The Church is the mother of all believers" (181).

The doctrinal riches underlying the awareness of the community as the context of catechesis are explored later in the *Catechism's* explanation of the "Catholic Church" and the "communion of saints" (748-962).

3. The Process of Catechesis: Integration

Chapter 3 of *Creative Catechist* describes the catechetical process of integrating daily experience with the church's living tradition. Drawing on an important scriptural theme found in both Testaments and in Vatican Council II, we call this a "process of discernment." Others call it "shared Christian praxis."

Just as we describe this process of relating daily life experience with the church's living tradition with the terminology of "signs of God's Word," the *Catechism* hints at this process in describing signs and symbols in the liturgy (1145). It explores "signs of the human world" (1146-1149) and how they relate to "signs of the covenant" (1150), "signs taken up by Christ" (1151), and "sacramental signs" (1152).

4. The History of Catechesis: Development

Creative Catechist briefly traces the key developments in catechesis from New Testament times to our own age. We are the beneficiaries of the experiences, insights, and practices of great catechists over some 20 centuries in various cultures and regions of the world.

The Prologue of the *Catechism* similarly encourages us to value and draw upon the important developments of the past, and cites some of the great catechists of earlier ages (8-9).

5. Content Source: God's Word

Creative Catechist follows the *National Catechetical Directory* in seeing "the source of catechesis, which is also its content" as "God's 'Word" (31). The content of catechesis embraces all the "signs of God's Word" described above: natural (life experience), biblical (Bible), liturgical (Liturgy), and ecclesial (Creeds, Doctrine, and Witness), together with the vital process of relating them to one another.

The entire *Catechism* deals extensively with Catholic Creeds, doctrinal and moral teachings, the bible, liturgy, Christian witness, and prayer. In its treatment of creation and God's gradual self-revelation (26-141), the *Catechism* recognizes that these are not the sole content of revelation or catechesis. It also hints at the importance of human experience and the discernment process: "Revelation is realized simultaneously 'by deeds and words which are intrinsically bound up with each other' and shed light on each other" (53).

6. Natural Signs: Life and Culture

Creative Catechist explores the riches of life experience and human culture as vital signs of God's Word, and therefore an important part of the content of catechesis. Drawing chiefly on Vatican Council II and the *National Catechetical Directory*, it speaks of the "natural signs," the "signs of the times," "voices of our age," and "seeds of the Word."

The *Catechism* suggests the same in its stress on the need to respect and take into account various local cultures (24). It more explicitly recognizes the experiences of daily life, human culture, and the created world as signs of God's Word in sections of its treatment of revelation (51-53) and creation (279-294; 299-301; 337-349).

7. Biblical Signs: Scripture

Chapter 7 of *Creative Catechist* explores the importance of the sacred scriptures, the "biblical signs" of God's Word, in catechesis, and ways to understand, respond to, and use the written Word of God. It provides a list of tools for accessing the fruits of modern biblical interpretation.

The *Catechism* is filled with quotations from and references to the sacred scriptures of Jews and Christians. It takes 31 pages of the Index just to list them. Early on (101-141), the *Catechism* addresses the nature and importance of the bible for Catholics, including guidelines for interpreting the scriptures. Part Four has suggestions for using the bible for prayer (2653-2654). Curiously the *Catechism* omits reference to the immense riches of modern biblical studies in describing how to interpret the bible (109-114).

8. Liturgical Signs: Worship

While *Creative Catechist* explores the place of the church's liturgical worship in relation to catechesis, and gives practical tips for catechesis before, during, and after the liturgy, the *Catechism* devotes the whole of one of its four major parts to explaining the church's official worship.

After a lengthy discussion of liturgy in general (1066-1209), Part Two of the *Catechism* explains each of the seven sacraments, as well as sacramentals, popular devotions, and funerals (1210-1690). The *Catechism* explicitly addresses the relationship of liturgy and catechesis, stating that the liturgy is "the privileged place for catechizing the People of God" and that "catechesis is intrinsically linked with the whole liturgical and sacramental activity" (1074).

9. Ecclesial Signs: Creeds and Doctrines

Chapter 9 of *Creative Catechist* describes the nature and importance of creeds and doctrines in the church's life and in the catechetical process of nurturing growth in faith.

As a compendium of Catholic doctrinal teachings, it is not surprising that the *Catechism* devotes the most space (some 263 pages) to its first part, or "pillar," "The Profession of Faith." The Apostles' Creed provides its organizational source.

In addition, the *Catechism* contains a large number of quotations from various creeds, councils, pontifical documents, ecclesiastical documents, and canon law—requiring 17 pages just to list them in the Index (720-736).

10. Ecclesial Signs: Witness of Christian Living

Creative Catechist recognizes the importance of saints and other saintly persons as signs of God's Word to us. The saints, with Mary as the foremost saint, are presented primarily as models and guides for Christian living, but also as miracle workers and intercessors. Chapter 10 also gives practical ways of helping people today recover genuine devotion to the church's saints.

The *Catechism* deals with the role of saints—including all of us—chiefly under "Christian Holiness" (2012-2030), the "Communion of Saints" (946-953), and "Mary" (954-975). In addition the *Catechism* provides a wealth of quotations from the writings of saints and other great Christians. Twelve pages (741-752) of the Index are devoted just to listing the references to the individual citations. It is unfortunate that lay persons, women especially, and modern saints are under-represented.

Part III of *Creative Catechist* deals with "Keys to Creative Catechesis" (Chapters 11-25). As noted earlier, the *Catechism* is not a catechetical textbook nor a guide to catechetical methodology. It needs to be adapted to various age levels, cultures, socioeconomic, and regional traits. So it is not surprising that it does not relate directly to all of the practical chapters in the last half of *Creative Catechist*.

However, the *Catechism* does throw light on some of the chapters of Part III. We will note them briefly.

11. Being Creative
The *Catechism*, in its treatment of creation, does not devote space to human creativity, but does so indirectly in sections dealing with the products of human creativity like art, media, and music (see chapters below).

12. Knowing the Learners
As we have seen earlier, the *Catechism* insists on the need to adapt it and its use to the particular needs, abilities, and traits of individuals and cultures. That assumes knowledge of and respect for those being catechized.

15. Using Textbooks and Planning Lessons
One of the primary purposes of the *Catechism*, as we already noted, is to be a guide in the preparation of catechetical materials like textbooks and of the actual catechesis itself.

16. Using Media 17. Using Pictures
18. Using TV, Video, and Film
The *Catechism* highlights the importance of the visual, first of all by actually using pictures to introduce each of its four parts. A visual symbol is on the front cover of every copy. Several sections stress the value of visual images, symbols, and sacred art, as expressions of truth through beauty in preserving and fostering faith (426-478; 1145-1152; 1156-1162; 2129-2132; 2500-2503; 3513).

The modern social communication media, which includes film, television, and video, receives limited mention in the *Catechism* under the Eighth Commandment (2493-2499; 2512).

19. Using Music and Song
The *Catechism* notes the beauty and value of music and song in expressing and nurturing faith, particularly in the liturgy (1156-1158). This applies as well to catechesis.

23. Praying
Perhaps the freshest, most inspiring, and most practical section of the *Catechism* is Part Four, "Christian Prayer."

Many have suggested that one begin reading the *Catechism* with this fourth "pillar." It explores what prayer is, gives biblical models of praying people, cites biblical prayers, especially the psalms, as well as traditional prayers (with explanations of the Our Father and Hail Mary), describes the chief kinds of prayer, and offers many practical suggestions for praying (2558-2865).

24. Educating for Compassion, Justice, Peace
Part Three, the third "pillar" of the *Catechism*, "Life in Christ," summarizes the central place of love and compassion in Jesus' life and in the church's life and moral traditions. It also stresses modern Catholic social teachings. A social justice perspective permeates the treatment of each of the commandments, which have often been viewed solely in individual, personal terms. See especially (1877-1948; 2401-2463).

Conclusion
The *Catechism of the Catholic Church* is not a replacement for present textbooks or *Creative Catechist*. It does not mandate or condemn particular catechetical methods. It has its weaknesses along with its strengths.

The *Catechism* is a rich resource for better understanding our Catholic faith in its fullness. It makes available in summary fashion the fruit of some 20 centuries of Christian experience from all over the world. As we move into the third millennium, the *Catechism of the Catholic Church* is a valuable gift to contemporary catechists.

We conclude with the words of the *Roman Catechism* as quoted in the *Catechism of the Catholic Church*:

> The whole concern of doctrine and its teaching must be directed to the love that never ends. Whether something is proposed for our belief, for hope or for action, the love of our Lord must always be made accessible, so that anyone can see that all the works of perfect Christian virtue spring from love and have no other objective than to arrive at love (25).

CORRELATION GUIDE

CREATIVE CATECHIST
AND THE
CATECHISM OF THE CATHOLIC CHURCH

Creative Catechist	**Catechism of the Catholic Church**

Part I: Catechesis: What? Why? Where?

1. The Goal of Catechesis: Faith Growth	3–4; 23; 26–184; 426–427; 903; 2226
2. The Context of Catechesis: Community	4; 7; 166–169; 181; 748–962; 1309; 1697
3. The Process of Catechesis: Integration	1145–1152; 1676
4. The History of Catechesis: Development	8–9

Part II: Content of Catechesis: God's Word & Its Signs

5. Content Source: God's Word	6; 53; 26–141
6. Natural Signs: Life and Culture	24; 51–53; 279–294; 299–301; 337–349
7. Biblical Signs: Scripture	19; 101–141; 513; 1094–1095; 2653–2654; Index, pp. 689–720
8. Liturgical Signs: Worship	1066–1209; 1210–1690; Index, pp. 738–740
9. Ecclesial Signs: Creeds & Doctrines	26–1065; 1691–2557; Index, pp. 720–736
10. Ecclesial Signs: Witness of Christian Living	905; 946–953; 954–975; 1697; 2012–2030; 2471–2474; Index pp. 741–752

Part III: Keys to Creative Catechesis

Note: The *Catechism,* as a "compendium of Catholic doctrine," does not deal explicitly with catechetical methodology or creativity. All of the remaining chapters of *Creative Catechist* fall under the necessary inculturation or adaptation of the *Catechism* to different cultures, situations, and individuals. See especially John Paul II's observation on page 6. See also #23–24 and 854.

More direct correlations between the *Catechism* and creative aspects of catechesis do occur in relation to some doctrinal, moral, liturgical, biblical, traditional, or cultural topics. See individual references below.

11. Being Creative	23–24; 854
12. Knowing the Learners	23–24; 854
13. Maintaining Discipline	23–24; 854
14. Using All Resources	23–24; 854
15. Using Textbooks and Planning Lessons	23–24; 854
16. Using Media and	23–24; 854; 476–478; 1145–1152 1156–1162; 1192; 2129–2132;
17. Using Pictures	2500–2503; 2513
18. Using TV, Video and Film	23–24; 854; 2141; 2493–2499; 2512
19. Using Stories	23–24; 854
20. Using Role-Playing, Drama, Dance	23–24; 854; 1674
21. Using Music and Song	23–24; 854; 1156–1158; 2678
22. Drawing, Writing, Questioning	23–24; 854
23. Praying	23–24; 854; 1674–1676; 1679; 2558–2865
24. Education for Compassion, Jus-Peace	23–24; 854; 1877–1948; 2401–2563
25. Evaluation	23–24; 854

RESOURCES

Here is a brief selection of available resources for further reading and study.

Church Documents

Catechism of the Catholic Church. USCC-Libreria Editrice Vaticana, 1994.

Congregation for the Evangelization of Peoples, *Guide for Catechists.* USCC, 1993.

Sacred Congregation for the Clergy. *General Catechetical Directory.* USCC, 1971.

National Conference of Catholic Bishops. *To Teach as Jesus Did.* USCC, 1972.

_____. *Basic Teachings for Catholic Religious Education.* USCC, 1973.

_____. *Sharing the Light of Faith*: National Catechetical Directory for Catholics of the United States. USCC, 1977.

_____. *National Pastoral Plan for Hispanic Ministry.* USCC, 1987.

_____. *Guidelines on Doctrine for Catechetical Materials.* USCC, 1991.

Pope John Paul II. *On Catechesis in Our Time (Catechesi Tradendae).* USCC, 1979.

The Congregation for Catholic Education. *The Religious Dimension of Education in a Catholic School.* USCC, 1988.

History and Trends

Boys, Mary C. *Educating in Faith: Maps and Visions.* Harper & Row, 1989.

Warren, Michael, ed. *Source Book for Modern Catechetics.* St. Mary's Press, 1983.

Theory and Principles

Berryman, Jerome W. *Godly Play: A Way of Religious Education.* HarperSanFrancisco, 1991.

Darcy-Berube, Francoise. *Religious Education at a Crossroads.* Paulist Press, 1995.

Downs, Thomas. *The Parish as Learning Community.* Paulist Press, 1979.

Dunning, James B. *Echoing God's Word.* North American Forum on the Catechumenate, 1993.

Greeley, Andrew. *The Religious Imagination.* Sadlier, 1982.

Groome, Thomas H. *Christian Religious Education: Sharing Our Story and Vision.* Harper & Row, 1980.

_____. *Sharing Faith: A Comprehensive Approach to Religious Education and Pastoral Ministry.* HarperSanFrancisco, 1991.

Harris, Maria. *Teaching & Religious Imagination: An Essay in the Theology of Teaching.* Harper & Row, 1987.

Hater, Rev. Robert J. *Parish Catechetical Ministry.* Benziger, 1986.

Hill, Brennan R. *Key Dimensions of Religious Education.* St. Mary's Press, 1988.

Hill, Brennan and William Madges. *The Catechism: Highlights and Commentary.* Twenty-Third Publications, 1994.

Jones, Nathan. *Sharing the Old, Old Story: Educational Ministry in the Black Community.* St. Mary's Press, 1982.

Kelly, Francis, D. *The Mystery We Proclaim: Catechesis at the Third Millennium.* Our Sunday Visitor, 1993.

Prieswerk, Matias. *Educating in the Living Word: A Theoretical Framework for Christian Education.* Orbis Books, 1987.

Ratzinger, Joseph Cardinal Ratzinger and Christoph Schonborn. *Introduction to the Catechism of the Catholic Church.* Ignatius Press, 1994.

Reese, Thomas J., S.J., ed. *The Universal Catechism Reader: Reflections and Responses.* Harper-SanFrancisco, 1990.

Walsh, Michael J., ed. *Commentary on the Catechism of the Catholic Church.* The Liturgical Press, 1994.

Westerhoff, John H. *Will Our Children Have Faith?* Seabury Press, 1976.

The Companion to the Catechism of the Catholic Church: A Compendium of Texts Referred to in the Catechism of the Catholic Church. Ignatius Press, 1994.

The Qualities and Competencies of the Religion Teacher. NCEA, 1983.

Methodology

Dues, Greg. *Teaching Religion with Confidence and Joy.* Twenty-Third Publications, 1988.

Glavich, Kathleen, SND. *Discipline Made Easy.* Twenty-Third Publications, 1994.

Hesch, John B. *A Primer for Catechists.* Paulist Press, 1988.

McCarty, Jim. *The Confident Catechist.* Brown Roa, 1990.

Manternach, Janaan with Carl J. Pfeifer. *And the Children Pray: A Practical Book for Prayerful Catechists.* Ave Maria Press, 1989.

Pfeifer, Carl J., and Janaan Manternach. *How to Be a Better Catechist: Answers to Questions Catechists Ask Most.* Sheed & Ward, 1989.

_____, *Questions Catechists Ask, and Answers That Really Work.* Sheed & Ward, 1993.

Schippe, Cullen. *Planting, Watering, Growing: The Volunteer Catechist's Companion!* Sandalprints Publishing, 1990.

Svoboda, Melannie, SND. *Teaching Is Like...Peeling Back Eggshells.* Twenty-Third Publications, 1994.

van Bemmel, John. *Take Heart, Catechist!: Twenty Stories for Guidance & Growth.* Twenty-Third Publications, 1991.

Vasiloff, Barbara, and Paula Lenz. *Discipline with Purpose.* 2457 N. 61st St., Omaha, NE 68104.

Walters, Thomas P., and Rita Tyson Walters. *Making a Difference: A Catechist's Guide to Successful Classroom Management.* Sheed & Ward, 1986.

Journals/Magazines/Newsletters

Alternative Models Newsletter. P.O. Box 310, Manchester, NH 03105.

Catechist. 2451 East River Road, Dayton, OH 45439.

The Catechist's Connection. P.O. Box 419493, Kansas City, MO 64141

Group's JR. HIGH MINISTRY. Box 407, Mt. Morris, IL 61054.

The Living Light. c/o Department of Education, USCC, 3211 Fourth Street, N.E., Washington, DC 20017.

Pace. Our Sunday Visitor, 200 Noll Plaza, Huntington, IN 46750.

Religious Education. 409 Prospect Street, New Haven, CT 06511.

Religion Teacher's Journal. P.O. Box 180, Mystic, CT 06355.

Shining Star: Practical Teaching Magazine for Christian Educators and Parents. 1204 Buchanan Street, P.O. Box 299, Carthage, IL 62321.

Today's Catholic Teacher. 1451 East River Road, Dayton, OH 45439.

Youthworker Update. 1224 Greenfield Drive, El Cajon, CA 92021.

Of Related Interest...

Jesus, I'm a Teacher, Too
Guidance and Inspiration from the Gospels
Melannie Svoboda
In this book, Sister Melannie offers more than 50 brief reflections for teachers and catechists based on the Gospel of Mark that demonstrate the similarity between Jesus' ministry and their own.

ISBN: 0-89622-645-X, 144 pp, $9.95

Discipline Made Easy
Positive Tips and Techniques for Religion Teachers
Mary Kathleen Glavich, S.N.D.
This book contains hundreds of tested methods as it reminds catechists that they are preparing students for life.

ISBN: 0-89622-598-4, 112 pp, $7.95

Teaching is Like...
Peeling Back Eggshells
Melannie Svoboda
In this book, Sister Melannie offers some 50 brief reflections that are intended to sustain enthusiasm, bolster morale and encourage teaching as a grace-filled privilege.

ISBN: 0-89622-613-1, 120 pp, $7.95

On Video
Empowering the Catechist
Skills and Techniques for Effective Teaching
Joe Paprocki
The emphasis in this six-part comprehensive video series is on development of the practical aspects of teaching: planning, lesson preparation, motivating students, leading prayer, discipline, etc.

Six-part video series, $99

Available at religious bookstores or from

TWENTY-THIRD PUBLICATIONS
P.O. Box 180 • Mystic, CT 06355
1-800-321-0411